SECRETS OF A LIFE ON STAGE...AND OFF

By
ED DIXON

First published by Dog Ear Publishing
4010 W. 86th Street, Ste H
Indianapolis, IN 46268
www.dogearpublishing.net

ISBN: 978-1-4575-1113-4

This book is printed on acid-free paper.

Printed in the United States of America

Foreword

KATHIE LEE GIFFORD - Omnipresent fixture in virtually every area of show business: *"My friend Ed Dixon is one of the most fascinating, talented and prolific people I have met in the theater world. His life experiences are profound, heart-wrenching and inspirational. He has not just survived, he has triumphed, and knowing Ed as I do, "We Ain't Seen Nothin' Yet."*

BEBE NEUWIRTH - Multiple Tony-winning star of Broadway, Movies & Television: *"Ed is as complicated as he is talented, and as perceptive as he is wry. Every once in a while he'll tell me a story of some event (or series of connected events) in his life, and my mind gets blown, my jaw drops, AND I'm thoroughly entertained. I look forward to any book Ed cares to write."*

CHRISTINE EBERSOLE - Multiple Tony-winning star of Broadway, Movies & Television: *"Ed Dixon is a force of nature, who does it all, with confidence, conviction, and character, and inspires all who venture on to his wonderful path."*

CHRISTINE BARANSKI - Multiple Tony-winning star of Broadway, Movies & Television: *"Good Heavens! I would love to be in on Ed Dixon's secrets on and offstage. What a brilliant, brave, varied, eclectic life he has led. I could go on... but let him..."*

HARRIET HARRIS - Tony-winning star of Broadway, Movies & Television: *"Ed Dixon is a beautiful singer, wonderful actor and a delightful raconteur. If the Devil is in the details; then the devil is surely in Ed. Whether recounting a particularly troubled Broadway opening or a report on what was eaten at breakfast Ed will delight and reward his reader."*

DOUGLAS SILLS - Tony-nominated star of Broadway & Television: *"He is one of a kind renaissance man equally comfortable in the decadent luxury of Turkish brothel or shooting the breeze about vegan cooking with Placido Domingo after his triumph in The Tales of Hoffman. I'd listen to him read my own diary, and be surprised and titillated."*

PROLOGUE

I was in a dingy room on the 14th floor of the Carter Hotel on West 43rd Street just blocks away from the Broadway show in which I was starring. I was doing handfuls of drugs with a transvestite and a staff writer from the New York Times, neither of whom I had met before that night. Suddenly the door broke open and a group of armed thugs poured into the room brandishing guns. Their leader, an enormous black man with a scar running the entire length of his face, dragged me to the stairwell. I bolted away from him and he caught me around the neck with a heavy cane which he was certainly not carrying for style. He pinned me to the wall with his mammoth stomach, told me that he had gone to prison for murdering a man and that he was going to rape me. I was 40 years old, had already received a Drama Desk Nomination for "Best Actor in a Musical" in a show I wrote myself and was currently in the biggest hit on Broadway. How on earth did I find myself in such a horrific position?

ONE

Getting Started

(Circa 1954)

HOW DO THINGS START? SOMEHOW they just do. In spite of everything, they just do. In 1948, I was born in the tiny southern Oklahoma town of Anadarko (Indian City). My father; a mean, fat, bald grocer—who I hated from my earliest memory of him—took on my mother's extreme fundamentalist Christianity, uprooted his little family and became an itinerant revival minister.

We moved from town-to-town in the depressed and barren dustbowl of 1950s Oklahoma, in poverty and hopelessness. By the time I was in the first grade, my parents were sending me door-to-door to tell my unsuspecting Oklahoma neighbors that they were going to burn in hell forever unless they joined our church. As soon as I could see over the pulpit I was leading the singing; though "singing" is much too grand a word for what we used to do in those meager services. At one point we drove a broken down school bus, painted a flat steely gray, all the way from Oklahoma to Manitoba Canada to bring "gawd" to the heathen. I had to help put up the tent, arrange the folding chairs and lead the singing. I also used to lie face down in the aisle of the bus trying to breathe in the exhaust fumes—since I felt suicide was preferable to life with my Bible pounding parents. I refuse to give any more details about the horrors of the revival minister circuit in 1950s Oklahoma.

In 1954, I entered myself in a talent contest without telling my parents. We were in a dingy suburb of Oklahoma City and I was 7-years old. I sang "Over the Rainbow" emulating Judy Garland's performance which I had seen

1

at the local drive-in. *The Wizard of Oz* made a big impression on me, partly because we had tornado warnings every week, but mostly because of Judy Garland. The word "gay" was not in usage in 1954, but if it had been, I'm sure my first grade rendition of "Over the Rainbow" would have met the criteria. The point is; I began to think of myself as a singer.

By the time I hit junior high school, I knew I had to get the hell out of Oklahoma—though I had absolutely no idea how. Then came a fortuitous accident. I went to the local high school to see their production of Meredith Willson's *The Music Man*. I have no idea why I attended that performance by high school students I didn't know; and I doubt that the quality of the Norman High School production of *The Music Man* was noteworthy, but it was the first live theater that I had ever seen and I was beside myself with awe. I began to fantasize escaping into the world of musical theater.

Shortly after this life changing event, I saw an offer to join a record club in a magazine and get a free stereo. My very first record from that "club" was *West Side Story*. The revolutionary musical style of Leonard Bernstein jolted my adolescent mind. I would sing along with the recording until I knew every rhythm and word. I didn't even notice that the lyrics were by a young fellow named Stephen Sondheim. I just loved Bernstein. So, now I had a new dream as well; to work with Leonard Bernstein. Fortunately, I had NO IDEA how unlikely that was.

A bit more about my record club; my second purchase was *The Merry Widow*, starring an American baritone named John Reardon—a confusing choice for a junior high school student, but not as curious as my third. I ordered *Turandot*, starring the Swedish soprano Birgit Nilsson, and became completely infatuated with her. Then I discovered the great Spanish tenor, Alfredo Kraus. I collected all their records and fell in love with them. Curious.

Seeing *The Music Man* caused me among other things to WRITE my first musical. Now, a more considered person might have thought of seeing a few more musicals before trying to create one—but not this eighth grader. I dashed one off and presented the manuscript to my chorus teacher, Mrs. Oliphant, a nice organ playing church lady. I think my composition was about ten pages long and based on the Little Rascals episode where they throw Darla into a papier-mâché volcano to appease the island God. I simply could not understand why dear Mrs. Oliphant was not thrilled with my opus and I was crushed when she told me that it would not be possible for Central Junior High to perform it.

Since I couldn't get my own musical produced, I decided to sing "Younger than Springtime" from *South Pacific* at the next school assembly. I could spend the rest of this book detailing how hilarious the junior high school students from Norman, Oklahoma found my performance of this song; but I would never be able to capture my surprise at the level of their derision. This is how one finds out the true nature of one's personality. Instead of retreating into my shell, I committed myself to an ironclad escape plan via the stage. As Oscar Hammerstein so beautifully said it, "Getting to Know You" or in this case, getting to know me.

Before I knew it, I was enrolled in Norman High School where I auditioned for and got the role of Freddy in *My Fair Lady*. Of course, I didn't know what acting was, or an English accent for that matter, but I was convinced that I was the greatest Freddy who ever lived. The next year found me playing the King in *The King and I*. Assaying that role; a man stronger and more powerful than anyone I'd ever met, taught me something absolutely vital about acting. You can be something greater than the sum of your parts. Useful information.

TWO

First Brush with Greatness

(Circa 1966)

I WAS ENROLLED IN MRS. Lucille White's chorus class at Norman High School. In 1966 we got a new student teacher from Oklahoma University, Scotty Salmon. He was what one might call "flam-boy-ant"—in Oklahoma parlance. I was slightly terrified by him, but not so much so that I did not ask him every question about music and theater that I could imagine. Of course, there was no way for any of us to know that little Scotty Salmon would become the original choreographer for *La Cage aux Folles* on Broadway; direct the Christmas Show at Radio City Music Hall and stage the Oscars and Grammies in Hollywood. He would also choreograph and perform in Ann-Margret's act and would be on stage with her when she suffered her now-famous forty-foot fall in Las Vegas. I'll come back to that.

Scotty told me that there was such a thing as summer stock. He told me about a place called Casa Mañana in Fort Worth, Texas where you could do one show after another all summer long, and they would PAY YOU! This was, for me, one of "those moments" in life.

I was already hanging around Oklahoma University because it had a large music and theater department. I would watch rehearsals and sneak onto the stage to sing in the darkness of empty theaters. On the bulletin board of one of their lesser buildings—it had the most peculiar smell, which turned out to be greasepaint—was a flyer from the very theater that Scotty had told me about, Casa Mañana.

The flyer described the upcoming season and the date, and location of their auditions. I recall that there were eight shows in their season, but I only remember one of them, *A Funny Thing Happened on the Way to the Forum* by Stephen Sondheim and Burt Shevelove. I remember it because it was the longest title I had ever seen. I wrote down all the pertinent information from the flier and determined that I was going to get that job.

The date arrived for the big audition and I got in my ramshackle 1954 Ford—which had only one working door—and set off for Fort Worth, Texas, a six hour drive. I sang, "On a Clear Day You Can See Forever" all the way from Norman to Fort Worth. I was going to get that job.

I was exhausted when I arrived at Casa Mañana—it was the furthest I had ever driven. But the sight of Casa Mañana's silver geodesic dome rising from the Texas plain like a giant spaceship revived me. I couldn't believe I had actually arrived at this Mecca of theatrical wonderment. I walked inside and found that the interior of the silver dome was gold and the seats were scarlet. There was a round white stage that was shaped like a wedding cake, in tiers, with several ramps leading up to it from the aisles.

But over the stage, suspended like a spaceship within a spaceship, was the light ring. It contained hundreds of Leiko lights with colored gels over them, in every shade of the rainbow. It was so beautiful to me that I burst into tears. I know it's sad, but this was singularly the most magical moment of my life so far.

It was only after this rather private reflection that I realized the auditorium was filled with people. This was the first time I had understood that all the people who were auditioning would be doing so in front of all the other applicants. I took a number and sat down. I saw a young woman walk up to the stage, clinch her fists at her sides and scream out, "Edelweiss" from *The Sound of Music*—like Ethel Merman trying to knock "Rose's Turn" out of the ballpark. I saw a young man do a sort of atonal rendition of "I Wonder What the King Is Doing Tonight" from *Camelot* and finish it with a back flip. I saw a young woman who looked like she was in a beauty pageant sing, "I Feel Pretty" and finish it with what was supposed to be a high C but was actually a dead on B natural. I propose that if you haven't seen an open chorus call for a summer stock company—preferably in Texas—you haven't actually begun your journey in the show business.

After a very long time, someone called my name. I started down the aisle in a high state of excitement, but when I got to the ramp leading up to the circular stage, something went wrong. The incline was much steeper than I had anticipated and I jammed my knee on my first step up. Then my other leg just didn't seem to want to go up the ramp. When I did reach the top and turned back toward the staff and other auditioners, something terrible happened. My right leg began to shake uncontrollably. Someone from the semi-darkness asked what I was going to sing and I whispered, "On a Clear Day." They yelled, "What?" I repeated myself a bit louder and the pianist started the introduction to the song.

By now, my right leg was shaking wildly and my whole body was flapping like a flag in a windstorm. I began clinching my torso to try and stop the shaking, but this was not helpful to my singing. As the number went on, I began to sweat and hyperventilate. A little voice in my head said that I wasn't "performing" and I had better do something about it. So, when I reached the penultimate line "You can see forever and ever and ever" on the word "You" I thrust out my right arm and pointed wildly into the darkness—causing someone at the back of the auditorium to burst out laughing uncontrollably. The song mercifully ended and a weary voice said, "Thank you."

I had seen enough auditions that day to know that I had been dismissed. But I couldn't just limp out, get in my '54 Ford and drive the 6 hours back home. So I sank down into a seat on the aisle and stayed there. I stayed there all day. Finally, the Stage Manager—a very large woman in overalls with a plaid shirt and sideburns—came over and laid a meaty hand on my shoulder. "You done real good honey" she drawled "you kin go home now." It was a very long and silent drive back to Oklahoma.

THREE

First Trip to New York

(Circa 1966)

INSTEAD OF MAKING MY SUMMER stock debut, I worked as a car hop in a Sonic Drive-In—something no one should ever have to do. But I saved enough money to see the first national tour of *Hello, Dolly* in Oklahoma City at the Shriner's Auditorium. It was 1966 and the show was fresh from Broadway. It was headlined by the original Dolly Levi, Carol Channing. And she was something I had never seen before, a genuine Broadway star.

I sneaked backstage afterwards and found her—still in her snow white curtain call outfit—having a business powwow with several very serious men in suits. I walked right up to them and no one even looked at me. She seemed to have light coming out of her. She was only about 40 years old at this point and luminously beautiful. I tried to speak to her but was unable. Eventually I muttered to one of the men, "Does she have time for an autograph?" To which he replied, "How the hell did you get back here?" Not exactly a successful interaction, but a near collision with a real star.

I began to save money to go to New York for a week and see some real Broadway shows. Somehow I scraped together about $200—by serving burgers & fries to hateful college students and juvenile delinquents. Nobody was nice and nobody tipped, but somehow I did get enough money to buy my first airline ticket. I don't know why my parents let me go. I think they had just given up.

I arrived in New York and was terrified by the sheer size of it all. I had never seen any big city before, much less Manhattan. By this time Scotty

Salmon was living in the theater district, so as soon as I got off the bus from the airport I called him. I was on my way to the Sloane House YMCA, but I was scared and wanted to see—if not a friendly face—at least one that would recognize me. I called him from a pay phone and he said I could come by for coffee. He gave me the address and I got on my first subway.

I stood on the 34th Street platform and saw signs that said "local" and "express." I assumed that the express train must be the fast one, so I took it. I watched the stop for Scotty's house pass by out the subway window, so I got off at 72nd Street. But by now I was late, so I really wanted the fast train, and jumped on the next express going back downtown—and passed his stop again. Finally, I got off and asked a man on the platform to help me. After he stopped laughing, he guided me to the "local" train.

When I arrived at Scotty's door, he saw my little suitcase in my hand and thought I was trying to move in with him. He turned white as a sheet and I found myself comforting him even though I was the one who was scared to death. Scotty went off to make some instant coffee and left me sitting alone in his living room. There was a bowl on the table next to me filled with buttons, each of which had a slogan on it. I picked one up at random and on it was written, "New York Will Break Your Heart, Baby." I started to cry—or rather leak. But somehow I managed to dry up before Scotty returned with the coffee.

During our brief conversation he told me that he was in the chorus of *Mame* with Angela Lansbury. I was awestruck. Then I noticed that right across the room he had a framed 8x10 glamour photo of Angela, autographed to him. But all he could do was complain about having to do the show over-and-over and said he wished that I could go on for him that night. "What an insane thing to say" I thought. Surely no one could become tired of doing a Broadway show! I left Scotty and checked into the YMCA.

That night, I bought my first ticket to my first Broadway show, *Sweet Charity*, at the Palace Theater. My very first actual Broadway show starred the amazing Gwen Verdon. I had long since memorized the cast album, and she delivered the same blockbuster performance in-person. She was a completely unique performer but there was another very interesting performance in *Sweet Charity* as well. Very soon I would meet her co-star, Helen Gallagher—but I'll get to that.

I saw eight shows that week. Top prices were only about $10 but I certainly couldn't afford THAT. I would estimate that I got all eight shows for somewhere around $40. I saw Angela Lansbury in *Mame* at the Winter Garden—she was utterly luminous and *Mame* was Broadway that made you think of the OLD days, even back then.

I also saw Ethel Merman in *Hello, Dolly* at the Saint James. I was in the top balcony for Ms. Merman. If you know that theater, you know that the expression "nose bleed section" was invented for the top balcony of the Saint James. The walk up is definitely not for people with heart conditions and the angle of the rake up there is not for anyone who is afraid of heights. I was very sad to be so far away from the stage, but Ms. Merman taught me something that night. You have to see a stage star ON THE STAGE. I had seen her in movies, on television and heard her recordings, but the phenomenon that was Ethel Merman happened in a theater.

While I was up there in the back of the upper balcony, I noticed that there was an empty seat on the second row, right down front. At intermission I moved downstairs and took that seat. As I sat there I thought, "My God, I'm going to see Ethel Merman do the Dolly number on this passerelle—the walkway built out in front of the orchestra pit—right in front of my nose."

I was just settling in for this amazing experience when a skinny old usher came up and demanded to see my ticket. She saw my stub for the upper balcony and took great glee in sending me packing. So, I did not have the experience of seeing Ms. Merman up close, even though I was only seventeen; had flown all the way across the country to do so and used money that I made from being a car hop. I'm sure that woman is long since dead, but I'm still holding a grudge.

Another amazing event of that first week was that I got to see Mary Martin and Robert Preston in *I Do! I Do!* at the 46th Street Theatre. I was more successful with my move-down attempt this time and ended up on the very front row for the second act. When Mary Martin sang, "What Is a Woman?" she was literally right in front of me. I could see the bridgework in her mouth. She made eye contact with me at one point and although I was scared to death—she had a very powerful gaze—I stared back at her for what seemed like a very long time. Thank God some over ambitious usher didn't rob me of that one. I would never see Mary Martin again.

I saw the original cast of *Cabaret* that week in the Imperial Theatre. It was fantastic to see Joel Grey plus I was lucky enough to see the great Lotte Lenya—I think the songs that John Kander and Fred Ebb wrote for her are the finest compositions of their many, many great songs. I wonder if maybe she scared them a little, as only the wife and muse of the great composer, Kurt Weill could do. Lenya was opposite the heavenly Jack Gilford—who I already loved from his Cracker Jack commercials—but it wouldn't be long before I would actually meet him as well.

I don't remember the other shows I saw that week, but I do remember the Sloane House YMCA on 34th Street. I understand that it's a very nice residence today, but it was certainly not a nice place then. I was warned by numerous people to "watch myself" at the infamous residence. Now, I was young and stupid, but I knew exactly what they meant. Nothing actually happened to me at the Sloane House—although a lot of old men leered at me—but I did see the oddest thing across the air shaft one night, a naked man holding a baseball bat. Then I realized it wasn't a baseball bat.

FOUR

University Life

(Circa 1967)

"HOW YOU GONNA KEEP 'EM DOWN on the farm, after they've seen BROADWAY?" It was very hard to return to my roots after that outing but it was inevitable. I enrolled in Oklahoma University and studied with the head of the voice department who, it turned out, knew nothing about teaching voice. I entered the NATS vocal competition (the National Association of Teachers of Singing); for which the requirements were to sing a German, Italian, French and an English selection. For the English selection, I entered a song cycle of my own composition—oh, yeah, I forgot to mention that I wrote three musicals; book, music and lyrics when I was in high school.

Everyone told me that using my own compositions would be a very bad idea and that I would be disqualified. I've never been very good at taking other people's advice. I won the NATS competition—largely on the basis of my own compositions—and was awarded a full scholarship to the Manhattan School of Music.

Everyone was very pleased, except my teacher who said that I would have no idea what kind of voice teacher I'd get up there. I just assumed they would be better than he was, so off I went. I had a brochure from the Manhattan School which in those days was on the Upper East Side in Spanish Harlem. There was a lovely picture on the cover showing only the front door of the building. When I arrived in New York I learned the reason. The broken down building was in a very bad neighborhood and the only part of the structure

11

that was presentable was that door. Inside was a cramped and inhospitable school with virtually no facilities and no practice space.

I was assigned a very prestigious voice teacher who had a career at the Metropolitan Opera and who knew nothing about the teaching of voice. This seems to be very common. The students and teachers were uninteresting and disinterested, with the notable exception of Catherine Malfitano, who even then was destined for a major career in the world of opera. She always knew where she was going and seemed to need little or no assistance in getting there. She has had, and still has, an enormous career in the operatic world. And happily, we are still friends today.

I was always a lousy student. The only things that ever interested me were performing and writing. I was attending a music school so I assumed they would feel the same way. They did not. At the end of the school year they invited me to seek education elsewhere.

One good thing came out of my time at the Manhattan School; I finally lost my virginity—to the first chair French horn player. At age 19, I was certain I was the last chaste person on earth. I don't think either of us enjoyed the event very much. It was like seeing your first orchestra concert and saying, "I don't know much about symphonies, but that can't have been a good one."

No longer a virgin and no longer in school, I began going to open call auditions. What is an open call? The two major theatrical papers; *Backstage* and *Show Business* would run little ads saying that they were looking for singers or actors of a certain type at a certain place at a certain time. And anyone could show up—ANYONE. And they did, by the hundreds.

FIVE

My First Real Job

(Circa 1968)

IN THE THEATRICAL WORLD OF the late 1960s, there were two audition/rehearsal hubs; Broadway Arts and Showcase Studios. Broadway Arts was the best we had—very shoddy by today's standards—but the best we had. It was over a Lincoln Mercury dealership on Broadway in the Upper Fifties with the smallest elevator in New York and the slowest door. Watching a whole chorus of dancers and singers trying to get up to the 4th floor by 10 AM was unchoreographed mayhem.

The rooms were too small to rehearse a large musical. There was no space in the hallways and only one little bathroom for each gender. Oh yes, and some very surly help behind a little sliding glass window, "How the hell should I know where your audition is?" Around the corner from there on 8th Avenue was Showcase Studios. That layout was better since it had an actual lobby, but the rooms were even smaller and apparently no one had ever heard of sound proofing. The tap class next door was always a part of your big ballad audition. Showcase Studios was pretty seedy and run-down, but those were the two apexes of theatrical activity in New York.

A big step down from there was Harlequin Studios on 46th Street. You had to walk up a flight of stairs that was so steep even dancers had trouble with it. The staircase had no landing it just went up and up and up until you got there. And "there" was a cramped and inhospitable space behind a strip joint—The Gaiety Male Burlesque was operational until only a few years ago—it was kind of like auditioning in a by-the-hour cat-house on the wrong side of St. Louis.

Around the corner from Harlequin Studios on 8th Avenue was an even worse place, called Jerry LeRoy Studios. There were holes in the walls of the tiny rehearsal rooms and you could see into the room next door. The walls looked as though they had been punched by someone's fist after a particularly bad audition. No one would dream of using their bathrooms, unless perhaps they were looking for a place to shoot heroin.

This is where I got my first job. I was cast by the inimitable Joe Hayes, founder and "artistic" director of Surflight Summer Theatre. He was short, fat, bald and talked a thousand miles an hour in a staccato voice that sounded like it was being put through a shorted out speaker. He congenially told me at my call-back—yes, I had to go there TWICE—that I would perform for the entire season; 10 shows in 11 weeks, and that I would receive room & board with a salary of $25 a week. He did not tell me that I would also be performing improvisational children's theater in the mornings—before rehearsal—or that all the men would sleep in one room on homemade bunk beds. What did I care? I was in SHOW BUSINESS!

One positive thing, I had never seen the ocean before, and Surflight was on the Jersey Shore. Both the theater and the cast house were only a block from the Atlantic Ocean. That summer, I got the only tan I have ever had in my life. I played Abner in *L'il Abner*; Emile de Becque in *South Pacific*; Billy Bigelow in *Carousel*; Aristide Forestier in *Can Can*; Nelson Eddie in an *Operetta Review* and small parts in the other five musicals. Of course, there was the improvisational children's theater and obligatory public appearances at Kiwanis and Elks Club lunches.

I was 19 years old. Try to imagine my Emile de Becque complete with white shoe polish in my hair. You also have to imagine the theater, which looked like a large storage shed with a corrugated steel roof, fantastic during a rain storm both for the noise and the leaks. Whatever the Surflight experience may have lacked in quality and financial gain, it made up for in sheer endurance and résumé building; and of course, the addition of an anecdote to my repertoire which put me in a very rare club. Surely, very few people have starred in *L'il Abner* and *South Pacific* in the same season.

I had my first real sexual experience that summer—I'm not counting the French Horn player—this was the real thing. But there was no place for us to go. So it was in the front seat of a car, parked under a bright streetlamp in clear view of the cast house, with someone else sound asleep in the back seat. I thought it was just perfect. I should have known right then and there that my tastes were not going to be catholic.

One other thing happened that summer. I became friends with Tracy Smith. She was in the chorus and her parents had a home on the island. They were everything my family was not: urbane, sophisticated, successful and educated. Mister and Missus Smith adopted me and took me into their bosom—as it turned out it was rather gin soaked—but a bosom nevertheless. I remained close with them for many years and eventually sang at both their funerals, which were unfortunately too soon and too close together. My friendship with Tracy survived the death of both her parents and would eventually save my own life, not in some figurative way, literally.

SIX

Casa at Last

(Circa 1969)

AT THE END OF THE Surflight season, I had no money and no scholarship to the Manhattan School of Music. So I returned to Oklahoma and went back to Oklahoma University. This might have been tragic had I not met Elisabeth Parham, the first actual teacher of my life. She is one of the only persons I have ever met in my journey through this world, who actually knew something about the teaching of singing. She loved music, she loved lyrics, she loved learning, she loved ideas, she loved theory and she loved people. I didn't know anyone who ever studied with her who was not changed by her. I regard her as the Mother of my artistic and intellectual life. It's not so much that she taught me everything; she taught me how to learn.

She transformed my voice and at the end of one year's study with her, I gave a very creditable audition at Casa Mañana. They hired me for the entire season, 8 shows in 16 weeks. Oh yes, these were 8 EQUITY shows. Being hired by a union house meant that I was eligible to join the actor's union—Actors' Equity Association. Since it cost virtually a whole week's pay to join, I did not really see the benefit of it at the time. But later on—oh yes, later on I most certainly would.

There is really no way to convey my joy at finally being in a real union theater making an actual living wage to do the thing that I had always been willing to do for free. And, I was about to work with my first star. Casa Mañana deviated from their normal business procedure by opening that season with a brand new musical on a pre-Broadway tryout. They had hired the

16

biggest star in Texas to play the leading role, Ruta Lee. I had never heard of her, but there was no question that she was a "star." She was always fabulously over-dressed, always coiffed within an inch of her life and she wore gigantic arena size false eyelashes to rehearsal at 10 AM—except once, when she over-slept and came tearing into rehearsal with curlers, a babushka and no make-up. This is when I learned that glamour is an accomplishment, not a gift.

The role that Ruta was playing was Texas Guinan, a world famous entre-preneur from the prohibition era. The show was called *Hello, Sucker*—a terri-ble title—derived from Ms. Guinan's trademark expression. Whenever she took to the stage of her famous speakeasy, she would exclaim to her customers, "Hello, suckers!" The show as I remember it, had little to recommend other than Ruta's performance, but there was a prophetic role in the girl's chorus. She was called Ruby and was meant to be Ruby Keeler, who had worked for Guinan before Ruby became a big Hollywood star. She was rumored to have met her first husband Al Jolson, in Guinan's club. We heard that Ruby Keeler actually came to see our little show—though I didn't get to meet her—but I certainly would, soon enough.

The rest of the season was pretty uneventful, except that I found myself standing by for the role of Cable in *South Pacific* a slightly more age appropri-ate part for me than Emile de Becque. The role was being played by Harry Danner—Blythe Danner's brother—who was a very fine tenor. As it turned out, Harry had to leave to fulfill a previous engagement and I got to go on in this role, my first big role in a professional theater. After the season ended I took the little dab of money that I had saved and my Equity Card and returned to New York.

I moved into a sublet and got hired to be in the chorus of the worst pro-duction of *My Fair Lady* that has ever been perpetrated on the theatrical pub-lic. It played in a converted movie theatre at the Paramus Mall in Paramus, New Jersey. There was a piano, a violin, a clarinet and a snare drum. That's it—I am not kidding. We had an Eliza, who was covered in freckles and could not sing, dance or act; the Higgins was from a soap opera; Freddie was a very operatic singer in a toupee; and Doolittle was a very respectable movie actor who just happened to be tone and rhythm deaf. The chorus, however, was fan-tastic. Three of them ended up at the Metropolitan Opera and both Walter Charles and I have had Broadway careers. By my count, we've done over 30 Broadway shows between us.

When this gig ended I went to another audition where something quite unique happened. I met Buster Davis. He was an amazing character who conducted, arranged and wrote incidental music for 22 Broadway musicals in his career (including the original *Funny Girl*, *Bells Are Ringing* and *Hallelujah, Baby!*). He was having an open chorus call for singers for a new musical of *Bus Stop* starring Paula Wayne, called *Cherry*. This audition was in a different locale from the normal audition venues, Nola Studios on 57th Street, a place usually reserved for more classical auditions.

When I arrived for the male chorus call, there was a mimeographed note from Buster on the door—not handwritten, mind you, mimeographed. It said, "One: If I say, 'thank you,' it means you were lousy and you can leave. Two: If I say, 'you're called back,' you should return next Thursday. Three: If I say, 'kiss me,' run for your life." In the world of 1969, this was an astounding piece of mimeograph paper.

When I got inside, Buster was short, thin and translucent—it's not just that he was pasty, you could actually see right through his skin. He was bald in the front, but the back of his head had blond hair that hung down his back. This also was not the norm for the time, and he spoke in a very high treble in which every sentence had some subversive innuendo attached.

I was very fond of singing Jerome Kern's "All the Things You Are" in those days. It was my favorite song, in fact. It never occurred to me that this old chestnut from 1939 might be considered old-fashioned or downright inappropriate for a musical version of *Bus Stop*. I proudly launched off into my favorite song and Buster stared at me bug-eyed. When I got to the end and did a big glissando—down from the high note to the last word—he said, "Where on earth did you learn to do that?" I didn't realize that what he meant was "What, did you just step out of a time machine?"

He didn't follow any of the rules on the door. He called me that night at my sublet apartment and told me that he had hired me for *Cherry*. I had my first Broadway show! I was jubilant—for about a week. Then Buster called me back and told me that they had lost their money and the show was cancelled. I ran out of money too and took a job at B. Blumenthal's Button Factory, the only "regular" job I ever had to take in my career except one; but that's a whole separate chapter.

SEVEN

Back to Casa

(Circa 1970)

I COULDN'T CONTINUE TO FILE back-orders in a button factory indefinitely. The way I saw it, I had failed in Manhattan. The only thing to do was move to Los Angeles. Of course, if I'd known anything, I would have known that a person who wants to do musicals has no business in Los Angeles, but I stupidly took off on this new adventure. My big plan was to stop off in Oklahoma and earn some money on my way across country. Once again, not very clear thinking.

When I arrived in Oklahoma, the U.S. government contacted me. It had never occurred to me that not being a student made me eligible for the draft— yes, we still had a draft in those days. We were right smack in the middle of the whole Viet Nam debacle. I was put onto a bus with a lot of guys who had made my life hell in school and we were collectively carted to Oklahoma City for our military physicals. I stood in various lines all day in my underwear and came to a startling conclusion: Standing around naked with a bunch of red necks can really clear your head.

I checked "the box"—the 1960s Draft Board parlance for saying "you're gay." When our papers were reviewed at the end of the day—by a large scary looking sergeant—I was called into his office for a private chat. He looked at me as though I was a maggot on a dead rat:
"This is just a phase yer goin' thru, right?"
"No, sir."
"You realize this is goin' on yer permanent record?"

19

"Yes, sir."
(*Almost too disgusted to speak*)
"Git outta here."

There were only three of us who didn't go to Viet Nam that day: A guy who was completely deaf; a man with a steel plate in his head from a construction accident—and me. It may not be something to do on a regular basis, but sometimes, honesty really IS the best policy.

I was declared Four F by the military and suddenly it was summer stock time again. I was accepted back at Casa Mañana and offered a couple of nice roles besides the chorus. I would be featured in *Take Me Along*—a little known show that was originally a vehicle for Jackie Gleason; and the even less known *Your Own Thing*—a rock adaptation of *Twelfth Night* that tried to capitalize on the success of *Hair*.

The brother in *Take Me Along* was a good fit for me, but a guy who favors "All the Things You Are" has no business playing a rock musician in *Your Own Thing*. The girlfriend in *Take Me Along* was played by a beauty pageant winner from Dallas. I don't think she had ever done a play or a musical before. She was, however, very pretty. She had a flat chest, straight brown hair and a retainer on her upper teeth. She could not speak above a whisper. You couldn't hear her even when you were standing next to her. I felt sorry for her. Later on—when she became very famous—I had to rethink my position. It was Morgan Fairchild. Never feel sorry for anyone; you have no idea where they're headed.

The star of *Your Own Thing* was also a beauty pageant winner, a statuesque blond from Fort Worth. There was a rehearsal space at Casa Mañana that had an old wooden telephone booth in the corner and an old wooden upright piano missing most of its veneer. On the first day of rehearsal for *Your Own Thing* this pretty blond woman made a phone call and then moved to the upright piano. It was 10 AM and none of us had had our morning coffee yet. She leaned her elbow on the piano, cocked her head sideways resting it on her palm and out came the most amazing sound I had ever heard. It was Betty Buckley. Immediately after this, she moved to New York and auditioned for—a very long shot of a show called—*1776*. The rest, they say is theatrical history (*Cats, Sunset Boulevard, Edwin Drood, Pippin, Eight Is Enough*, etc.)

Later I was passing through the rehearsal room, someone stuck their head out of that old wooden phone booth and shouted that there was a long distance call for me. I couldn't imagine who it might be since I had not given that number to anyone. I picked up the receiver and heard a very high pitched voice say, "Hi honey. Ya wanna do a Broadway show?" It was Buster Davis.

He told me that they had reached capitalization to revive an old chest-nut from the 1920s called *No, No, Nanette* with a bunch of old stars and he remembered me from the *Cherry* audition. In particular, he remembered my genuinely old-fashioned way of singing. Then he asked me if I could tap dance. "All my life!" I replied—I had never even touched a tap shoe. He told me that I had the job and it would start in September as soon as the season ended at Casa.

It turned out he had called the Actors' Equity Union looking for me; they had my contract on file from Casa. When I got off the phone, I announced to anyone who was within earshot that I had just gotten my first Broadway show. Of course, I didn't actually have a contract and was more than a little dubious about Mr. Davis and his potential interest in me. If I'd known more about life—or more particularly Buster's life—I would have known that he wasn't interested in any young man who hadn't spent time in reform school or prison. But that was slightly beyond my level of sophistication.

With my meager Casa savings, I bought a beat-up Volkswagen van that looked like a troop of hippies had lived in it for a decade. I think I paid $50 for it. I loaded my hippie van and prepared to drive across America to make my Broadway debut. In my first couple of years in the theater, I had amassed almost 30 musicals and I was on my way to Manhattan to make my Broadway debut! I took with me a blond surfer from the crew who wanted a free ride to Manhattan. Someone from wardrobe said, "Can't you see he's just using you?" After I stopped laughing, my blond surfer and I drove off into the sunset. But that's another story.

EIGHT

Rehearsing No, No, Nanette

(Circa 1970)

THERE IS NO WAY TO describe my elation about returning to New York City to be in a Broadway show. To me, it was the most important thing in the world. I literally felt sorry for everyone who wasn't me. "Poor President Nixon, he can't sing a lick"—it could be said that this period of my life, like so many others, was lacking in perspective.

I arrived at Broadway Arts Studios at the appointed time and was extremely thankful that everything was on the up and up. A contract was waiting for me. I was very relieved when I signed it and no one put their hand on my knee. The room was filled with young people. It was the largest chorus that had been assembled in many years. The old tradition of a separate singing and dancing chorus had been revived, so there were a lot of us; which meant that I didn't have to tap dance after all. Whew!

There were only two big rooms at Broadway Arts and we more than filled them both. Getting everyone crammed into the tiny lobby elevator—that held maybe four at the most—took a long time. If you came to rehearsal at the last minute, you would definitely be late, and being late was no laughing matter. We had two stage managers from the old school. May Muth—a withered crone with blazing red hair and a face like a bowl of oatmeal—was infamous for having stood by for Celeste Holm as Ado Annie in the original *Oklahoma*. The word was that when Ms. Holm had fainted in the middle of "I Can't Say No" May had stepped over her body and continued the song on the next line. I cannot testify to the veracity of that story, but based on my observations of her, it seems likely to be true.

Her second-in-command Bob Schear, was the good cop to May's bad. But he had one of those five o'clock shadows that was in full swing by 10:00 AM, so he didn't give the impression that he was likely to take any crap. The two of them were formidable ship stewards and God forbid you should break any rule of stage decorum in their presence. Bob would do a great favor for me later on, but I'll get to that.

I am ashamed to say that the principal players in this extravaganza were mostly unknown to me. I had little knowledge of theater or Hollywood history but was about to get a crash course. Overseeing the entire show was Busby Berkeley, the historic movie making pioneer who had invented the overhead shot and made a series of gigantic extravaganzas during the depression, most of them starring Ruby Keeler. Now, I was just past 20 years old, so anyone over 30 years seemed "ancient" to me, and here was a director in his late 80s. Well, in actual fact, he wasn't going to end up being the director, Burt Shevelove was about to assume that role.

Busby was "supposed" to be the director but when he arrived in New York, the producers met him at the airport—he came in on a flight that had one of those push up stair units—and when Busby got to the bottom of the stairs, he just kept on going down and down until he was face down on the tarmac. Then they took him to a restaurant where he had a cocktail and slipped under the table—literally. In the early days of musical staging, Busby had the juvenile and ingénue against the back wall singing their hearts out while all the chorus kids were standing squarely in front of them. When one of the producers whispered in Busby's ear, "Mr. Berkeley, no one will be able to see them way up there." He croaked, "It's okay! There's going to be a close up!" This apparently was the last straw.

Burt Shevelove, who was already engaged to rewrite the ancient and creaky book, was bumped over in the driver's seat. Busby stayed on, but mostly sat at the back of the room, unmoving and completely mute. There were a couple of notable exceptions, however. One day, the ensemble was being particularly frisky and hadn't noticed that Donald Saddler, the award-winning and extremely genteel choreographer, had entered the room and was attempting to address us.

Now, Mr. Saddler was very soft-spoken so, the singers and dancers took no notice of his presence and failed attempts to call us to order. I happened to be looking at Busby when he struggled to get out of his folding chair, wobbled to his feet and barked out, "QUIET!!!" The sheer exertion of which caused him to fall backwards and collapse into his chair like a pratfall in a Chaplin movie. When people turned around to see who had spoken, Busby was again comatose and only I knew the source of the reprimand.

Another time, Buster Davis was swishing across the room and Busby rasped out, "Butch! Butch!" When that got no response Busby belched out even louder, "BUTCH!!!" Buster turned slowly and gave the whole room a Jack Benny reading of, "Well, that's the first time anybody's ever called me THAT."

Irving Caesar, the lyricist and only surviving member of the original creators of *No, No, Nanette* was a contemporary of Mr. Berkeley. I never saw him without a cigar clenched in his teeth. Unlike Busby, Irving liked nothing more than to regale anyone who would listen to him with show business stories. I was so oblivious to this treasure trove of theatrical lore that I literally ran away from him whenever I saw him coming. To me, he was an "ancient boor covered in cigar ash." When I look back on it I just can't imagine that I was not able to override my aversion and ask him questions about Irving Berlin, Tin Pan Alley, the Gershwins—anything. But alas, I did not.

NINE

Ruby Keeler and Company

(Circa 1970)

I DIDN'T REALLY KNOW WHO Ruby Keeler was when we started rehearsals. We didn't have old movies available to us in those days, and it had been many years since I had seen *42nd Street* or *Gold Diggers of 1933* or *Dames* on TV. The woman who arrived at Broadway Arts Studios was a nice, suburban mom who spoke in a whisper and was 60 years old. In 1970, this was regarded as very old. She also seemed to be scared silly and mostly stood in the corner with her old friend from Hollywood, Patsy Kelly. She kept her cloth coat on as if she might bolt for the door at any moment.

Of course, I didn't know who Patsy Kelly was, either. She had been in a slew of movies at about the same time as Ruby, playing the same wise-cracking maid that she would be playing in *No, No, Nanette*. She looked like Ruby's mother—though she was actually a couple of years younger. Patsy was "full figured" and "liked a cocktail." She was also notorious for being Tallulah Bankhead's long-time companion in life and booze. The two of them scandalized both coasts with their drunken antics. This is how young I was; I didn't know that anyone who looked the way that Patsy looked—like a sack of potatoes—could be good on stage. It never occurred to me that she was a great comedienne and her brilliant performance would win the Tony the next year.

I had at least heard of Helen Gallagher, and had, in fact seen her in *Sweet Charity*, the first day I set foot in New York. She was fast, sharp, hard as nails and above all, businesslike. There would be no idle chit chat with Ms. Gallagher during the breaks. All three of these women were tough Irish Americans who had grown up in an immigrant environment without cash or privileges and any one of them could have easily taken on a pit bull. My money would have been on Helen.

Helen was a well-known teacher—surprising since she is one of the least maternal people I've ever met—but she was a very good teacher and gave me some instruction that I still use to this day. Helen had made her Broadway debut with Phil Silvers in *High Button Shoes* the year before I was born. She used to say that "there were so many musicals on Broadway back then that all you had to have was one song and a time step, and you'd never stop working." Gone are the days.

The delightful Hiram "Chubby" Sherman was cast opposite Ruby. I didn't know his work either, but he'd been in 20 Broadway shows before I ever met him and he was a consummate performer and comedian. Everything he did was funny, and he—unlike the other stars I've mentioned—was very easy to talk to and get to know. But he was going to surprise us all.

One cast member was not present the first few days of rehearsal, Bobby Van. I was informed that he had been a Hollywood song and dance man, but I had never even heard his name. We spent a few days rehearsing to be in the background of one of his big numbers, all the while looking forward to meeting him and imagining what he would be like. When he finally arrived, he walked into the room as we were rehearsing his number and angrily quipped, "I thought this was supposed to be my SOLO!" It was not a successful introduction. Later on, I would see his famous on screen routine where he jumped up and down for five minutes. I failed to see how it had earned him his fifteen minutes of fame.

The remainder of the cast was filled out with the three girls who were mistakenly involved with Chubby's character: Loni Zoe Ackerman, who belted in a crazy guttural way; Pat Lysinger, who played the violin while singing soprano and K.C. Townsend, who had "the biggest talents" on Broadway and couldn't carry a tune in a pushup bra.

K.C. played the part that everyone referred to as "the tits girl." She had once appeared on *The Tonight Show* during the run of *Henry, Sweet Henry*, wearing only a small white towel and high heels. K. C. was easily 6 feet tall without heels, was platinum blond and spoke in a parodying rip-off of Marilyn Monroe. She was a huge hit with Johnny Carson.

When I tell you that twelve people were fired on the first day of rehearsal, I am not exaggerating. The "just cause" rule had not yet been instated in the Actors' Equity Rule Book and anyone could be fired at any time for any reason, or no reason—Martin Charnin would change all that many years later when he fired all the little girls in *Annie* on a fateful Friday afternoon, giving the Just Cause Clause the nickname "The Black Friday Clause."

I must say that it shook all of us up a bit to lose so many people on the first day. When poor Carole Demas—who was playing the role of Nanette—was fired a few days later, we went into a state of panic from which we never recovered. "You're firing the title role during the first week?" Here was a dear little 1920s musical about sweetness and light, and it was anything but. In actual fact, it was a very good training program for a life on the Great White Way.

TEN

Producers and Other Stuff

(Circa 1970)

THE WHOLE IDEA FOR THIS charming "lighter than air" affair had come from a producer named Harry Rigby—mind you, this is what Harry said—Cyma Rubin, the other producer tells a completely different story. This concept of pulling an old, forgotten show out of mothballs and peopling it with a lot of old stars was very radical for the time. We had already had *Hair* and *Jesus Christ Superstar* on Broadway, so the idea of standing around singing, "Tea for Two" was, well—preposterous.

We were all looking for other work even as we were rehearsing. NO ONE thought it was going to be even a moderate success. The fact that it had been conceived by Mr. Rigby—a very slight and aquiline man with the highest voice ever heard on this planet—did not inspire confidence. I was never able to hear Harry's voice without feeling somehow that he was putting us on. That just couldn't have been his real voice. He made Tiny Tim sound like Arnold Schwarzenegger.

Nevertheless, to assist him in raising money, Harry took on Cyma Rubin, a Manhattan socialite married to the formidable Sam Rubin—a financier. Once again, I hasten to say that this was Harry's version of the story. This could be construed as a major tactical error on Mr. Rigby's part, as Ms. Rubin was—ambitious. Her ruthless firings and public diatribes against anyone or anything she found even slightly objectionable quickly earned her the title, "The Black Witch of Broadway."

If you even looked at her cross-eyed you could find yourself out of a job, or worse, facing a law suit. During the run of the show, there were countless firings and litigations. So many in fact, that a production assistant penned a show business memoir *The Making of No, No, Nanette* chronicling some of the specific carryings on. However, when I read it I found it lacking in both teeth and accuracy. He simply didn't know the most unpleasant—or interesting— events.

Before we left town on our multi-city pre-Broadway tryout, Susan Watson took over the title role of Nanette. She was pretty, could sing, dance, act and was a lovely person. Ms. Keeler, as I mentioned before had been very reserved, stand-offish and fearful. But as the weeks went by, she gained in confidence and it began to become clear what a dear and charming person she was. A transformation began to occur. She stopped clutching her coat and standing in the corner with Patsy. Then, one day she came in wearing make-up and the producers sent her to Vidal Sassoon, one of the most expensive hair salons in New York. She returned with a spectacular bob. Ruby then began to pull out her higher end dresses and shoes. And finally, one fantastic day, she walked into the rehearsal room in a full length mink, looking like a true Hollywood star. We were thrilled, both for Ruby and for ourselves. It would be inaccurate, however, to say that we began to feel hopeful for the future of our show. We did not.

The rehearsals were overseen by Burt Shevelove and Donald Saddler, the director and choreographer, respectively. Burt, a very likeable if slightly abrupt fellow, had a style that none of us particularly understood. He was very fond of addressing us like dim-witted children, "The show is a bubble. It has no substance. It's a bubble and we all have to keep it in the air. We have to KEEP IT IN THE AIR." This played all right the first time we heard it, but the tenth or fifteenth time we were so admonished, we began to glance sideways at each other with that "what the hell is going on here" look in our eyes.

Donald Saddler, an extremely refined and soft spoken gentleman—I never saw him when he wasn't impeccably dressed in navy blue and gray— never spoke above a whisper. He liked to take his time. He would stand staring at the floor silently immobile for long periods of time, waiting for an idea. This prompted us to coin the expression, "*No, No, Nanette*: The first show to be choreographed by rumor."

His assistant was Mary Ann Niles—Bob Fosse's first wife and dance partner. She looked exactly like Bette Davis in tap shoes. She would have made a great movie character as the wise-cracking, drunken secretary who manages the entire office while chewing gum, chain-smoking and sneaking a flask. She was a whirlwind of manic, self-deprecating energy. I don't think the show would have opened at all had it not been for Mary Ann's tireless and unacknowledged efforts.

By some cosmic accident, I actually choreographed one tiny section of the "Peach on the Beach" number. The four lifeguards—yes, I was a lifeguard—were left in a room with some oars and told to make up something. I came up with this twirling routine in which we tossed the oars back and forth and threw them under our legs while kicking as high as we could, like drum majors. I was amazed when Donald Saddler came back into the room and said, "Yes, do that."

During one performance, my oar flew out of my hand into the audience like an airplane propeller, bounced off the orchestra rail and hit the drummer. After official complaints were made to the musician's union, the lifeguards and "my choreography" were moved to the back of the stage. Ruby later told this story on *The Tonight Show*—the closest I ever came to being on Johnny Carson.

No, No, Nanette was one of the last big shows to get the real "out-of-town tryout" treatment like the old days. We were scheduled to go to Boston, Toronto, Baltimore and Philadelphia before our New York opening. I can't say that any of us seriously expected to make it back to the 46th Street Theatre in the fall. We were just glad we hadn't been fired yet.

ELEVEN
Out-of-Town
(Circa 1970)

WE ARRIVED IN BOSTON AND checked into the Avery Hotel, en masse, with the exception of Ruby. So the entire company was crammed into a rustic little hotel—where I spent the first night with our extremely pretty and utterly insane Italian hairdresser. After a particularly energetic and noisy first-date, I was awakened the next morning by an elegant chorine in the next room whispering through the wall, "Ed, what time is rehearsal today?" Oops.

The show began loading into the historic Shubert Theatre along with a million dollars' worth of gorgeous sets, costumes and fabulous arrangements. It had never occurred to any of us that they would be so gorgeous. The designs by Raoul Pène Du Bois, were spectacular, as were the arrangements by Ralph Burns. I had never seen or heard anything like them, and neither had anyone else. There were two grand pianos in the pit—a la Ferrante & Teicher—and the ravishing overture played in front of a drop-dead gorgeous art deco show curtain. We began to feel cautiously optimistic, although the old fashioned subject matter and corny jokes still seemed beyond salvaging.

A few more speeches about keeping the bubble in the air from Burt and we were ready to open to our first preview. It was a matinee at the Shubert Theatre. Everyone knows that matinee audiences tend to be older and less responsive, so we were steeling ourselves for the worst. The overture played and to our surprise, the audience burst into applause when "Tea for Two" and "I Want to Be Happy" started. They remembered these songs? Then the act curtain flew up and Patsy walked out pushing a giant vacuum cleaner that exploded and belched out black smoke. To say that Patsy did a double take would be dishonesty by omission. It was not even a triple take, it was a quadruple take—no one who had been born after the age of Vaudeville could have attempted such a feat. Long after the endless take was finished, her multiple chins continued to vibrate wildly as her eyes bugged out of her head. The laugh from the audience lasted something like a full minute. "I HATE THIS JOB!" she rasped loudly and the audience laughed for another sixty seconds.

Then, Helen Gallagher came on the stage to entrance applause and sang, "Too Many Rings Around Rosie." The audience cheered. Finally, at the top of the staircase, Ruby Keeler appeared. No one could have been prepared for the reaction of the audience. They went wild welcoming back a lost treasure from their collective past. They simply would not stop applauding. Ruby paused on the landing halfway down to wait for them to finish—they would not stop. She had to turn upstage, overcome with emotion. This caused Helen, of the cast iron constitution, to lose it. She too had to turn upstage until they calmed down.

Then it was time to start "I Want to Be Happy" Ruby's big dance number with the entire company. Donald Saddler had constructed this number from all the steps that Ruby said she was able and willing to do 8 times a week at age 60. What we hadn't seen about Donald Saddler's brilliance was that, though he worked slowly and quietly, he had constructed an arc to the number that built and built and built as one line of dancers after another joined Ruby in all her favorite steps. Her taps, by the way, were PERFECT. The sounds she produced were like a riveting machine run by a computer. She had an odd style because, as she told us, there were no female teachers when she was growing up. She was taught by men who danced on the concrete pavement—hard. But even though she danced like a man, all elbows and knees, she was charming as hell.

She wore a sheer peach organza dress and her beautifully cut gray hair fell into her eyes as she tapped in that magical masculine/feminine way to the conclusion, where all the lines of dancers joined together. Suddenly, everyone froze and Ruby began to do trenches—a highly energetic step where you run frantically in place while extending your arms and legs out first in front and then behind you as if you were being chased by a locomotive. The line behind her joined in doing the exact same thing, then the line behind that and finally those of us who could dance the least, and were confined to the stairs on either side of the stage, joined it. Ruby, who was three times older than most of us, started the step, so she had to do it the longest. Even though doing it for just a few moments was exhausting—she went on and on and on. The taps and the orchestration reached a spectacular climax.

The number ended triumphantly and everyone froze in the final pose. The response from the audience was mass hysteria. They leapt out of their chairs and threw their programs in the air—no, really—they threw their programs in the air like graduation day at West Point. They would not stop applauding; the ovation went on and on and on. It was a good thing since now we were ALL crying. We had just realized that not only were we not in a bomb, we were in a hit—a great big gold-plated mega-money-making Broadway hit.

TWELVE

On the Road

(Circa 1970)

THAT FIRST CURTAIN CALL WAS as crazy as you would expect it to be. At the perfect moment, we all pulled ukuleles from behind our backs and began playing "I Want to Be Happy" in unison. This blatant showmanship did not go unrewarded; the already screaming audience went nuts. It was one of the ideas that actually did come from Busby—he wasn't JUST senile. He also came up with the idea of girls dancing on giant beach balls during the "Peach on the Beach" number, which turned out to be one of the biggest successes in the show.

The curtain call was amazing, and so was the opening night, but we still had to make it past the critics. Thinking that you know what they're going to do is like thinking you know what a mad bull will do after sitting on a campfire. There's no such thing as safe but we did feel pretty confident, which was pretty amazing considering where we had been only a few weeks before.

The opening night party was at Ruby's hotel The Ritz-Carlton, which was right off the Boston Commons and quite beautiful. It was a night of firsts. I had never seen Beef Wellington and I had never seen so many people so drunk. At one point, Burt Shevelove grabbed me on a staircase and gave me such an inappropriate kiss that I nearly fainted. My eyes must have bugged out of my head because Burt very quickly scampered away like a pooch who knows he has destroyed the Sports Section of the Sunday Paper. I had no idea that people in their 60s even had sex, much less made advances to people a third of their age. It was uncomfortable enough that Mr. Shevelove came up to me at rehearsal the next day, looking quite hung over and said, "Uh, I guess I, uh...owe you an apology." I tried to be gracious but I probably wasn't.

The reviews were just what you'd want them to be if you wrote them yourself. Now, our success was virtually assured; unless you recall that "critics being like mad bulls sitting on a campfire" business. You would think that things would have calmed down after that—but no, more people were fired and rehearsals became more and more unpleasant. They adopted a very unfortunate attitude that I have since seen managements use on far too many occasions. They would call the entire company in for every hour of rehearsal that the union would allow, which was a lot. We would stand on stage while Burt would make his "keep the bubble in the air" speech—which we had taken to mouthing along with him—or while somebody tried to think of something for us to do. Of course, mind you, we were doing 8 shows a week, as well.

We went to the airport to fly to Toronto, our next tour city, and got in one long line with our boarding passes. Suddenly, the Company Manager walked over to the chorus boy standing next to me, tapped him on the shoulder and said with no emotion whatsoever, "You can get out of line, you won't be going to the next city." We had all been frightened before, but now we were terrified.

In Toronto we played the O'Keefe Center, a house that seated thousands and was more suited for a hockey game than our little show. It was a huge success anyway. We continued to rehearse and people were constantly threatened with being fired. The morale was terrible even though we were in a huge hit. Then we flew to Baltimore.

Baltimore in 1970 was dangerous. When we arrived at our first hotel, we paraded off the bus into the lobby of a dilapidated whorehouse. We all just turned around and got back on the bus without saying a word. The Company Manager did some tap dancing of his own and we very quickly we were on our way to a sweet little old world hotel that was a very long way from the theater—nowhere near downtown. The stars all stayed at a very expensive Hilton next door to the theater but all the rest of us were in this charming little hotel. It did, however, have something slightly odd about it.

It turned out that the city of Baltimore was using our hotel to house some of the overflow from a mental institution. On Christmas day, an aged woman in an intense state of dementia, crashed through the connecting door between her room and mine, knocked over my Christmas tree and cried "They're coming for me! They're coming for me!" I managed to get her back into her own room and move a chest of drawers in front of our shared door. It would be twenty years before I would have a worse Christmas than that. (Drugs would be involved.)

The Morris Mechanic Theatre, where we were booked in Baltimore, had been built by an architect who had apparently never seen a theater. The outside was quite modern and very attractive, but inside, two-thirds of the theater seats did not face the stage. The seats in the middle of the orchestra faced the stage but the ones on the sides faced inward toward the center of the building. There is a theater in Philadelphia built without dressing rooms for the actors—we were about to play it—but a theater in which the audience does not face the stage? That's one for the books.

You remember K.C. Townsend, the tall, leggy blond with the amazing tatas? There were many rumors about her, rumors that I did not understand. They said she was dating the Mafia. Not someone IN the Mafia—THE Mafia. Some rather unkind chorus girls referred to her as "The Holland Tunnel" and they said she was a "pill freak." I had no idea what that meant—literally, no idea.

After a few days, K.C. got a call from the management saying that they did not trust her to stay in the rustic little hotel with the rest of the company. They wanted her to move downtown next door to the theater with the other stars. She was furious and wanted to spend Christmas with the rest of us. But the management was absolutely insistent. By a curious stroke of fate, I happened to be standing on the street in front of our hotel at the very moment that Ms. Townsend made her exit to a waiting cab in a state of high dudgeon.

She flounced down the walkway of the hotel in 4-inch heels with her luggage under both arms and cursing aloud to herself along with anybody who would listen. She passed me on the sidewalk—as if I was invisible—and headed toward the cab that was parked at the curb on a very steep incline. Just as she made it to the door of the cab, still cursing to high heaven, the latch on her overnight case gave way. The bag swung open and out poured hundreds of multi-colored pills that began rolling away. They weren't even in bottles; they were just loose in the case. She threw herself onto the ground and began scooping them up and throwing them back into the bag all the while continuing her non-stop flow of obscenities. I can't say that I quite understood any of the vision that I had just witnessed, but I filed it away for future reference.

Once again, like the other cities, we were a big hit in Baltimore and moved on to Philadelphia and the famous Forrest Theater, the one with no dressing rooms. It had an underground passageway like an escape route from a castle under siege. You had to duck down and run through the passageway to the building next door to get to its makeshift dressing rooms. We were a big hit in Philly our last out-of-town tryout city. Now, we only had to come into New York and claim the prize that surely awaited us there. But before we got our great reviews and left Philadelphia, two very interesting things happened.

Ruby Keeler's second dresser—she had two—a diminutive, pockmarked and rather unattractive Hispanic man named Henry, was secretly a well-known drag queen. It was 1970, and being a drag queen was not something that ever came up on the news, TV, in plays, movies or anywhere. However, word got out that Ruby's dresser had gotten himself booked into a local gay bar and was going to do his notorious "Salome's Dance of the Seven Veils." The entire company showed up. There in this seedy dive on a back street in Philadelphia sat Ruby Keeler, Patsy Kelly, Hiram Sherman, Bobby Van, Helen Gallagher, Burt Shevelove, Donald Saddler, Buster Davis and the whole ensemble of *No, No, Nanette*.

First up was a very large and masculine man in a green satin dress who could sing exactly like Eydie Gorme—not lip-sync—he actually sang like Eydie Gorme. Then, his music changed, he dropped his voice two octaves and launched into "Old Man River" as a bass. The place went wild and he had to repeat the whole thing from the top. Next up was a very beautiful young man who was halfway through a sex change. He had smallish bosoms and an amazing rear end. His act was composed mostly of turning his back to the audience and making his tush vibrate at speeds that were in the jet-engine range. This also had to be repeated numerous times. The applause was so massive that poor little Henry must have had some idea that something out of the ordinary was going on; but when he walked out, the look on his face was priceless.

And who could have dreamed he would be so beautiful? He looked like Gina Lollobrigida. But he was stuck and had to actually go through with his very graphic routine—which involved removing all of his veils and humping the head of John the Baptist. Henry was a big hit that night. Ruby did not go back to his dressing room, but I happened to be there the next day when she congratulated him at our theater like one old movie star meeting another. After she had complimented him sufficiently, she asked demurely, "And who was the young gentleman with the very attractive behind?" Ruby was a delightful woman.

The other thing that happened in Philly was not so delightful. To put it in context, the threats and firings continued. Girls were told they were too fat or too ugly. Boys were told they wore too much make-up or not enough. Law suits were starting to pile up. Many costumes and sets—gorgeously designed by Raoul Pène Du Bois—were not used after they had been ordered and created. Some sets were simply left sitting out on the street, deserted. Raul was not paid for the work of designing them. Counter suits were filed. Cyma Rubin began trying to oust Harry Rigby and take over the show, when the entire thing had been Harry's idea—that is, if you believe Harry Rigby.

Of course, we continued to rehearse all day, every day and when I say rehearse, I mean stand around all day with Burt and Donald trying to think of something for us to do while the staff argued. People began to be very unhappy and talk subversively in corners, stairwells and hallways. One particularly long and tiring day, we had been standing around on stage for hours when Hiram Sherman—who was fantastic in the show and had been superbly reviewed in every city—stepped forward and shouted into the house, "I am a very old man. I cannot take any more of this. I am going to my dressing room. Come there and fire me!" Of all the zaniness we'd seen so far, this took the prize.

We never saw him again. His pronouncement was even stranger since, by my count he was only 62-years old and we were only weeks away from coming into New York in a pre-made hit. His understudy took over and did a terrific job, believing that his show business ship had finally come in. But when we arrived in Manhattan, Jack Gilford took over the role. Jack was a delightful, lovely and talented man, but the part had been tailored by Burt Shevelove to the particular comic genius of Hiram "Chubby" Sherman. I absolutely came to love Jack Gilford, but in all honesty, after Hiram left, the part was never as good again.

THIRTEEN

On Broadway at Last

(Circa 1971)

FINALLY, WE RETURNED TO NEW York and moved into the historic 46th Street Theatre (now the Richard Rodgers) in the dead of winter. There were more people in *No, No, Nanette* than had been in that theater since the depression, so a boarded up storeroom on the 7th floor had to be opened and turned into a dressing room for the male ensemble. There was a tiny elevator that only held one person, but that didn't matter since it didn't work anyway and was being used for storage—I don't think it was legal. Not only did we make-up on the 7th floor, we did all our costume changes there as well. So we went up and down multiple times per show. We were young and healthy and took the stairs three at a time. I can tell you one thing, we all had great legs.

The dressing room was a complicated scene. I said that we were all young and healthy, but that's not entirely true. There was one old, jaded queen who had been in 12 Broadway shows dressing side-by-side with a bunch of kids who had never been in 1. He worked out every day— which most people did not do in those days—and he was tanned like an alligator. He put "beading" on his eyes; an old world show business practice of heating some kind of black goo in a spoon—like a heroin addict—and slathering it onto your eyelashes with a brush. He only spoke as Bette Davis. He could make "What time is rehearsal?" sound like, "What a dump!" I was terrified of him and terrified that I would turn into an old alligator like that just by being around him. One day, I was out with the flu. When I returned he snarled:

"Where were ya?"

"I had the flu."

"Don't do that again!"

"I had the flu."

"DON'T do that again."

He was old school.

In the opposite dressing room corner from him, was a pair of guys who had been shacked up together since the first out-of-town city. However it was still 1971, so they both claimed to be "straight." After keeping up this façade for some time, they got into a lover's spat right in front of us all. The tougher of the two crammed the other one into a large trash can—butt first. He did it so forcefully that it took several of us to remove his boyfriend. We were all afraid that management might "trash" any one of us at any moment. It was not a very nice place. I put a little sign on my mirror that said, "K.Y.M.S." (Keep Your Mouth shut) but, of course, I didn't.

Our Stage Manager, May Muth began standing in the offstage wings—out of audience view but in plain sight of the cast—shouting out editorial comments, "You can't dance! You're lousy! What the hell do you think you're doing out there?" This made me very angry. I decided to do something about it. I got some paper and envelopes and with my left hand—I'm right-handed—I wrote one sentence in a heavy slant, the opposite of the way my handwriting goes. The sentence read, "Please investigate the behavior of the Stage Manager." It was one simple daring sentence that I copied and sent to each producer, the director and the musical director—just for good measure. I thought I had secretly done a good deed for us all. But a day or so later, word began to circulate that someone was sending "poison pen letters" and they were going to find them and fire them on the spot. "Are you kidding me?" I thought, "The Stage Manager is yelling insults to actors on stage during the show and management is trying to find out who wrote the letter—or rather, sentence?" I didn't have that much knowledge of management at that point.

There had been rumors that Cyma Rubin's daughter Loni, was conveying information to her mother, but there was never any proof. However, a day or so later, we were all sitting in our 7th floor "penthouse" when Loni arrived before the show. She had never visited our dressing room before—hers was several floors below—so we were all pretty surprised. She had an LP album of *No, No Nanette* in her hand and told us that Leopold Stokowski—the famous conductor—had seen the show twice and was such a big admirer that he wanted us all to write a little something to him on the album, and not just our names, a whole sentence.

Honestly, you would have thought creepy music would have played behind her and Peter Lorre would have appeared in the stairwell. She stood right there and waited for us to sign. So I used my real handwriting with my right hand and slanted it in the right direction. I know now, that my handwriting is very, very recognizable and there's no way they didn't know it was me. But, for whatever reason they did NOT fire me. And of course, they didn't fire May Muth either.

FOURTEEN

The Opening of Openings

(Circa 1971)

EVENTUALLY THE BIG DAY ARRIVED, as big days have a way of doing. It's worth mentioning that at this point in theatrical history an "opening night" actually was just that, one night. Today, the critics come as much as a week before or a week after the so-called opening and you get as many as sixteen chances to get it right. However, back then, the critics all came to just one performance. As you can imagine, having one night to get it right ensured that the cast had a phenomenal case of nerves. The audience was made up almost entirely of critics. Imagine singing, dancing and telling jokes to a group that is silently looking down and taking notes.

For a person who had never experienced it before, it was overwhelming. The backstage area and the dressing rooms were so filled with flowers from well-wishers that they had to be put in the hallways and onto the stairs. Staircases were literally lined with floral arrangements—all seven floors. Presents and telegrams from anyone who was anyone in show business, were littering dressing tables and taped to mirrors. It was very festive and people were extremely nervous.

No, No, Nanette had kept its original antiquated form, performed in three acts rather than the usual two. So, there were two intermissions, each with enormous set changes and big expanses in which to become even more nervous. The sets were unit designs that didn't move during the course of the act, so they were big solid constructions. There was no room for these sets backstage—off-stage wing space at the 46th Street Theatre is minimal—so they had to be hoisted up by wenches and chains until they were utilized. Each giant set piece was hanging above our heads like a *Sword of Damocles*.

In spite of our nerves, opening night was going fantastically. Patsy got her huge laughs; Ruby got her big welcome back to Broadway applause and the tap number landed like a stage full of dynamite. All was well with the world—until the end of the second act. This is when K.C. Townsend was to make her first big entrance that closed the second act and set up the show for the third.

The entire chorus, in beautiful colorful costumes, was lined up across the back of the stage in a semi-circle and all the principals were down stage in a line across the front. We all looked stage left for K.C.'s big entrance. She wasn't there. Silence—and then more silence. When she finally did appear, she came staggering onstage in a state of near unconsciousness.

We later learned, she had been sitting in her dressing room very nervous, on her usual regimen of pills, which she was perfectly capable of handling. But to calm herself she had decided to down one of those little complimentary bottles of booze that are sometimes given as gifts—the kind you might get on an airplane. When that little bottle of vodka hit her load of pills, K.C. went into something like a coma. Since she had a private dressing room, no one knew this until it was time for her entrance and the end of the second act.

For her entrance, K.C. had on very high heels and a fringed dress cut so low that every time she put it on at least one person said to her, "Aren't you afraid you're going to come out of that dress?" To which she always replied, "Tip o' the iceberg, honey. Tip o' the iceberg." Her staggering walk caused her enormous bosoms to undulate more than usual—sending the fringe beneath them into hurricane mode—and the audience began to laugh uproariously. We on the other hand were shitting our pants—our beautiful Raoul Pène Du Bois, art deco pants.

Eventually, she came face to face with Jack Gilford just left of center. She tried to stop but the weight of her pendulous tatas pulled her onward; her very high heels came off the floor and she listed forward onto the balls of her feet. We thought she was going right over on her face, but at the last moment she flopped back on her heels and came down hard, causing another mammary upheaval. She managed to slur out her one and only line, which may have only been, "Hi, Jimmy," but it sent the audience into paroxysms of laughter and the second act was over.

The curtain had no sooner hit the deck when Bobby Van streaked across the stage and slapped K.C. right in the kisser—hard. She immediately went down to the floor and he leapt on her like a wild animal and began throttling her. This was after all, his one and only chance at a Broadway come-back. The stagehands and some other cast members separated them and the stage managers hustled K.C. off stage right. Most of us just stood there with our eyes bulging out, not fully comprehending what had just happened. I didn't know where the stage managers had put K.C. until the banging started.

They had shoved her out into the alleyway behind the theater and locked the door behind her. Now she was wearing a skimpy little silk fringe dress and it was January; the wind was freezing with snow flurries in the air. You could hear her muffled cry "Let me in. What did I do? Let me in" all the while banging her naked lily white arms against the cold metal door. I honestly think she didn't know what everyone was so upset about.

The third act opened with a big song and dance number featuring Bobby Van and the three girls called "Telephone Girlie." It was decided that there was no way K.C. could attempt a dance number in her current condition. So they began dividing up the lines and dance moves between Loni Ackerman and Pat Lysinger during the fifteen minute second act intermission.

Pat later explained to me what happened next. The act three curtain went up and Pat was seated on the settee stage right next to Loni, trying to get her thoughts together and more scared than she had ever been. She was just about to say K.C.'s first line when she heard the click of the door latch on stage right. K.C. had gotten back in somehow and had entered the scene already in progress.

No one knows how K.C. made it through the number—apparently the cold air in the alleyway had been of some assistance. K.C. had made it through her most difficult material in the act, other cast members took over and the show ended with a rousing standing ovation. The reviews the next day were love letters, with many favorable mentions of Ms. Townsend's "hilarious" performance.

K.C. was not fired; perhaps it was her notices. Pretty amazing when you consider that maybe fifty people had been fired at this point for no reason. We heard that Bobby Van brought her up on charges with the union, but we also heard that he received a phone call in the middle of the night from someone with a raspy Italian accent, "I suggest youz drop da charges." He did.

FIFTEEN

Being in a Hit

(Circa 1971)

PEOPLE KEPT TELLING ME HOW lucky I was to be in a big hit my first time out on Broadway. There's just no way to have perspective on a concept like that, until years pass. I now know how true that is. Not only were we a success, we were a unique success, of a completely original genre. No one had ever pulled off anything like it before; dragging an old clunker like *No, No Nanette!* out of mothballs and turning it into a mega-hit.

It felt like the entire world came to see our show. Over the next few weeks a parade of old Hollywood stars passed through the audience and through the backstage door of the 46th Street Theatre. We had Joan Crawford, Lucille Ball, Joan Blondell, Joan Fontaine, Fred Astaire, Ginger Rogers, Liberace, Gene Kelly, Van Johnson and Donald O'Conner to name a few. Every old Hollywood star still ambulatory paraded through. We would all stand on stage, form a reception line and they would shake hands with each and every one of us. Some cast members got sick of this routine and started skipping the "star portion" of our assignment. Not me.

One night, we met Richard Nixon—and yes, he was just as creepy as he appeared on TV. His face actually looked like a Halloween Mask; one of the most amazing noses I've ever seen—like two Bob Hope schnazolas stuck together with Krazy Glue. I should have said, "You tried to kill me in Viet Nam but I went to Broadway instead!" But I just muttered, "Nice to meet you."

Joan Blondell went to Jilly's with us after one show—Frank Sinatra's old hangout. Joan and Ruby were lifelong friends and they sat around chattering like school girls. One of the boys knelt down to snap their picture and Joan yelled out, "Stop!" in such a loud voice that the entire party ground to a halt. Then—with the whole room listening—she intoned with baritonal authority, "Never shoot a woman over forty from BELOW." Or a woman over sixty, apparently. Lesson learned.

Seated at the same table with them was Gertrude White, Ruby's sister. Of all the people I met during this period, Gertrude was my favorite. I can't explain it. I simply adored her from the moment I met her. The crazy thing was Gertrude was Ruby's primary dresser. There was a moment during the show that I was privy to every night. I would be standing in the wings waiting for my entrance, when Gertrude would get down on her hands and knees and buckle on Ruby's tap shoes. Then Ruby would hike up her peach organza dress and straighten her hose—exposing the entirety of her 60-year old flawlessly beautiful legs. I knew that it was an amazing thing to be a witness to this ritual every night, but I always wondered why Gertrude—who was Ruby's equal in every way—took on this subservient position.

One day, a very cheeky chorus kid asked her why she dressed her sister. Gertrude matter-of-factly replied, "Ruby kept the whole family alive during the depression. It's the least I could do." (Gertrude is in all of Ruby's movies.) Many years later there was a *No, No, Nanette* reunion where I took Gertrude aside and whispered confidentially, "You know you were always my favorite." She slapped my arm like a flapper and quipped, "I know, dear." Years later I wrote to her reminding her how special she was to me, but the letter came back. I had waited too long.

A couple of other favorite *No, No, Nanette* audience memories: Diahann Carroll was so beautiful in 1971, that I could actually see her from the stage sitting in a special reserved house seat. Her luminous face looked like it had an electric light on it—even out in the darkened house. And later, another great star caught my attention in the exact same seat.

It was my ultimate idol, Birgit Nilsson, the great Swedish soprano. Back in the days when I was living on $25 a week, I spent $50 on a ticket to see her at the Metropolitan Opera in *Die Walküre*. By that time I had purchased all her recordings, and she was simply my favorite person alive. A lot of people didn't stay around to meet Madame Nilsson the night she came to see the show because they had no idea who she was. Of all my nights at *No, No, Nanette*, the night that she came, was my absolute favorite.

I mentioned earlier that Bob Schear, the *Nanette* Assistant Stage Manager, would do something kind for me. He had been a Stage Manager for Madame Nilsson, and when we were in Philadelphia, Bob got me a signed program from her concert there. It was at the same time as one of our performances, and Bob warned me not to call in sick or I would be out of a job. Apparently, while stage managing another musical, Bob had taken a night off to see a Nilsson concert. He found himself seated next to a chorus boy—who had called in sick—from the same job. As the lights went down, Bob whispered, "I hope you enjoy the concert, you're fired."

Nilsson was at the height of her fame in 1971 and she showed up wearing a fabulous red pants suit with gold threads running through it, very high heels and her trademark brunette glamour wig. When I finally got to meet her, I took her hand in both of mine and said very deliberately, "Madame Nilsson, you are my favorite woman in the entire world." This massively powerful woman who had conquered the entire world, transformed into a little Geisha before my very eyes. She whipped her head to the side, covered her mouth with her hand and giggled like a 6-year old. A perfect first meeting.

A few months later I met another idol of mine—Leonard Bernstein. He was seeing singers for the premiere of his *Mass*, which was to open the brand new John F. Kennedy Center for the Performing Arts in Washington, D.C. When I went to the first audition, without Bernstein of course, I felt that a chorus boy from *No, No, Nanette* had about as much chance of opening the Kennedy Center in a new work by Leonard Bernstein as—well, you come up with a metaphor.

I was called back to meet Bernstein himself and told to bring every kind of music imaginable from pop to jazz—Bernstein loved jazz, something that confused me terribly. I have never sung either pop or jazz—not then, not now—but I wrote an arrangement of one of my favorite songs "Come Back to Me" from *On A Clear Day* into what I thought was "jazz-like." Of course, it wasn't jazz, but it WAS very different from the original version—it was slow. I put every song I liked into a satchel and went off to meet Mr. Leonard Bernstein.

The callback was at Nola Studios where I had first met Buster Davis, but this time, it was in the biggest of all their rehearsal spaces. I walked into the room and behind several long tables pushed together sat: Leonard Bernstein; Alvin Ailey (the world famous choreographer); Gordon Davidson (the world famous director); Roger Stevens and Schuyler Chapin (the world famous producers) and a whole row of "suits" (the money). Seated next to Bernstein was a casually dressed very young man, younger than me. I thought, "Oh my God, he's brought his little boyfriend to the audition, how kinky!"

I walked up onto the stage—this rehearsal room had an actual recital stage in it—and put my huge sheaf of music on the Steinway. Bernstein asked me what I wanted to sing. I really could hardly believe it! Leonard Bernstein, the composer of *West Side Story*, was asking me what I wanted to sing for him? Surprisingly enough, I can't remember what that choice was—weird when you consider my memory for minutia—but it was probably "All the Things You Are." After that, I went through Italian Art Songs; German Lieder; Musical Theater Songs and a few other things. I couldn't imagine what else he could ask for. I was near completion of my entire satchel repertoire when the young man next to Bernstein asked in a very bored way, "Do you have anything CONTEMPORARY?"

I absolutely could not believe that Bernstein's "trick" was addressing me at my audition. I thought of my arrangement of "Come Back to Me" and rather haughtily answered that I had that. He, even more haughtily replied, "Oh, you mean da, da, da, da, da, da." He was mocking the Broadway up "tempo-ness" of it all. I, even more haughtily retorted, "No, as a matter of fact, not," and proceeded to do "my" new, very slow version of the up-tempo standard. At this point Bernstein said "Thank you," and it was over.

I left the room and felt that I had blown my big chance to work with Leonard Bernstein by getting in a tiff with his boy toy. I became physically ill and missed the show that night. Actually, I think this was the occasion that I referred to earlier when I told the scary chorus boy I had the flu. Oh, and by the way, the "trick" sitting next to Leonard Bernstein was Stephen Schwartz. Who, although he was one year younger than me, had *Godspell*, *The Magic Show* and *Pippin* running simultaneously on Broadway that year. He was providing some of the lyrics for *Mass*. (Today, of course, he has *Wicked* running worldwide, which is one of the most successful musicals of all time.)

A day later my phone rang and my agent told me that I was going to open the Kennedy Center as a soloist in Leonard Bernstein's *Mass*. Words cannot express—no, seriously—they cannot! To literally make your dream come true? Priceless.

I went back to the glamorous snake pit that was *No, No, Nanette* and turned in my notice. I had not been fired over the "poison pen" episode and now, here I was the first person to leave under his own volition—except for Hiram Sherman. I told everyone my fantastic storybook tale of being hired by my idol and my escape from the chorus. In the third act, I put on my gorgeous, perfectly tailored tuxedo and prepared to stand in the French doors behind Helen Gallagher and sing, "ooh...ooh...ooh" while she belted out, "Where Has My Hubby Gone Blues."

Just as I was about to walk onto the stage, May Muth—everyone's favorite stage manager—came over to me with a big Cheshire Cat grin and whispered, "You're on a 6-month rider, we're not accepting your notice." With that, she shoved the handwritten notice back into my hand and I made my entrance. I took my position in the doorway behind Helen like a zombie. When the music started I began to cry. I just stood there and cried through the entire number. Not one single "ooh" came out of me.

However, the next day, good old Actors' Equity stood behind me and declared that the *No, No Nanette* Company could not hold me to a Chorus contract when I was being offered a Principal role. What can make you happier than making a dream come true? Defeating the Wicked Witch of the West while you're doing it.

SIXTEEN

The Kennedy Center

(Circa 1971)

WHEN I ARRIVED AT THE newly constructed Kennedy Center in Washington, D.C.—rising like a giant marble box of Kleenex on the Potomac—I went directly to the top, walked out on the observation deck and looked out over the river at the Washington, Jefferson and Lincoln Memorials for the first time in my life. I was about to inaugurate a magnificent new hall; create a role in a new Leonard Bernstein composition; work with Alvin Ailey and his entire company; the Norman Scribner Choir and the Berkshire Boys' Choir. All the living Kennedys were going to come to the premiere, and we were going to record it with Bernstein himself conducting. I was 23-years old. Did I have any idea how unusual all this was? Of course not; I was 23.

I mean, I knew that it was great and that I was lucky to be there, but I had no idea that something like this happens once in a lifetime. I somehow thought I had earned my place in the world, or some such silly notion. Just as it was impossible to understand how rare it was to open on Broadway in a huge smash hit the first time out, it was equally impossible to grasp that something like opening the Kennedy Center was utterly unique. To a youth, everything is unique, so everything is normal.

Each rehearsal space that we used in that new building was an inauguration since we were the first people in each one. In them, I met my co-soloists: David Cryer (a well-known Broadway regular—now known as Jon Cryer's father); John Bennett Perry (a television actor—now known as Matthew Perry's father); Marion Ramsey (a spectacular singer—now known from the

Police Academy movies); Kay Cole (the "At The Ballet" girl from *A Chorus Line*); Walter Willison (a well-known juvenile who had just been nominated for a Tony); Larry Marshall (a well-known "Sportin' Life" and cabaret performer); Alan Titus (an attractive young man with a guitar who would become a well-known opera star) and a few others. We all met each other, played some theater games together, and then worked separately on our own songs with various coaches and pianists. While the Alvin Ailey Company worked in their own space and the separate choirs worked in their own halls. There was also a jazz combo, a symphony orchestra and a marching band—this *Mass* was HUGE.

The result of working this solitary way was that none of us had any idea what the piece was about. Bernstein was literally writing parts of it as we went along. Although we each knew our own little bit, the very premise behind the work remained a secret. And which brings me to my next topic; the size of our solos. We had all been promised a great deal when we signed on—and make no mistake, it was great to be there—but most of our parts were, well—small, or at least, so we thought. The constant mantra was, "Wait for the Secret Songs at the end." The "Secret Songs" were apparently the last part of the *Mass* structure—a fact of which I was unaware. Bernstein was writing them as we went. So as each day passed, we became more anxious for the arrival of those "Secret Songs."

I had several small parts in *Mass*, but my best solo was part of a larger piece called "I Don't Know." My lyric in its entirety was as follows:

WHAT I NEED I DON'T HAVE.
WHAT I HAVE I DON'T OWN.
WHAT I OWN I DON'T WANT.
WHAT I WANT LORD,
I DON'T KNOW, NO, NO, NO.
I DON'T KNOW.

It was not a gigantic opus, but it was in a very good key for me and I sang it for all I was worth at every single rehearsal. Once, at a party after hours, some hippie-dude stage manager asked me how I managed to get so much out of such a small piece of music. I—taking myself much too seriously—looked him dead in the eye and proclaimed, "Because that page of music is the only time in my life when I'm truly alive." He stared at me for a few seconds and then whispered "that's pathetic." This was the first time I realized that crew members could be much smarter than performers. There would be others.

Besides my own part, I was standing-by for David Cryer—who had a much larger role. He had a long and very complicated solo in twelve-eight time. Every single note had a dot or a slur or a triplet on it and it was, well…hard. I worked on it mostly on my own and was quite certain that I was ready to go on at a moment's notice.

Then, one day, Maestro Bernstein suggested that we go into one of the brand new rehearsal rooms and go over that particular solo. Just to point up who he was to me at this point—I had never actually been able to speak to him—he was just too rich, too famous and too exalted. I had been left alone in the wings with him at one point and was completely mute. Once, he had stood next to me at the urinal in a new and gorgeously appointed restroom in a $2,000 suede suit—that's $2,000 in 1970s money! He chatted away to me over his shoulder while I seized up like a—well, like a person who can't pee. And now, here we were, just the two of us in a small rehearsal room. He was seated at a Baldwin upright and I was standing over his shoulder with the assignment of singing his song back to him. Frightened as I was, I was also extremely excited about showing him all my hard work on it. "I'll bet none of the other soloists know their covers cold like I do," I thought.

Bernstein played the intro and I proudly sang the first measure. He stopped and pulled his hands off the keyboard. "No," he said, "this note is dotted and this one is a sixteenth, you see." "Oh." I said, and we went back. I started again. "No," he said, "the dot is too short and the sixteenth note is too long." "Oh," I said, and back went. I started again. "No," he said, "these three are triplets, not dotted." "Oh." I said, and back we went.

This kept up for what seemed an eternity—it was probably only half an hour. Until finally, he gave up on the first part of the piece and we went on to the middle section, without ever having his approval on the first. Now, I got to my first high notes and was positive that he would be pleased with this bit. "No," he said, "your G flat is more like an F sharp." I didn't even know what that meant. I assumed it meant that I was flat—something that I had never really considered a problem of mine. To my mind, there was no difference between a G flat and an F sharp. So, what was I supposed to do? I tried to be as clearly in the center of the pitch as I could. "Much better." he said, but I had no idea why.

This went on for an hour and we only got through part of the song. At the end of this work session, I was not the same person. I was changed forever that afternoon. This little coaching with Bernstein changed the way I learned music from that day on. Previously—in my desire to interpret and add my own stamp to music—I had worked more from feeling and intuition than from slavish detail work, which I had regarded as lacking in creativity and self-expression. From this time on, I began to break songs down into the smallest fraction possible. And as I worked on them, I became obsessed with pitch. I didn't have any terminology for this, but years later in an interview, I heard Maria Callas refer to this habit as straight jacketing—the exacting detail work you do before you add any of your own interpretation. I wish I'd heard that interview sooner. Of course, I probably wouldn't have listened. There's nothing like being called on the carpet by a world famous genius to raise your consciousness.

SEVENTEEN

Opening the MASS

(Circa 1971)

FINALLY AFTER ALL OUR INDIVIDUAL preparation and a bit of group work, we were brought into a brand new rehearsal hall, the largest so far—it was VERY large. The entire creative staff; Leonard Bernstein; Alvin Ailey; Oliver Smith (set designer); Alvin Ailey dancers, both adult and children's choirs and all soloists were finally together for the first time. We began at the first note of the piece and stitched it together in its entirety for the first time. We all found out at the same moment that there was a plot, a theme, and an overarching idea behind it: A crisis of faith.

It was also the first time we saw Judith Jamison and the rest of the Ailey dancers do their thing. Ms. Jamison, particularly, had a series of staggering variations in a wonderful flowing costume. We were all suitably amazed. But shockingly, we also found out that we were all there in the service of the star— Alan Titus. Yes, that attractive young man with the guitar, who had been off rehearsing separately, had ALL the music, all the drama, and a tremendous mad scene at the end entitled, "How Easily Things Get Broken."

There was a moment when we were supposed to fall to the ground at the end of that piece. We had been told that Alan would tear off his vestment, smash the host and chalice to pieces and we would just lie there. That's all we knew. What we didn't know was that Alan would launch off into this aria—rivaling the mad scene in *Lucia*—while we just remained motionless. Alan did a terrific job. We'd really never heard him sing full-out, only a little crooning with a guitar before this. Here he was singing over a two octave range and running the full range of dynamics from pianissimo to forte to Sprechstimme (speak-singing).

The piece finished and then the oddest thing happened—unprecedented really. Someone started to cry, then someone else, and then slowly the entire room began to weep out loud. It would be forty years before I would see anything like it again. I don't know if it was because it was so powerful; or because we were in the presence of Bernstein, an undisputed genius; or because we were all jealous of Alan Titus; or because we were furious that our parts were so small—or all of the above. But, EVERYONE was crying. Bernstein himself was crying and going around kissing everybody—as he was wont to do. It was common knowledge, that if you were around "Lenny" for any length of time, you were bound to be slobbered on.

There was one person who definitely was not crying. Mari Kajiwara, the great Alvin Ailey dancer, found the whole display of emotion utterly repugnant and rolled her eyes like a cartoon character. Mari was a tough cookie. I once was struck dumb by her "Fix Me, Jesus" solo in *Revelations* at City Center in Manhattan. And when I told her afterwards how amazing she was, she just rolled her eyes in that droller than droll way of hers and said, "Naaaah, I was off my balance all night." Recently I discovered that she passed in 2001. What a terrible loss.

By the way, the "Secret Songs" finally did arrive, and they were something like a tag at the end in which several of us took part, singing, "Lauda Laude." It was about sixteen more bars for each of us—hardly the great opus for which we had been pining. Of course, it was VERY beautiful, but it was also a half-step higher than I could actually sing. You haven't lived until you've sung sixteen bars that are a half step too high for you with Leonard Bernstein and a symphony orchestra—unless, of course, you've recorded it for Columbia Records.

When the day of the Kennedy Center grand inauguration finally arrived, the security was fantastic. You couldn't go anywhere without a plastic pass around your neck. The stage door was swamped with press. The brand new scarlet red opera house was truly a thing of beauty that managed to make a 2,000-seat house seem somehow intimate. The acoustics were terrific—which is always iffy in a new hall. And we were all very excited. By the way, the dressing rooms were fantastically appointed, and believe me, this is not the norm. A dressing room with well-lit mirrors, space to stretch out and a private bathroom—is heaven.

The glittering audience was packed with celebrities, politicians and all the living Kennedys. The performance went fantastically and there was a lot of positive reaction at the ends of numbers. Then, we reached the climactic moment when Alan Titus, standing atop a seemingly endless staircase—Mr. Smith had designed it in a forced perspective so that it seemed to go up into infinity—smashed the plaster host and chalice to the ground and broke them into a thousand pieces.

We all fell to the ground expecting to hear Alan's first note, but what we heard was a woman screaming from the back of the auditorium in a very high and shrill voice, "Theees ees a sacreeleeege! Theees ees a sacreeleeege!" I took the accent for Armenian. She kept this up until the ushers literally carried her from the building. Alan then began his mad scene and we finished the piece to a great ovation. (By the way, the "Armenian" woman came back three more times and did the exact same routine including the being-carried-out-of-the-building part. Someone should have told her that it would really have been more dramatic if she'd only done it once.)

A fantastic exchange happened in the boxes on that opening night. Maestro Bernstein was seated in one box—Maurice Perez was conducting that night—and the Kennedys were in the next. The only separation between the boxes was a short partition—not even three feet high—so they were quite accessible to each other. During the gigantic ovation, flashbulbs were flashing, film crews were rolling and Leonard Bernstein was full on weeping. He reached across the partition to embrace Rose Kennedy, but she thrust up a bony hand between them and hissed, "My MAKE-UP!" Now, that's a matriarch.

EIGHTEEN
The Recording
(Circa 1971)

I HAD MADE ONE RECORDING before *Mass*, namely *No, No, Nanette*. But in *Nanette* I had not one moment that was my own, not one peep. So the recording of *Mass* was a big deal to me for hosts of reasons: It was a premiere original work; written and conducted by Leonard Bernstein; and I had solos. Also, by one of those curious strokes of fate my part was about to become larger.

Works like *Mass* are always done, as they say, for scale—this means that the management knows that you are desperate to do it, so they won't offer you any money above the minimum rate required by the union. When everyone has to settle for exactly the same salary—this is called favored nations. Scale and favored nations are two things no performer wants to hear. But the reality is that if you're not a huge Hollywood star and a project is prestigious, you do it—for scale.

There was one young soloist whose agent had apparently not heard about this rule and was holding out for more money. So without even bothering to tell him, the management came to me, and a couple of other soloists, and asked us to learn his parts for the recording. This is how I ended up on the "God Said" portion of the recording as well as the "Letter from a Young Soldier." Those two bits, together with my own "I Don't Know" solo and the "Lauda" section, meant that I would actually be featured on the recording, something that had never occurred to me.

Certain parts of the recording were done in the yet to be inaugurated symphony hall at the Kennedy Center and the rest were recorded in Columbia Studios. It wasn't until I had actually gone into the studio to record these new sections that the young man who should have been doing them, found out that he had been removed from the recording. I just happened to be standing there when he came running into the building and crashed into the studio doors—which were glass, two inches thick and locked. He stayed there until Bernstein finally went out and spoke with him, but the train, as they say, had left the station. I felt terrible for him—but I still recorded his solos.

We were in the Symphony Hall when it came time to record my favorite bit the "I Don't Know" section—you know, "the only time I was truly alive" one. There were a lot of people in that hall. At one point I saw Bernstein speaking with Aaron Copland on the stage. I could kick my ass around the block for not going up and shaking Aaron Copland's hand. He is one of my favorite composers and many critics said that the best parts of *Mass* sounded like vintage Copland. He and Lenny were, of course, great friends. But all that aside, this was a unique opportunity that I missed. I just didn't know how precious moments were then. I would never cross paths with Aaron Copland again.

What I'm trying to convey is that there was an entire symphony orchestra on stage; a bunch of cutthroat soloists; a couple of large chorales; random famous people standing around and I was coming to my ultimate moment with Leonard Bernstein on the podium conducting. It was a big deal to me and as we got closer and closer to my big moment, I became more and more nervous. Then, just as we reached the measure where I would burst into song, the orchestra contractor called a break.

Orchestra breaks are not like actor breaks. There's none of this "take five" business for orchestra members. When they stop, they're going to be out for 20-minutes, at least. But eventually, every torture must end and we all reconvened. Somehow, I was going to have to start this very agitated solo from a dead stop. Maestro Bernstein mounted the platform, clicked his stick on the stand, turned his head back to me and in a loud and clear voice pronounced in front of all these people, "Mr. Dixon, as only YOU can." I don't care why he did that, or what he meant by it. He may have only been trying to get me back up to the place where I needed to be to sing his song, but it was a hell of a moment and I did my solo in one take. Even today, I am rather pleased with it.

Leonard Bernstein gave each of us the first page of our most major solo on opening night with an inscription for each person who had introduced it.

Mine was, of course, "What I Need I Don't Have" and under those lyrics, he wrote, "But what I needed I did have, exactly you! Eternal thanks, Leonard Bernstein." How could I ever have imagined this when I opened my record club copy of *West Side Story* all those years before in Norman, Oklahoma?

None of the reviews for *Mass* were what we expected. Bernstein had reached a kind of mythic plateau where nothing he ever did was regarded as worthy of what had gone before. Also his political leanings were very out of step with the mainstream and he had made many enemies. They were merciless to him in the press and didn't bother to mention any of us at all. What a curious introduction to the big time. To be in *No, No, Nanette*—a nostalgic pabulum, which was canonized, followed by *Mass*—a lofty endeavor, which was castigated. Good preparation for a life in the theater.

Something besides *Mass* happened during our run at the Kennedy Center. One day, some company members who were staying at the very pricey hotel next door, came in complaining about their lavish digs. They were paying all this money for the beauty and convenience of a first-class hotel—I was several blocks away in a much lesser establishment—and they were practically being held prisoner. It seems that the Secret Service had overrun them and was making life impossible in the lobby, elevators and hallways. The confused tenants were angry and it would be some time before their questions would be answered. Their hotel was, of course, the Watergate. And to think only a few months before, I had shaken hands with the man at the center of that scandal—he with the perpetual five o'clock shadow and comic book nose. Yes, I was actually present for the demise of Richard Nixon. The man who—had it not been for a disgusted Oklahoma City army sergeant—would have sent me to die in Viet Nam.

Mass went on to the Philadelphia Academy of Music, a gorgeous, rococo, old world hall with near perfect acoustics, and then to New York and the Metropolitan Opera. In just a few short weeks, I had gone from the Kennedy Center to Lincoln Center. How do I describe my first entrance backstage at the Metropolitan Opera to my gigantic dressing room behind that massive stage? Heady? Exhilarating? No—crushing. As I cleared security, an older, jaded soloist hissed at me, "Enjoy it now, 'cause you'll NEVER be back here!" Wow, guess her career hadn't been all she had hoped.

It was the most amazing dressing room I had ever seen, or would ever see, for that matter. There were two gorgeous make-up mirrors with light booms that could be adjusted any way imaginable. A Persian Carpet, a piano of my own, and a chaise lounge! I shared this "palace" with Hector Mercado—

the fantastically handsome and muy macho Alvin Ailey soloist. You could never tell if Hector had just come from a ballet barre or a knife fight. One day, one of the company members suggested that Hector "spend the evening" with him and his gorgeous fashion model wife. Hector was incandescent with rage. "Ah tell you one ting. When ah have sex weeth hees wife, he ees definitely NOT gonna be dere."

The most interesting part for me every day was singing the "Lauda" section into the amazing auditorium of the Metropolitan Opera. I would stand there doing a beautiful piece of music with a symphony orchestra and singing one half-step higher than I was actually able to sing, into a hall where the greatest singers in the world sang on a daily basis. Now I know that there have been many famous singers who were singing things a half-step higher than they wished at the Met, but I didn't know that then.

We played a full month at the Metropolitan Opera House. Then, just as amazingly as it had started, this heady world came to an end. A few of us did a brief television appearance with Maestro Bernstein on a PBS show called "The Great American Dream Machine" and then, it was over. I was just another unemployed actor/singer living in Hell's Kitchen.

One night, many years later, I fell asleep with the radio on and was awakened in the middle of the night by someone singing beautifully. I became conscious and thought to myself, "Wow, I wish I could sing like that!" And then I realized that it was me! They were playing the "Lauda" section of Leonard Bernstein's Mass. Perhaps my high A natural had been better than I thought.

NINETEEN

The Student Prince

(Circa 1973)

DURING *NO, NO, NANETTE* I had taken a little apartment at 515 West 48th Street. When people would hear the address they would say, "Five Fifteen? Is that in the Hudson River?" It was very far west—between 10th and 11th Avenues. It was three rooms for $78 a month—a cold-water, railroad flat with the bathtub in the kitchen. It would easily rent today for $2,000 a month. The times, they are a changin'.

During this period a new facet of my life developed. A dancer from the chorus of *No, No, Nanette* asked me to help him with his singing. Let's just say singing was not his thing. I thought, "What harm can I do? I can't make it any worse than it is." So I took him on as a student. He was taking Helen Gallagher's performance class. She noticed that his technique improved noticeably under my tutelage, so Helen began sending me "damaged" voices. Soon, I had a whole studio full of the most excruciating noises you've ever heard, some of them belonging to people three times my age.

(A friend asked me to insert a brief description of "the teaching of singing" here. To put it succinctly; one gets a student to vocalize until the voice can be stretched over two octaves. Sometimes this alone is a very long process. Then they must learn to do this on all ten vowels in the English language—other languages have more. And then they must study diphthongs, when two or more vowels are connected together—a major stumbling block in English singing for many singers. Then you find the best area of a person's voice—which in some cases is confined to only two or three notes—and try to expand that "good" area over the whole two

octaves. Only then do you start breaking down lyrics and finding out how to make the vowels and diphthongs function to their full capacity while pronouncing the words on pitches—then the act of "interpreting" begins. When people try to interpret before they've established a working instrument, unhappiness ensues. That's as brief as I can make it.)

I got a gig singing the works of new composers at Lehman Engel's BMI Workshop. BMI (Broadcast Music, Inc.) was the alternative union to ASCAP (American Society of Composers, Authors and Publishers) for composers. Lehman, a well-known conductor and composer—he was particularly known for conducting operettas—had created this workshop to foster young composers and lyricists. For something like $50, I sang the works of several new artists. But one of them stuck out easily from the rest. This particular composer had written a musical version of *Casanova* and I debuted a new song for the title character, "In the Middle of the Eighteenth Century." It was by a young and then unheard of composer, Maury Yeston. Twenty-five years later after he won the Tony Award for *Titanic*, I called to congratulate him—he still had the same phone number. He was extremely gracious and said, "May what happened to me happen to you." Maury's song got a standing ovation on the BMI Workshop, a first for me in New York or anywhere else for that matter. But I was still unemployed.

Then, I got a curious phone call—from Lehman Engel—about a new staging of *The Student Prince,* which he himself was mounting and conducting. It seemed that at the audition, because they were seeing so many singers, they had used numbers instead of names to keep track of the applicants. When they cast the role of Detlef—the young man who sings the famous "Drink, Drink, Drink" song—they had used the wrong number and hired the wrong person. It seems that this "wrong person" arrived at the first day of rehearsal unable to sing or dance or act—at all. The show was about to go on an extended tour of the U.S. and was booked to come back to the Winter Garden Theatre on Broadway. Lehman wanted to know if I could replace the Detlef and leave on tour the next week. "Yes, Lehman, yes I could."

I don't know that I've ever seen a group of people so glad to see anyone as the cast of *The Student Prince* was to see me that first day when I walked into Broadway Arts rehearsal studio. "Drink, Drink, Drink" is a very high and very difficult song. The cast was very gracious to me. The two leads were Bonnie Hamilton—a glorious soprano who is now a famous opera teacher; and Harry Danner—a wonderful tenor and the man I had replaced as Cable in *South Pacific* at Casa Mañana. But the actual star of the show and the engine behind the entire production, was the man playing Lutz, the comic lead; a man I would come to regard as the greatest character actor of the 20th century—George Rose.

I didn't know who George Rose was. In fact, I didn't know what a character actor was. Before he arrived, people were telling me what a great actor he was. Imagine my shock when in walked a rather fey unprepossessing man of medium build and no particularly defining characteristics. "What good could he possibly be?" thought I, in my youthful wisdom. Then, he walked to the center of the room and turned this absolutely "nothing" role of Lutz into the *raison d'etre* for the entire production.

Lutz was one of those roles regarded as a Vaudeville turn—someone from the old comedy circuit hired for their own particular brand of "schtick." George had it put in his contract that he could say or do anything he wanted in this part with no regard for text or staging. Such was his star power at this point—and he hadn't even won the first of his several Tony Awards. He could take the most uninteresting piece of script and whip it into a soufflé of side splitting humor.

I couldn't stop watching him and I was absolutely terrified of him. On tour I would stand in the wings and watch him in every scene—I had no idea that I would ever become a character actor myself—I just found him and his whole skill set an utter amazement. He had this uncanny ability to tear the fabric of the fourth wall—that invisible barrier that separates the stage from the audience—and intrude. He could take the sleepiest Mid-western audience, shake them to full attention and reduce them to weeping with laughter. His talent was simply staggering.

I became friends with George on that tour in my own timid way—it's hard to imagine that I was actually timid, but that was the way I saw myself at the time. I would drop in on him in his dressing room unannounced, and though I never felt he was particularly happy to see me, he would tell me amazing theater stories then barrage me with questions: "Who is your favorite Slavic soprano? What is the principle behind the jet engine? Who is the worst American politician?"

His knowledge of virtually all things seemed to verge on the infinite. He was an avid reader and political activist—I believe he was a socialist, although he never actually said so. He always had the most curious newspapers on hand with the most salacious political headlines. He seemed to love knocking people off-balance. And, since he scared the crap out of me, I was an easy mark. Nevertheless, I spoke with him whenever I could.

I was very upset when we arrived at the Canadian border and George unceremoniously left the tour. There was some problem about him having something in his possession that could not cross the border into Canada. He was traveling in a Winnebago. What on earth could he have had in there? I assumed it was an immigrant grocery clerk or some such companion, as George had alluded to his affection for "coffee colored boys."

Well, whatever the reason, he did leave the tour and was replaced by Ray Walston, famous for *My Favorite Martian* on TV, and for having created the role of the devil in the original *Damn Yankees* on Broadway, for which he won a Tony Award. To say that Mr. Walston was a disappointment would be a monumental understatement. Not only did we all love George, his performance raised our little operetta to the level of something actually noteworthy. Mr. Walston was not even remotely funny, was not a nice person, and he sunk our show like a stone.

Whatever had driven Ray Walston to stardom in the old days, had died. It was my opinion that booze was to blame—though I have no proof—but a lot of alkies are funny. Mr. Walston was not. He also had developed a curious eye ailment that made him averse to bright lights, so whenever his character—the comic relief—would enter the stage, the lights would dim. Comedy poison. He never got a laugh in the show except when he put moves on all the young women in the wings. Yeah, he was a real delight.

At his first performance, he walked onto the stage where my character is supposed to be asleep with my head down on a table. Without any warning, he picked up my head by my hair, and then slammed my head back down onto the table—hard. I did not appreciate this. But it's verboten to talk to another actor about his performance, so I went to the stage management—and asked them to take care of it. Apparently they were none too circumspect about their presentation of my complaint because the next day I was confronted in the wings by Mr. Walston, who screamed in my face, "I thought we were all ACTORS here!" I believe that was our last heart-to-heart.

Luckily, when we returned to the United States, Mr. Walston departed and dear George Rose rejoined the tour—amid much Winnebago speculation. To celebrate his return to the company, George decided to throw in one of his best onstage surprises. Since he could say and do anything he wanted, he was very fond of trying out new jokes, especially when we, the student corps, were all standing at attention and unable to react. For his re-entry into the company, he worked out a routine with Ted Tinley—the ancient character man who played his butler.

Ted appeared to be 90-years old and weighed about 90 lbs. Ted was very fond of gin. All of the students, being in the 25-ish age range fully expected poor little Ted to die before the tour ended. One day in Dallas, we were waiting in the wings to go on stage and Ted fell over on his face, like a board. "Oh, my God, he's dead!" lisped a wispy tenor. But Ted, already scrambling back onto his feet muttered, "No, I'm fine. I'm fine." He was dead all right—dead drunk.

As a comic bit, George would pile every bit of luggage onto Ted for every entrance. It was empty and weighed virtually nothing, but the sight of George's long-suffering servant carrying all those "heavy" bags, was hilarious. On that particular night, George began playing his departure scene with Ted as if the two of them were lovers and that Ted was leaving him after a particularly nasty quarrel. We were all standing at attention throughout this entire scene, unable to react. While Ted struggled to leave the stage with all the heavy bags, George whined:

"How could you leave me? How could you leave me after all our years together?

"What?"

"After all the lovely presents I gave you?"

"You...never... gave... me... nothin'!"

"What about that lovely canary I gave you in a cage?"

"That... canary... had... only... one... leg."

"Well, it was a singer not a dancer."

I don't know how long it was before the scene could go on, but it was quite some time.

One thing about Lehman Engel: he was mean. At our dress rehearsal in the Winter Garden Theatre, with a full house, he stopped the orchestra in the middle of Harry Danner's serenade and yelled to him on stage, "BLEAT...LESS!" Harry did have a fast vibrato—but then so do a lot of great singers—and to do this in front of an audience—unforgivable.

A bedraggled acne ridden chorus boy immediately began having a "relationship" with Lehman. The boy fancied himself a composer and would have done anything to get ahead. Lehman was short, fat, bald, sick and old—not the perfect consort for a very young man—oh, and did I mention...mean?

There was a really embarrassing moment when we arrived in Washington, D.C. Lehman had been off the tour for a couple of weeks doing another job, so he hadn't seen the kid for a while. This bedraggled boy and Lehman were the only company members staying at the Watergate, while the rest of us were in a much cheaper hotel. When the tour bus stopped at the Watergate to let this poor kid off, he came walking down the aisle of the bus with all Lehman's luggage—shades of Ted Tinley.

Lehman was already at the hotel and standing in the portico. The youth, who had recently begun a new complexion treatment, stood hopefully before Engel. Lehman looked him up and down and croaked, "Oh, I didn't recognize you without your acne." I regard myself as ambitious, but I never wanted ANYTHING enough to sidle up to the likes of Lehman Engel.

I can't leave *The Student Prince* without telling one rather complex but obscure little story. There was a curious practice among the chorus boys of that show—they were very fond of taking songs from the show and changing the lyrics backstage. For instance, they liked singing the line, "Blossoms drop from the trees" and substituting the word "dildos" for "blossoms." For whatever reason, the boys found this constantly amusing no matter how many times they heard it. On stage one particular night, a rather ungainly tenor decided to sing that particular lyric for his own amusement. Now, the rest of the very large ensemble, including all of the principals, was singing the correct lyric. But by a cruel turn or fate, Lehman just happened to be looking at this one misbehaving lad. Mr. Engel called the entire company together afterward and gave this poor schlub a public dressing down, the likes of which I had never heard. It continued long after it had become pointless and embarrassing. To make matters worse, not one day later, this errant fellow discovered that he had contracted hepatitis from his rather prodigious sexual efforts on the tour. Not only did he have to depart, yellow and in shame, but all the rest of us had to have inoculations at the company's expense. It was how you say—embarrassing.

However, there was a rather disheveled baritone on the tour who was something of an über-nerd inventor. He came up with a truly inspired send-off idea. He bought a dry cell battery and attached it to an imitation tree procured from an HO miniature train store. Then ran metal wires out the branches and attached small nails to the ends with the heads of the nails facing outwards. He took other small nails, covered them with putty and formed them into miniature dildos. He turned on the dry cell battery and when electricity ran through the wires to the attached nails, they became magnetized and held the little dildos in place. Once his invention was set, he called the departing yellow tenor into the green room with the rest of the company. About forty people strong and in 4-part harmony, we all sang "DILDOS DROP FROM THE TREES!" He pushed a button and all the miniature dildos rained to the ground. It was a very kind and very extreme gesture—the likes of which I never expect to see again. This nutty inventor was the Yin to Lehman Engel's Yang—a kind of healing through "nerdery."

I could have used a little healing myself. I had a messy on-going entanglement with one of the cadets, which had me in quite a state. My parents dropped in unexpectedly in Dallas and I refused to see them. (I don't think I saw my parents more than three times in my entire adult life.)

The tour ended and a few weeks later I was back in New York. As I was strolling down Greenwich Avenue in Greenwich Village, I saw George Rose walking his two dogs. They were Schipperkes—very beautiful and totally hateful creatures. They barked, snipped and snarled at everyone and everything— including each other—but they had beautiful coats, like black minks.

I was very happy to see George, and we stood on the corner chatting away. Suddenly, George stopped talking and watched a couple passing us on the street, a very fit young man with a gentleman at least twice his age. George watched them for a bit and then remarked, in that extremely cultivated English accent of his, "Well, you know, when a woman gets older she has to open her purse." It was the first time I had ever thought that George considered me a close enough friend to joke with me in that way. Immediately after that an extremely pumped-up muscle man swaggered by in a shirt much too small for his bloated physique. Once again, George stopped talking and watched him disappear down the street. Then he turned back to me and mused, "You know, whenever I see a man like that I always think, I'll bet he's got a dick like a summer rosebud." After I stopped laughing I thought to myself, "Wow, I'm friends with George Rose!"

He invited me back to his apartment for tea. I didn't care for tea, but I was thrilled at the prospect of spending more time with George, so I accompanied him to his apartment on Bank Street. The building was post-war modern and his apartment was large, yet rather dingy. It was spare to a surprising degree and besides seeming pretty beat up; it had a peculiar odor—of cats. Odd I thought, since I had just seen him with dogs. He told me to sit on his rather ratty sofa while he went off into the kitchen to boil water. Just then, the door to the bedroom opened. How odd—he didn't tell me he had a roommate. Then, into the room strode a very large adult mountain lion.

The thing was 4-ft. long, not including the tail. Its paws were 5-inches across and they made a little thumping sound as it padded intently and directly across the floor toward me. The lion had me fixed in his glistening golden eyes and I was utterly immobile, unable to speak or even twitch. The creature moved slowly and inquisitively toward me until his nose bumped unceremoniously up against my frozen knee. I had honestly never experienced this particular kind of terror. At that very moment, George came popping out of the kitchen and exclaimed, "Oh, you've met!" His off-the-cuff remark in no way masked the amusement he was taking in the whole proceedings. George gave the lion a piece of meat and it took a swipe at him with its mighty paw. He reprimanded it and it returned to the bedroom. I noticed for the first time numerous deep scratches on his hands. The naughty glee George exuded let me know that the whole thing had been a set up—he knew perfectly well what the animal would do when he left a guest with a strange scent sitting alone in the living room.

It turned out that there was actually a second mountain lion living in his normal, two-bedroom apartment. The second lion was a female, apparently the less aggressive partner of the male I had just met. She remained in the bedroom during our entire visit. It turned out that among George's many political leanings, he was an avid animal rights activist. He had rescued these two mountain lions from some terrible situation and they had been living with him in his Winnebago on tour. This is why he was unable to cross the border into Canada. I had been thinking much too small with my grocery clerk suspicions. Perhaps if I'd had less respect for George, this would have been our last meeting. But my admiration for him was so great that his eccentric behavior just added to his whole mystique. We would be friends for many years.

TWENTY

The Santa Fe Opera

(Circa 1974)

I HAD ALWAYS FELT CONFLICTED about my operatic leanings versus my musical comedy self, so after *The Student Prince* closed, I auditioned for and was accepted into the apprentice program at the Santa Fe Opera. I thought to myself, "Now I'm finally in the world of art." You may notice a theme here. I often make ridiculous assumptions.

I arrived in hot, dusty, run-down Santa Fe, New Mexico. Yes, there is the glamorous jet-set, Jacuzzi-next-to-the-pool Santa Fe; that's not where I was. Without credit cards, a salary of $75 a week and no savings, my Santa Fe prospects were grim. And to make matters worse, room and board were not included with my salary. I checked into the cheapest housing available, the De Vargas Hotel, and my hope died like an opera heroine. It was a ramshackle wreck of a place, with a strange gnome-like man behind the broken down reception desk—he looked like an extra from *Night of the Living Dead*. The place was not air-conditioned—in the desert.

The mere act of getting to my dingy room was a very strange journey in itself. I had to climb up half a staircase, walk down a long hall that was so twisted—ala *The Cabinet of Doctor Caligeri*—that you couldn't see the other end of it. When I reached the end of the hall, I would walk down half a flight of stairs and come to the worst couple of rooms in the place. One of them was mine. The wooden door didn't look like it could withstand a slight nudge without bursting open. The room was barely furnished, and yet, not clean—it had that peculiar hotel mildew smell that nothing will remove. It overlooked a gravel parking lot. Ghosts seem to be in every shadowy corner. I would not have restful sleep at the Hotel De Vargas.

The next morning, I was picked up in a school bus to be taken to rehearsal. I had heard about the glories of Santa Fe before my arrival, but that ride across the desert to the Opera House may as well have been across the surface of Mars—the hot side. The yellow conveyance was filled with other apprentices, one more ungainly than the next, except one; he had been selected by the management for his beefcake value. One slight downside to Mr. Beefcake, he was denser than plutonium.

The first conversation I heard between three very large fellow apprentices went something like this:
"Have you heard my high C?"
"YOUR high C? What about MY high C!"
"Well, if you want to talk high C's…"
It was going to be a long summer.

I was given the tiny role of Nepomuc in *La Grand-Duchesse de Gerolstein*, starring the marvelous British mezzo, Ann Howard. She had the most amazing sense of humor and the most amazing figure, displayed to its utmost in very low-cut ball gowns. Other than playing this small part in a funny operetta, I was bored out of my mind. The first time I actually sang on the Santa Fe stage, I walked off into the wings and went right down to the floor. I had forgotten about the altitude. (Note to self: Just because you're in the desert doesn't mean you're at sea level.) The Santa Fe Opera is at 7,000 feet.

The management, in their infinite wisdom, hired a British tenor to play opposite Ms. Howard. He was not an attractive man. He did not know the role. He could not speak French. He could not sing. All in all, perhaps not the ideal choice.

During vocal rehearsals, he would bury his face in his book. And when it came time for him to sing, he would mumble in a sort of half falsetto, "Mu bu du su ne pas du," instead of the French text. I remember thinking, "Wow, he must really sound great when he sings out, or surely he would not be here." Then came opening night; Ann Howard was knocking her part out of the ballpark, she was very well known for her Duchesse and she really delivered the goods. But, when the tenor made his entrance, he walked to center stage, put his head down and murmured inaudibly, "Mu bu du su ne pas du" just as he had done in rehearsal. After that performance he came to the opening night party, got very drunk and made passes at all the chorus girls. We never saw him again. He was replaced by an absolutely marvelous American tenor named John Walker. John was not just good, he was very, very good, but he was already playing Tamino in *The Magic Flute*, and the Painter in *Lulu*. This meant that he was doing three very large, very hard parts in revolving opera repertory.

I was standing by for the Painter. I had learned it with a pitch pipe in my dusty room at the De Vargas. There were, of course, no pianos available to learn an atonal role in one of the hardest operas in the world. Alban Berg wrote *Lulu* in the tone-row system—a way of composing that absolutely guarantees that there will be no recognizable harmonies as known in Western music. Also—unlike his his *Wozzeck*, which keeps a constant rhythm for long stretches—every measure of *Lulu* is in a different time signature, so you can never quite catch your balance. The idea of learning it with a pitch pipe is simply insane. However, learn it I did. I was that bored—and that poor. I couldn't go out for a drink or movie even if the opportunity presented itself, which it did not. The one night I actually managed to come up with a "date," I was confronted by the desiccated gnome at the front desk who demanded that I pay extra. I moved out instead and lived in a broken down mobile home.

I had a private coaching with one of the assistant conductors. He was astounded that I actually knew the part of the Painter—apparently none of my compatriots with the stunning high C's had learned their *Lulu* covers. He reported my feat to the management. I should probably note that I had been something of a pain in the ass all summer. I was hot, tired, poor and had been promised a lot of perks before I arrived. No perks appeared and I was damned angry. I had words with Richard Gaddis, who ran the apprentice program— he was wound tighter than a rubber band around Pavarotti's midriff—and I got the impression that no one had ever spoken frankly with him about anything, much less his apprentice program.

So, imagine my surprise when the ancient phone in my dusty room rang and Mr. Gaddis, in a rather unctuous voice, inquired if it was actually true that I had learned my *Lulu* cover. It seems that the valiant John Walker had finally succumbed to his work load and did not feel that he would be able to sing the Painter that night. I had actually had a part of one rehearsal with the wonderful singing actress Patricia Brooks, who was playing Lulu, when John was held up at another rehearsal. That's PART of one rehearsal. I have never believed in saying, "No" (except to the draft), so I told Richard Gaddis that I would indeed save his ass. Actually, I just said, "Yes."

I was picked up by a limo—not exactly what I had become accustomed to in my Santa Fe life—and taken to the theater. Every step I took backstage, someone would race up to congratulate me, always with the codicil, "Do you ACTUALLY know it?" I was starting to question whether I really did or not.

I was on my way to wardrobe—of course, I had no costumes, wigs or make-up for the part—when I heard a commotion in the hallway that connected all the dressing rooms. I went out to find John Crosby, the founder and artistic director of the Santa Fe Opera (and the conductor of *Lulu*) in full white tie and tails standing on his head in the middle of the concourse.

I should explain a bit; John Crosby was crazy. I am not a psychiatrist and am not medically trained to make informed diagnoses of mental patients, so I cannot specify if he was schizophrenic, bi-polar or manic depressive, but John Crosby was crazy. I don't mean it like when a friend of yours is acting silly and you say, "Oh, he's so crazy!" No, John Crosby was <u>crazy</u>.

He could be in the middle of conducting a very lively scene—in *La Bohème*—and suddenly flip to a dirge-like tempo appropriate for say, Tristan's death. Or, he could be in the middle of addressing the company and suddenly fall silent and begin looking up at the sky with his lips still moving as if he was hearing some kind of spirit voice. He could start screaming at someone, anyone, for anything at any time with no provocation whatsoever. It is enormously impressive that such a man managed to raise millions of dollars and build his own opera company in the middle of the desert so that he could conduct operas. That being said, John Crosby—was crazy.

So, there was the conductor of *Lulu* standing on his head in full evening attire in the center of the concourse of the Santa Fe Opera. He waited until the entire company had silently gathered to stare at the exhibition he was making. Then, he slowly righted himself, sauntered over to William Lewis—the illustrious other tenor of the evening—and whispered quite audibly in his ear, "Have you noticed, that the statues on the set, have not been circumcised?" Then, he ambled slowly and silently toward the pit.

It would be incorrect to say that I was frightened—there's actually not a word for what I was at that moment. I was about to perform an extremely difficult (and high) role; in an atonal, tone-row opera; that I had not rehearsed, been staged into, or had an orchestra read-through; I hadn't even met the rest of the cast; and yet—I was willing. Perhaps that's why the theater Gods at that moment caused John Walker to decide that his laryngitis was not as severe as he had previously believed. He went on and the whole thing was lifted off my shoulders. It would have made a better story if I actually had gone on and muddled through *Lulu* somehow, but that's not what happened. No limo was provided for my return. I got on the school bus and went back to my hovel.

Although the whole Santa Fe experience was excruciating, the management did ask me to repeat my little role in *La Grand-Duchesse de Gerolstein* when that production went to Baltimore. I stayed in a much nicer hotel than my first Baltimore experience with *No, No, Nanette* and the opening night went without a hitch. Then, I was taken to the opening night party in a car driven by a handsome young blond apprentice from the theater—who I just happened to be "dating." Who else was in the car? John Crosby.

At the party, they ran out of food before we arrived—someone had apparently gotten the catering numbers wrong. We left quickly, quietly and very hungry. We drove along for maybe a mile in silence, when suddenly Mr. Crosby wheeled on the young apprentice—who had nothing whatsoever to do with the opening night party—and screamed at the top of his lungs, "DO YOU THINK THIS IS ANY WAY TO RUN AN OPERA COMPANY? DO YOU?" We sat in stony silence all the way back to my hotel. As I got out I realized that Mr. Crosby was staying in the same hotel that I was, so I couldn't invite the apprentice upstairs. John and I slowly exited the car, silently crossed the lobby and entered the same elevator. The doors closed and we tentatively pressed our buttons. The elevator lurched as he leaned his face close to mine and whispered in a voice that sounded like Freddy Krueger in *A Nightmare on Elm Street*:
"Would you like—some peanuts? I have peanuts—in my room."
"No, thank you."
"I have peanuts."
Just then, the elevator doors opened and I ran out. I did not stop hyperventilating until my door was double-locked behind me. I decided to take a little break from the world of opera.

My second grade photo from Hollis, Oklahoma
wearing what is probably my favorite shirt of all time.

Rehearsing *The King and I* at Norman High School with Mabel Ritzman who introduced me to
the world of theater. Yes, I shaved my head... and I also painted that set.

Here I am at the Paramus Mall Theater in the world's worst production
of *My Fair Lady*. I did love that hat though.

My first professional headshot, taken by Van Williams during my time at *No, No, Nanette*.

The recording session for *No, No, Nanette* (my first) standing between
the fabulous Jack Gilford and the remarkable Patsy Kelly.

The climax of *Leonard Bernstein's Mass* at the Kennedy Center in Washington D. C.
I am the first guy on the right. Wish I had kept THAT shirt.

In *Berlin to Broadway* in 1975.

Taken by the great George Rose on a boat in the Dominican Republic.

The Lord Chancellor in Gilbert and Sullivan's *Iolanthe,* one of my favorite roles of all time.

As Thenardier in the original production of *Les Miserables* on Broadway with the marvelous Jennifer Butt.

A private backstage moment with Ozzy from the original Broadway
production of *The Scarlet Pimpernel.*

At the opening night party (at Tavern on the Green) for
The Iceman Cometh with Kathleen Turner.

Onstage with President Clinton after *The Iceman Cometh* on Broadway.

Rehearsing *Gore Vidal's The Best Man* for the Broadway revival. Shot by fellow cast member Jordan Lage.

TWENTY-ONE

Very Good Eddie

(Circa 1976)

THERE USED TO BE A running joke: If you wanted to make an actor nervous, you told them that David Merrick was in the audience. He was the most powerful producer in the theater when I arrived in New York and he remained so for many years. (*Hello Dolly; I Do! I Do!; Gypsy; 42nd Street,* countless more…) The mere mention of his name would make people tremble. It's hard to imagine something like that today. It's also hard to imagine how he ended up palsied, incoherent and incontinent after the sway he held for so many years. (As Tosca declares over Scarpia's dead body "E avanti a lui tremava tutta Roma" (And before him all Rome trembled)).

Merrick moved a decrepit Jerome Kern show called *Very Good Eddie* from the Goodspeed Opera House to Broadway. I saw it when it first opened. I could not understand for the life of me why he brought it in. He put no money into the sets, costumes or orchestrations, so it arrived looking and sounding just as it had on the tiny stage of the Goodspeed. It did have in it a staggeringly funny performance by Virginia Seidel, who seemed to be channeling Betty Boop via Molly Picon through Marilyn Monroe. She was absolutely hilarious, and in material that was clearly not. The critics embraced it unanimously—one of the great mysteries of that season. They had just slaughtered the delightful *Something's Afoot* that same week. "Who can explain it, who can tell you why…?"

I needed a job, so I auditioned for and got the national tour of *Very Good Eddie.* The catch was that this was not a singing part, it was a dancing part. I somehow made it through the extremely rigorous dance call and was cast as M. de Rougemont, the comic dancing lead in the show. I had to helm a gigantic dance number where I partnered with the very lovely Candy Darling—not the drag queen—the real girl. She was engaged to Meatloaf at the time, so I met him. The way you're imagining he would be—he was just like that.

My job was to portray a zany Frenchman with an accent you could cut with a knife and to perform this period dance number called "I've Got To Dance!" That number was such an aerobic workout it left me near retching every time I did it. Then, I would have to shout, "Encore!" and do the whole thing again. I never got used to it.

The show also had an amusing stunt in it that I executed twice at every performance. I've always been very limber, thank God, because I had to do the splits—twice—once on the floor and once on a staircase, 8 shows each week for a solid year. I got so used to it that I was able to stir it up on several occasions in later life when everyone—including myself—would have thought it quite impossible. You never know when something ridiculous is going to come in handy.

There was another performance—other than Virginia's—that I was very fond of in the show, by veteran comedian and old movie star, Benny Baker. He had replaced Jack Gilford on Broadway in *No, No, Nanette*. He always referred to himself as "The Old Jew" and I communicated with him for years using that moniker of his own choosing.

We shared a dressing room for most of the tour and he kept me in stitches. He would do things like bend over the sink to wash off his make-up, always in baggy underwear, and look nervously over his shoulder saying, "I ain't turnin' my back on you." His feigned fear that his 70-year old honor was imperiled by my presence, never ceased to make me laugh. He also had an uncanny ability to land in a new city and find the best greasy spoon and most authentic barbecue joint—neither of which he could digest. I think it was a divining skill he picked up on the Vaudeville circuit. I have particularly fond memories of being with him at the Royal Alexandra Theatre in Toronto because it was so old world—with winding metal staircases leading up to old dressing rooms and landings that overlooked the stage—just like the ones he had played on the Orpheum Circuit.

While we were in Toronto I was constantly listening to my new Sony Walkman—a brand new invention at the time. I always had on a tape of Birgit Nilsson, my favorite soprano. One day, after listening to her sing the impossibly difficult *Die Freischutz* aria on my little machine, I was so overcome with admiration that I sat down and wrote her an impassioned fan letter. I told her, among other things, that I was grateful to have been born in the same lifetime with her. Imagine my surprise when just a few days later, I received a beautiful piece of stationary delivered to the Royal Alexandra Theatre from the Metropolitan Opera. It was a handwritten note from Madame Nilsson, wishing me good luck with the show and hoping that I was enjoying the touring. She was at the absolute height of her fame at this point and it's unbelievable that she answered me the same week. Now, THAT'S a star.

I never tired of watching our own star, Virginia Seidel give her remarkable performance in the show. One performance, in some less than major city, I was finding the audience sluggish, while Ms. Seidel was getting huge rolling laughs. I stood in the wings watching her; she was just a tiny little thing in a frilly white dress. She stood motionless, her dainty hands dangling from her relaxed arms like a rag doll as she knocked joke after joke right out of the ballpark. When she walked off into the wings, I said, "My God, Virginia, you're absolutely killing them and you're in a state of complete relaxation. Your hands are just dangling off the ends of your arms like they're not even attached." She looked at me quizzically and said in a voice almost too high for the human ear, "Well, I'm not very strong." God, she was funny.

Reality is always the funniest joke. One day I was waiting for my entrance off stage left and a poor little chorus girl, direct from Georgia, sidled up next to me. She had just gotten her Equity union card and this was her first show and her first tour. She looked sad, so I asked her what was wrong. Almost tearfully she replied, "Before I come up North, I always heard about stage door Johnnies, but I always thought they was waitin' fer the GIRLS!" I almost missed my entrance.

I was having a fling with the most psychotic chorus boy in the company—I always had a soft spot for pretty psychos. He was in a long-term relationship with a Broadway star—who shall remain nameless, since he's STILL a star. For pure meanness, the chorus boy called up the star—who was headlining in a big Broadway hit—and told him that we were having a serious relationship. We weren't. The poor star ducked out on his matinee and flew to Chicago in tears, where I accidentally ran into him in the lobby of our hotel. Embarrassing. Interestingly enough, the psychotic chorus boy was also having a dalliance with the Georgia chorus girl from the previous story. No wonder she was confused.

We were terrorized by David Merrick's appearance in the audience on several occasions. People were always telling the most frightening stories about him, but I would not get my own genuine Merrick story until many years later. I was in the audience on opening night of *42nd Street* on Broadway—the night he kept Gower Champion's death a secret so he could announce it during the curtain call for added publicity. (Mr. Champion was the director *of 42nd Street*.) Merrick paced back and forth wringing his hands like a bad actor assaying Shylock. Being a showman doesn't necessarily mean you should be on the stage. In his old age, he married an ambitious chorus girl with whom I was acquainted. He then had a stroke and she had him committed to an institution. He escaped in a wheel chair during a torrential rainstorm wearing only his pajamas, had the marriage dissolved and limped on for years in a greatly diminished yet equally cantankerous state. Later I worked with Merrick's ex-wife and all she would say of these events was "Why doesn't he just DIE?" "E avanti a lui tremava tutta Roma."

I'm glad I got to meet David Merrick, a theatrical legend and I'm glad I did *Very Good Eddie*—the only time in my life I was ever the principle dancer. Thanks for the paychecks, Mr. Merrick, and thanks for those splits—they would prove useful at a later date.

One more thing about *Very Good Eddie*—I met my first "bad boy" on that tour. I suppose that my extreme fundamentalist upbringing had left me with a penchant for anything naughty, and I found the idea of meeting a "gentleman of the evening" the most exciting thing imaginable. I went back to New York and found my very own bad boy, fresh off the bus from Georgia at a dive called The Haymarket—a real den of iniquity. His name was Johnny (as in "stage door") and I saw him for the next EIGHT YEARS.

TWENTY-TWO

By Bernstein

(Circa 1975)

IN 1975 I GOT TO work with Leonard Bernstein, again. The Chelsea West-side Theater was doing a review using music cut from all of Lenny's previous shows. The book and concept were by Betty Comden and Adolph Green. (*Singin' in the Rain, The Band Wagon, On the Town, Wonderful Town...*) I thought my relationship with Bernstein might help me get the job. It did.

I was cast along with Janie Sell, who had just won the Tony for *Over Here!,* and Patricia Elliot, who had just won the Tony for *A Little Night Music.* They were both terrific; the show was not. It was great to be with Lenny, Betty and Adolph, but the show, based on flop songs from hit shows, was not a great idea.

There were about 7 of us in the cast all together and a couple of weeks into the process, we all went to a Chinese restaurant together for lunch. Some-how, the topic turned to how nervous we all were about opening a new show in New York with no out-of-town tryout. How much tension we felt rehears-ing in front of Bernstein, Comden and Green, and how we were all afraid of being fired.

Ted Thuston, the elder statesman of the group and a wonderful old char-acter man (*L'il Abner, The Most Happy Fella, Kismet*), spoke up and chided us, "What are you young people going on about? You're all so talented and none of you are going anywhere." When we got back from lunch, Ted was fired. Beside our upset at losing Ted, the man that they brought in from New York

City Opera to replace him was nowhere near as good. From that day forward the project was cursed.

Comden and Green, true show business royalty, could be slightly—self-concerned. Once, during a group photo, they literally shoved me out of the shot to get a better position. Betty came storming up to me after a preview performance and yelled, "Young man, you have too much make-up on your eyebrows!" I replied quietly, "I don't have ANY make-up on my eyebrows." "Oh," she replied and went on to the next person. One morning around 10 A.M., she got up on stage—it was only about a 4-inch rise—to address the company. She had obviously been having cocktails the night before, and although her make-up, hair and grooming were impeccable, it was clear that she was seriously nursing her head. She raised a hand to begin her address when suddenly she went over backwards like a board. It was like that scene in a cartoon when a character falls backwards and bounces like a basketball. We were all too stunned to move for a moment. But before we could, Betty leapt to her feet and resumed speaking as if it had never happened.

Adolph kept criticizing my diction on "Ring Around A Rosy," a very difficult and wordy number cut from *Candide*. Finally, Bernstein spoke up and said that it had over a two octave range and no one else could sing it at all, so he should just lay off. After rehearsal that day, I found myself in tandem with Adolph—whom I could never seem to engage in even the smallest conversation—out of nervousness I asked him if he would like to share the cab that I was currently hailing. "No, thank you." he replied. Then he walked up one car-length and took my cab.

One of my favorite Betty moments was at a rehearsal during previews. We put in an absolutely enormous amount of changes and no one knew how on earth we were going to remember them at the performance that night. There is a famous expression that people use during an out-of-town tryout when many changes are happening. They say, "Well, that's what we're on the road for." Betty Comden addressed the company and quipped, "Well, that's what we're in town for."

But over and above these amusing anecdotes was the fact that their book for the show was just an assemblage of cocktail references as if they were writing a 1950s Hollywood Movie. "Another Manhattan, anyone?" was out-of-sync with the production and the times. Worse than that however, was seeing the condition that Bernstein was in at this point. He was chain-smoking in the most disturbing way—absolutely without ceasing, and he had a young graduate student from Yale following him around with expensive Scotch and a bucket of ice on a silver tray. No, seriously, that was his job; he followed Bernstein around with Scotch on a silver tray.

It was an object lesson in stage craft to watch Janie Sell and Patricia Elliot avoid the pitfalls of the dicey material. And in spite of everything, I enjoyed the experience. I had a beautiful song that had been cut from *Peter Pan* called "Dream with Me." I recently obtained a pirated copy—you can get anything these days—and was reminded what a beautiful song and beautiful arrangement it was.

Well, I don't have to tell you that the show opened and was savaged by the critics. The cast mercifully was spared. But once again, they saved their big salvos for Lenny himself, most of them saying that he should be writing NEW material and not recycling his old. Of course, second rate material from Bernstein is better than first rate material from just about anyone else. Lenny had long been castigated in every review for throwing a party in his own home for the Black Panthers. I think the critics finally got tired of mentioning that just before he died. Legends always take on a different patina when the schlubs finally start to realize that we're all only passing through.

The show closed and I used my new nighttime freedom to go see some shows. I went to a preview of Sondheim's *Pacific Overtures* at the Winter Garden, and as I walked into the crowded lobby, there was Lenny surrounded by a large entourage. I had such a terrible feeling of separation seeing him "way over there." With the closing of *By Bernstein*, I was no longer a member of his coterie. Just then, Lenny saw me from across the crowded lobby, waved to me and shouted out, "Sorry about that, Ed!" He was apologizing for the untimely demise of *By Bernstein*. "Very Cool, Lenny! Real Cool!"

TWENTY-THREE

A Little More Summer Stock

(Circa 1976)

BY NOW I WAS GROWING rather weary of constantly going back to summer stock. It was holding less and less charm for me and I wanted to do new works. But I hadn't ruled it out just yet. I went to the North Shore Music Theatre to play Mr. Snow in *Carousel*, for which I was much too young, and the boy in Tom Jones and Harvey Schmidt's *Philemon*, for which I was much too old.

I had already performed *Philemon* once—damned odd—since it's a very rare work. I had forged a relationship with Jones and Schmidt (*The Fantasticks*) early on, and performed in several workshops in their own theater, called Portfolio in Hell's Kitchen. I can't remember just how we met, but Tom married Susan Watson's sister, Janet—Susan Watson was Nanette in *No, No, Nanette*—and very early on, we all just knew each other.

At one point Harvey Schmidt asked me to do some music copying work for him. Harvey, one of the most brilliant pianist and composers who ever lived, couldn't write down his own music. He composed it, but he played by ear, so someone else had to write it down. I was so young and stupid that when he asked me to work for him I was actually insulted. I remember thinking something like, "I have my OWN career to think about, damn it!" Young people can be very silly.

One of the workshops I did at Portfolio was *Philemon*, and now, here I was doing it at North Shore with Paul Sorvino, Christine Andreas and John

Reardon! (John Reardon's *Merry Widow* was the SECOND record I got from that record club.) We had a scene together, just the two of us, and I couldn't believe I was standing on stage singing with the man who had introduced me to operetta.

Paul Sorvino, who was not yet famous, kept telling us he was the greatest singer since Caruso and kept doing push-ups to show how strong he was. One night, we were in a very small Italian restaurant in this very small town and Paul—after a lot of vino—got down in the middle of the floor and did push-ups for all the clientele; while he sang a Neapolitan song. I am rarely speechless. I was that night.

One afternoon, I was in the car with Paul and his wife when they announced to me that they were having another baby. Some terrible political situation was going on in the world—as usual—so I mused out loud, "How can you bring a child into a world in this condition?" I was never able to keep my thoughts to myself—obviously. Paul looked knowingly at his wife as he condescendingly answered, "Someday, you'll understand." Well, thirty years later when Mia Sorvino won the Oscar and dedicated it to her dear old dad, I finally did understand.

Also in *Philemon* was Vanessa Shaw (from the all-black Broadway version of *Kismet* called *Timbuktu*) one of the most beautiful women I had ever seen. She "came out" of her very skimpy costume by accident on opening night, and since it was a theater-in-the-round, there was no place for her to hide her exposed bosom. Beverly, Massachusetts was agog. Later that night, we got together with another beautiful girl in the company—a blond—and went to see Dizzy Gillespie at a local club. None of us could believe that the great Dizzy was playing this miniscule little dive in Beverly, Massachusetts, so we just HAD to go.

Because I was with two gorgeous women, we were seated up front right next to the stage and right in front of Dizzy. Now, I'm not saying that Mr. Gillespie was ON something, but I am saying that Mr. Gillespie APPEARED to be on something. And a great deal of it. He spent the entire set sweating, blowing his cheeks out like a mating frog—which he was known for—and staring directly at Vanessa Shaw. It was fairly clear what he had on his mind, and it wasn't jazz—well, not the musical kind.

When the set ended, Dizzy ran back to his dressing room and Vanessa ran out of the club, because she had a date. Meanwhile, the blond moved over into Vanessa's seat to have more legroom. Just then, Dizzy came racing out of his dressing room at 100 miles an hour, aimed directly at the chair where Vanessa, only moments before, had been seated. He was about 2-inches in front of the blond's nose when he finally realized that something was wrong. Bug-eyed Dizzy blurted out, "What happened to the colored girl?" I guess when you're playing jazz clubs your whole life nobody sends you the latest politically correct phrase book. We tried to tell him we enjoyed the show, but he was already gone. Dizzy knew what he wanted.

John Reardon was too old to be playing Billy Bigelow, though he was still singing marvelously. (At one matinee, an ancient woman on the front row was so overcome by his "If I Loved You" that she passed out and slid down to the floor at his feet.) I was too young to be playing Mr. Snow. The sight of me with all those children and white shoe polish in my hair, and John with a too young Julie and black shoe polish in his hair—just wasn't very nice. But, the role of Julie was perfect for the very beautiful Christine Andreas.

She told me one afternoon that she thought she was going to be cast in the enormous revival of *My Fair Lady* being planned for Broadway. I thought she was out of her mind. I mean, she was perfect for it, but she had basically no credits and was very young. How could she possibly be cast as the lead in the FIRST major revival of *My Fair Lady*? Well, she was; Christine Andreas was Eliza Doolittle in that revival and she won the Theatre World Award.

George Rose was cast as Doolittle in that production, but meanwhile he was with us at North Shore playing Noah in *Two By Two*. So, I got to see him again, though this time when I saw his Winnebago parked out back, I knew exactly what was inside—or so I thought.

When *My Fair Lady* opened on Broadway, George's performance was absolutely staggering. This was truly George in his element. He was born into poverty in Lancashire, England, so he knew everything about the underside of British life. Not only did he stop the show dead with "Get Me to the Church on Time," his eyes did the most amazing thing during it; they seemed to have light pouring out of them which darted around the auditorium like some crazy 3-D movie. I've never seen anyone do anything like it.

When I went back to his dressing room afterward, he slammed the door behind me like a naughty child and demanded in a whisper:
"What did you think of Ian Richardson?"
"Not good."
"No, poor dear. No one can play Higgins who was born after the war."

I nodded in agreement, trying to look hip, but inside I was thinking, "WHICH WAR?" To this day I regret that I tried to act cool instead of asking him what the hell he meant. I thought Richardson was charmless with precious little voice for a Shakespearean actor. But I don't know what that had to do with any war.

When I asked George what on earth he was doing with his eyes during "Get Me to the Church." He looked like an even naughtier child and said, "It's very simple, dear. You just look at the lights." I laughed, but I knew perfectly well it was a great deal more than that. It was a GREAT performance. He won the Tony that year.

George had been so angry the previous year when he was nominated for Best Supporting Actor in *My Fat Friend*, with Lynn Redgrave—his part was actually larger than hers—that he had refused the nomination. Refused it, mind you! So this year, when he actually WAS playing the supporting role, they nominated him for BEST ACTOR and he won it over Ian Richardson. I guess George WAS born before that war.

TWENTY-FOUR

Brel, Identity and Schnorrers

(Circa 1977)

THINGS WERE NOT GOING MY way. I just wasn't getting the parts I wanted, I certainly wasn't getting them in New York and I wasn't getting any younger. I was almost 30! The only thing that appeared on my horizon was a little tour of *Jacques Brel Is Alive and Well and Living in Paris* in upper Massachusetts or some such place—maybe it was Rhode Island. Wherever it was, it wasn't where I wanted to be. I was very frustrated—very.

When I got the score, it seemed to me that Mr. Brel had also been very frustrated, judging by his material. And the score to *Jacques Brel* is published in some sort of handwritten chicken scratching. It takes an archeologist with a Rosetta Stone to make head or tail of it. But when I deciphered it, I found the ravings of a very angry man who felt just like I did. I LOVED working on it. Brel's music began to tap into something in my own psyche in a profound way. I knew that he was very ill and dying in Paris and I began to meditate in an attempt to communicate with him. I became convinced that he was communicating back in some booga-booga way and that he was guiding me. Never mind if this sounds insane. That's what I thought in 1977.

I was working with Elly Ellsworth, who replaced Elly Stone in the show off-Broadway. A very young Meg Bussert (*Camelot, Brigadoon, The Music Man*), was the second woman and Thom Christopher, a well-known soap actor, rounded out the cast. Joseph Rescigno, now a highly respected conductor and the nephew of Maria Callas's maestro, Nicola Rescigno, was our pianist and musical director.

One day, during a particularly slow moving rehearsal, I was seated back-to-back with Elly in folding chairs on stage. She calmly leaned over her shoulder and whispered, "What are we doing in this tired old show?" She had done twelve productions of it previously. "We should be doing something new and original." A light bulb clicked on.

I started writing my own show right then, based on the ideas that I was getting from working on Mr. Brel's material. He wrote about the mundane things that were going on in his life. I wrote about the mundane things that were going on in my life. I also wrote about one thing in my life that was definitely not mundane. I was having an affair with a married crew member and our behavior was salacious even by my laissez faire standards. That, incidentally, produced the best song in the show that I was writing—one that I would eventually transplant into another show many years later, while I was doing something even more scandalous.

I began wearing black all the time and pretending that I WAS Jacques Brel—an embarrassing and puerile affectation. But when the show opened, I actually did seem to be channeling old Jacques and it was what I would call the first big success of my performing life. For the first time I was doing something that was actually expressing my feelings. Even though I was in the middle of nowhere, in an old show, in a small venue, I felt that I was finally accomplishing something.

Opening night, I walked out to do "Amsterdam," a fantastic fireball of a number, and I had an out-of-body experience. I saw myself from the outside, standing right beside myself. I was being a conduit for all the rage and frustration, not only of my life, but of everyone in the audience. It was a profound experience. The audience went wild. The critics went wild. I went wild. If you ask me, it was my first real theatrical experience. I had been working professionally for 10 years.

I finished my own work, *Identity and Other Crises* and when I arrived back in New York, I found a producer and got it produced Off-Broadway. Saying it like that makes it sound so easy—and that's exactly how it was. I had just finished it and Barbara Beck, who was just starting to produce, heard it and offered to put it up. She asked me where I would like to have it done and I said that my dream venue would be Barbarann's Cabaret on 46th Street. I saw Maltby & Shire's *Starting Here, Starting Now* there, several times, and it's where I wanted my show to be. That's where it went.

Looking back, it's amazing to me, that when things like this happened in my early life, I was never particularly stunned at the miraculous unfolding of events. I always seemed to take note of the parts I didn't like, while ignoring the amazing course of things. I wasn't happy with the response to the piece; with the audiences we got; with the money that was made; with who came and who didn't come; or the fact that it didn't have a long run and make me a million dollars. Nevertheless, I had been produced in New York. I also had a little fling with my leading lady; one of only two such departures in my adult life.

With my new courage, I auditioned for—I'm sure I wore black—and was cast in the role of Belasco the fop, in a new venture by Judd Woldin—the composer of *Raisin*—called *King of Schonorrers*. It was based on a short story by Israel Zangwill. I thought it was the worst title I'd ever heard. "Schnorrer," is Yiddish for scoundrel—a person who lives by cheating others. The role of the head scoundrel would be played by Lloyd Battista, a soap opera star.

Lloyd Battista and I became friends. However, Lloyd was so famous from his soap that you could hardly walk down the street with him. I had never really understood the power of the soaps before this experience. I assumed that since they were of no importance to me, they weren't of any real interest to other people either. Big mistake.

King of Schnorrers was actually based on several stories by Zangwill and I was to play several parts—though the clothing-obsessed Belasco was my favorite. The show was to open the brand new Harold Clurman Theater on 42nd Street, recently reclaimed from its sordid history as a house of ill repute. The restoration was so new, that when we moved in we were afraid to touch anything for fear it might not have been disinfected. There was still an obscene hand-painted mural on one wall when we arrived.

Grover Dale was the choreographer and director (original cast of *West Side Story*). Grover was one of those choreographers who can only work on your body. If he wants to create a piece of choreography, you have to keep doing it until he sees something he likes. We worked on the opening number every day for the entire rehearsal process. It changed every single day, and not a little bit, it changed radically. After just a couple of weeks, I had so many versions of the opening number in my head that I couldn't remember which side of the stage I was entering. And we were poor people in merry old England, so we had baskets of fruits and vegetables strapped to our waists, one on each leg. They were made of wood and wire. After dancing for only a few minutes in these contraptions, they would cut into our legs. One chorus member quit the show over this opening number. The rest of us just complained and kept dancing. I had a great number in the second act with my wardrobe closet. No way was I quitting.

One of the upsides of the rehearsal process was that Grover Dale was married to the incredible Anita Morris—famous for her star turn in *Nine* on Broadway. No one who saw her do her thing in that musical will ever, and I mean ever, forget it. It didn't matter if you were old; young; male; female; gay or straight. When she came out in those 4-inch heels and that invisible lace body stocking and tied herself in a human knot while singing a high C upside down, you had been "had." It was hilarious watching the audience come unglued. If you saw Anita Morris in *Nine,* she had you.

Not only did we meet her at rehearsal, Grover invited us to their home and she cooked for us. One of those crazy occasions when you meet someone in real life and find out they are EXACTLY like they were on stage. Amazing. She was from another planet.

King of Schnorrers opened with no fanfare whatsoever, but it got a fantastic review in The New York Times. Suddenly, it was impossible to get a ticket and then we were informed that we were moving to Broadway. I was going to get to do that fantastic song on Broadway. Belasco's song, "I Have Not Lived In Vain" was a preening fop's love song to his wardrobe. The clothes came to life during the song and danced with me. The number built and built until finally I broke into a cadenza, a cadenza that went from a low F up the scale in a furious chromatic run, three octaves, to an F above high C—I would think that I was making this up, but recently I came upon a pirated recording of the show, and by God, there it was, a three octave run. I imagined how great it would be to do that on Broadway with a big orchestra and with proper sets and costumes. However, when we moved into the 48th Street Playhouse, we moved the show exactly as it had been at the Harold Clurman; small and tatty without one additional set, costume or orchestration. A disastrous move.

We kept rehearsing and changing the opening number every day, up to and including opening night on Broadway. I simply could not believe it when Grover put changes into that poor overworked number on opening day. I walked out that night in front of the critics and did the choreography from two days earlier; or was it three? It did not go well. The show did introduce a wonderful new leading man to Broadway, a very young and absolutely gorgeous John Dossett. But the poor little show looked and sounded ridiculous in a big house and it was soon gone.

TWENTY-FIVE

A Psychic from Hawaii and Other Things

(Circa 1979)

I WAS TEACHING A GREAT deal by this time and making a very good living. My clients ranged from virtually the entire cast of *A Chorus Line* on Broadway; to bored wealthy housewives from the Upper East Side; to a stripper from Brooklyn—Tammy-Temptation-and-her-Terrific-Terrier. Tammy was one of my favorite New York characters of all time. I had an 8-by-10 glossy photo of her on my wall, which had her in pasties and fishnets bending over and making a circle with her arms and her trained terrier jumping through them. It was right between my framed music from Leonard Bernstein and my letter from Birgit Nilsson.

One day after her lesson, we left the building together and were confronted by paramedics removing the lifeless body of my downstairs neighbor on a gurney through the hallway, with her white hair and bloodless arms trailing outside the sheet. My neighbor was well into her 90s, so it wasn't particularly upsetting, just unusual. As we waited for them to pass, I whispered to Tammy, "In a city as crowded as New York, it's amazing how seldom you see something like this." Tammy's eyes bulged out and she whispered back in a voice as high as Virginia Seidel's, "Well, thank heaven fuh small favuhs."

A wealthy East Side matron, who had been studying with me for some time, told me one day that she had a present for me. She knew a psychic who was only in town briefly from Hawaii, and she had paid for a session on my behalf. I had never visited a psychic and was quite skeptical. But a present was a present. So I went.

96

I had been meditating a lot, trying to clear my head of the hundreds of singing clients I was seeing. Teaching singing is a lot like being a psychoanalyst—people tell you a great deal, even when they don't intend to and their condition gets all over you. I felt like a psychic sponge. I needed a special meditation; the one I was using involved lying on the floor and imaging an inverted pyramid of protective energy over me.

I walked into the psychic's apartment and the first thing she said was that she saw an inverted pyramid over my head. I was intrigued. She told me a number of things about myself that I found quite interesting. She told me that I was likely to have a drug problem. I only smoked marijuana, a habit I picked up from the first and second chair violinists from the Manhattan School of Music. I didn't even consider marijuana a drug. (I do now, by the way.) So I thought she was way off base.

Then she told me that I was about to write a piece for the theater. I had not mentioned my writing to her. Instead of noting how amazing it was that she knew that, I simply thought she was wrong, since I had no ideas in development at that time. I told her so. She responded, "You will." She told me that there would be numerous people involved and that it would begin with a lone voice singing a sustained high note and that it would be done in New York.

She also said that the inverted pyramid was the symbol for the Archangel Michael and that he was going to channel the piece through me. Now I knew she was flying blind, because I was not into angels or archangels or channeling. I left the session not feeling good about the whole thing.

A few days later, I was meditating on the floor of my living room when an idea sprang into my head. "What if I wrote a theatrical piece based on the scenes of the Requiem Mass—I had just been listening to the Verdi *Requiem*—and what if it was about someone who was ruthlessly rising to power in the world of show business but becoming soul-dead in the process?" I jumped up from the floor and thought, "How many scenes are there in the Requiem Mass? Please let there be enough scenes to base a theatrical work on, and let the topics be interesting enough to build a play!" I grabbed the libretto out of my LP box of Verdi's *Requiem*. (Remember LPs?) I saw immediately that there were plenty: Dies Irae: Day of wrath; Tuba Mirum: Sound the trumpet; Liber Scriptus: Written in the book; Rex Tremendae: Mighty king; Ingemisco: I am guilty; Lacrimosa: Day of tears; Libera Me: Set me free; etc.

Within weeks I finished a draft of the piece; including the songs, choral arrangements and libretto. I had never experienced anything like the sheer volume of material that flowed through me, and of course, it began with a lone high voice singing, "Requiem." I thought that could have just been auto-suggestion from the Hawaiian psychic's remark, but there it was on my piano, a completed work in only a few weeks. After I finished notating the final moment, I flipped idly through the libretto to check some spelling and noticed a tiny footnote at the bottom of one page, "The overseer of the Requiem Mass is the Archangel Michael." I fell right off the piano bench.

The show was called *Oliver Quade Triumphs at Last*. I showed my draft to Lloyd Battista. He said he wanted to direct it, but he hated the title. He insisted that I call it *Oliver Quade*. I didn't want to change what had come to me in such a miraculous way, but Mr. Battista was VERY persuasive. I changed the title.

Lloyd was friends with EVERYONE, which included Art D'Lugoff, who ran the Village Gate. Art came to my apartment in Greenwich Village with Lloyd, listened to me perform the whole thing while accompanying myself on the piano and offered us a slot, once or twice a week on the set of a pre-existing show. The Village Gate was where the original *Jacques Brel Is Alive and Well and Living in Paris* had played. This was getting spooky.

However, Lloyd did not feel this was a good deal and thought we could do better, so he invited his friends from the American Jewish Theatre to look at the work. They agreed to give us a proper slot in a proper theater. We took it. A Jewish Theater had taken a piece written by a non-Jew, based on the text of the Catholic Requiem Mass and channeled by the Archangel Michael—highly unlikely.

The show was my first real foray into creating a complete book musical in a serious way. I could hardly believe that I was getting it produced in New York and was starring in it. There was a moment at the end when the entire ensemble was singing an anthem to Oliver, based on a little melody that he had always sung to himself in the beginning of the musical. The ensemble was made up of characters he had betrayed in one way or another—I borrowed an idea from the conclusion of Poulenc's *Dialogues of the Carmelites*—and had the voices drop out of the chorale one by one until only Oliver was left singing. Then, the accompaniment dropped out as he realized that he was utterly alone. The lights went out. It was quite chilling.

But once again, the show seemed to take place in a vacuum with few people knowing or caring about it. I mean, it was amazing that it was being done at all, but it just wasn't getting the attention I felt it should. What on earth do you have to do to actually make people pay attention to your work? More than you think when you start down that road. More than you think.

TWENTY-SIX

Ex-patriotism

(Circa 1980)

IN 1980, I WAS SO furious about the way things were going for me and so upset with the political climate in the old U.S. of A. that I decided to give up my American citizenship and move to Germany—okay, I never said this was a sensible decision. It's just where my head was in 1980.

I had done several opera gigs, interspersed with my musical theater career in the previous decade. I had my infamous interaction with the Santa Fe Opera that landed me in *La Grand-Duchesse de Gerolstein* at the Baltimore Opera playing a character tenor role; I had played Doctor Falke (a baritone) in *Die Fledermaus* with the scandalous Providence Opera Company, where I cashed my check before I left town and those who didn't never got their money; I played Raoul de St. Brioche (a bari-tenor) in *The Merry Widow* with the divine Mary Costa, on tour; I did a New York City Opera tour, overseen by none other than Beverly Sills; I played Doctor Grenvil (a bass role) in a production of *La Traviata* featuring the premiere of Jerry Hadley as Alfredo (I thought Jerry was the most talented singer I had ever shared a stage with. The young Jerry Hadley sang like Gigli. It was like standing next to someone from the golden age reborn. I had never known anyone personally who sang so beautifully. If anyone had told me he would die by his own hand, I would never ever have believed it. But he did indeed take his own life after years of depression and alcohol abuse. What a squandered treasure.); I played Deacon Thumb (a tenor) in Carlisle Floyd's *Bilby's Doll* at the Omaha Opera and was the star tenor for them in *Operetta!*, a review put together by the international opera director, Christopher Alden—this piece also featured the amazing singing actress, Sheri Greenawald, who sang all over the world and now runs the Merola Program at the San Francisco Opera—we did the premiere of *Operetta!* at the creation of the Manhattan Theatre Club when it was still in a bowling alley on the Upper East Side—my dressing room was an empty lane in a deserted bowling alley.

If you find this mishmash of types and vocal facts confusing, imagine how I found it. My voice—like my inner child—was all over the place. I could sing really high and really low, but I never felt at home in any particular assigned range. I just sang what I felt like or what caught my fancy. This is not a good career move. Nobody knew what to do with me and I didn't know what to do with myself.

And so it was that I packed my little bag and set off for Germany to find the cradle of Opera and Operetta. By a bizarre twist of fate, my beloved teacher, Elisabeth Parham, was on a sabbatical at the same time and decided to go with me. She had a very successful student, Roberta Knie, a famous Wagnerian soprano who had a villa in Lassnitzhoehe, Austria—just outside of Graz—where we were invited to stay. Who runs away to Germany and finds themselves staying in a free Villa on the side of a mountain with their beloved old teacher? That would be me.

It turned out that Roberta, who had been living and singing in Europe for 20 years, building a huge international singing career, was from Cordell, Oklahoma—one of the terrible little towns I lived in as a child. In fact, we were there at the same time, when I was in the 4th grade. Then, she was known as Bobby Nigh and all these years later she still had her rural Okie accent— even when speaking in German.

She soon departed on tour and left us the villa to ourselves. It had an indoor swimming pool that produced its own waves, but I was not to take advantage of this or the many other amenities there. I was off immediately on an audition tour through Germany and Austria. I was taken on by an opera agent in Vienna, Der Herr Doktor Rudolph Rabb—they like to use as many titles as possible in Austria. I started going from one town to another on Der Herr Doktor's submissions and singing for opera companies all over Germany and Austria.

It was insane. Reviewing music on the train; vocalizing in the bathroom; sleeping in my audition suit; and working in a foreign language can be quite daunting. I studied German at university and knew many nouns and verbs, but auditions are a whole other matter. You stand on stage and an opera director yells things at you from forty rows back. And you have to make it work. I mean, an audition in English is hard enough, but German!

In some town in the middle of industrial Germany, around Koln—a truly ugly smokestack-filled area—I took the stage expecting to hear, "Wie Heissen Sie?" (What is your name?) as I had heard on so many other occasions. But this director yelled at me, "Irren Namen, Bitte?" from the back of the house. I didn't quite make it out, so I asked, "Bitte?" (Please?) He yelled louder, "Irren Namen, Bitte?" and I, now, really confused asked again, "Bitte?" (Please?). Finally the accompanist—clearly English and gay—turned around and whispered, "He's asking for your name, dear." There's no way to describe how embarrassing this was or how impossible it was to explain in a foreign language to a man—half a football field away—that I actually knew a lot of German. And that even though I had not understood a sentence that a 2-year old would know, I was not stupid. This single moment changed forever the way I feel about all non-English speakers trying to muddle along in our language.

In Regensburg—an ancient walled city in Bavaria—I saw the most frightening audition scenario play out. A young woman went on before me as I was waiting in the wings. She sang "Marten Aller Arten" from Mozart's *Abduction from the Seraglio*. It is a very hard aria. She should not have been singing it. I heard the director yell to her from the back of the house in English—very unusual:
"You are American, ARE YOU NOT?"
"Yes."
 "You sang here last year, DID YOU NOT?"
"Yes."
"YOU SING VERY BADLY. DO NOT COME BACK!"
At that point, she left the stage visibly shaken and my name was called. I don't even remember how I sang that day, I was just glad when it was over.

In Bielefeld—a city in the middle north of Germany—I had a very good audition. The director of the company asked me to come into his office and speak with him. I thought, "This is it. I'm moving to Germany." We sat down and he explained to me that he thought I was going to become a great singer, but that I needed a couple of more years to develop and then, he would like to hire me as a Wagnerian. I was completely crestfallen. He saw this and asked me, "Do you understand what I'm saying to you? This is a very good thing." I understood, but it really did not help me. I was almost entirely broke.

The next call I got from Der Herr Doktor Rudolph Rabb made me very happy. I had an audition back in Graz, Austria. So, I could see some people I knew and sleep in a Villa on a mountainside instead of on a train. I was in very good spirits as I journeyed to that audition on a gorgeous sunny day. I had sung for so many opera houses at this point that I felt capable to deal with anything that came my way in English or German. I sang well. I was rested for a change. They asked me to sing something else and at the end of my second aria, the director came down to the edge of the stage. This had never happened before.

He asked me if I knew the role of Prince Gremin in *Eugene Onegin*. I said that I had once done it in college many years before—this was a bold-faced lie. I had never even heard a recording of *Eugene Onegin*. He said that they had an opening and they would like me to do it in ten days. TEN DAYS? They gave me a copy of the score that was printed in Russian, but they were doing it in German; so the German words were scribbled above the Russian. Not only were they illegible; it was impossible to tell which note went with which word. The good news was that the role of Gremin was basically one scene and one aria, so it was something that I actually could learn in ten days. I can be VERY lucky.

TWENTY-SEVEN

Opera in Graz

(Circa 1981)

I BEGAN FURIOUSLY STUDYING THE role of Gremin, which fit me quite well. There were many idioms and antiquated words in the text that I had never seen or heard, but I was able to get around that with some coaching. It was an invaluable help to have my favorite teacher of all time with me. I would take the bus back and forth down the mountain to Graz to work with the Stage Manager. *Eugene Onegin* was already in their repertoire and they weren't going to waste any time or money putting me into it. In a rehearsal room I worked with this lovely young stage manager on the blocking and discussed the nature of the part with her. She spoke not one word of English. Imagine trying to grasp the inner workings of a psychological situation and acting problem, in a language in which you're basically only prepared to order a hotel room or talk about the weather—I had done a bit of "dating" with this kind of German and that engendered some pretty amusing scenarios as well.

One afternoon as I was leaving the rehearsal space behind the theater, I saw a woman in a full-length leopard coat and very high heels coming out of the stage door. It was Birgit Nilsson! She started toward what I thought was an unusually small car for such a big star and I blurted out, "Madame Nilsson, may I speak with you?" I had no idea what I was going to say. She turned toward me and, with a stride like a general in the army, came straight toward me and stopped about a foot in front of my face with her eyes unflinchingly riveted into mine. For whatever reason, she decided to give me her full attention; it was considerable.

To me this was like meeting Abraham Lincoln, John Kennedy or Martin Luther King one-on-one—I was utterly disarmed. This was not at all like the prefabricated format of seeing her backstage at *No, No, Nanette*, surrounded by the show and other cast members. This was just two people on an empty street. I did not feel that I could hold up my end. I managed to say that I had once written her a letter and that she had been kind enough to respond. "I get a lot of letters. Which one were you?" she queried in that unmistakable voice of hers.

I wanted to tell her that I was the one who said that he was glad to be born in the same lifetime with her, but I just couldn't. I mumbled something and she asked me what I was doing here. I told her that I was about to sing Gremin in *Eugene Onegin*. She asked me when I had auditioned and I told her ten days before. She looked shocked. Most opera contracts—even in small companies—are set up a year in advance. Our little conversation came to an end and she started for her car. Suddenly, she turned around and shouted, "Mr. Gremin! What is your name? If you are making your debut after only ten days, I should know your name." So I shouted my name across the parking lot to Birgit Nilsson. And she got into her tiny compact car and drove away. I stood there thinking, "I could have asked her to tea. I could have asked her to lunch." Instead, I could hardly say my own name. It's hard to talk to a living legend.

Birgit was there doing a Wagner recital with orchestra, something she did a lot at the end of her career. Of course, I attended. It was fantastic to see her on stage again and in a much smaller venue than I ever had before. But for the first time she seemed human. Graz is not a first-rate house—the smallish auditorium could have used a coat of paint. It's not that she wasn't great she simply wasn't as great as Nilsson had been. I felt a kind of sorrow, the kind of melancholy you feel on a gorgeous autumn day when you know that winter will soon be upon you.

During my rehearsal period, I went to see an operetta that was in the current repertoire at Graz. I thought to myself, "At last I shall see operetta in the land that gave birth to the operetta!" I think it was *The Bartered Bride*. The utter lack of class and charm that this production exuded makes it impossible for me to recall. The singing, the sets, the costumes and the direction were execrable. At last I understood how Germany and Austria had an opera house in every city. They operated at the level of American summer stock, or dinner theater. I thought I had come to the cradle of art, but what I found was the same thing I had left behind. Just in a different language. This was not a small revelation.

Eventually, it was time for my own performance. I was very frightened and rightfully so. I got a cold. It did not stop me from singing; it just added to the whole tension-filled air of the event. As I took the bus down the mountain to my debut, it suddenly dawned on me. This was not like singing German songs on some college recital or in an American opera house. These people were Austrian; German was their native language. I imagined myself sounding the way Zsa Zsa Gabor or Charo do to an English-speaking crowd—more nerves.

I was finally put into wig, costume and make-up. I guess they wanted me to look A LOT older because there was A LOT of make-up. It was starting to sink in on me that I had never had an orchestra rehearsal; in fact, I hadn't even met the conductor. I hadn't met any of the singers and I had never seen the set, only a diagram in a rehearsal room. I was led backstage to a large set of double doors that two stage hands were about to page open for me. I found myself standing in the dark next to the diva soprano of the company—I had seen her photos all over the lobby. She turned to me and whispered, "Sind Sie Nervos?" (Are you nervous?) "Nein," I replied. "Sie lugen," she replied. (You're lying.) And she was right.

They paged the doors for me and I walked onto the stage. Suddenly, the sound of the orchestra hit me and I realized how surreal the whole situation actually was. Hearing the musicians, seeing other cast members for the first time, in front of an audience, in an opera I had never heard before and had lied to become a part of. One has to be rather foolhardy to find one's self in any kind of show business, much less this kind of insanity.

I began making my way to stage right as the Stage Manager had taught me. What she had not taught me was that the stage would be revolving and that it would have four giant statues on it, at evenly spaced intervals that would be hurtling toward me. Now, she had explained to me that people would be dancing. But I hadn't thought that the women would be wearing gigantic hoopskirts that took up all the space not occupied by their partners, and, the enormous statues, all of which needed to be dodged and circumvented.

Eventually, the revolving stage stopped and I arrived at stage right and planted my feet. I caught the conductor's eye for the first time, steadied myself, heard the introduction to my aria and prepared to begin singing. Just at that moment, the stage began revolving again and to my horror, I discovered that my right foot was off the revolve but my left foot was still on. So, I began doing the splits involuntarily. I stepped off the revolve, once again connected with the conductor and took off into the singing portion of my assignment.

It went surprisingly well, given the circumstances. I knew what I was saying and I was in very good voice for a person with a head cold. I made it past all the idioms and antiquated German and arrived at the final moment where I would plunge downward, end on a low F sharp and hold it for a long time. I went for the note and nothing came out. I had often heard the expression, "My whole life flashed before my eyes," but I always assumed that it was just that, an expression. No, every situation in every chapter that I have just written flashed before my eyes. Then the note kicked in and I finished the performance.

We hadn't discussed the curtain call. Suddenly, stage hands were pushing me out in front of the curtain. Gremin isn't in the last act, so he takes a solo curtain call after his aria. No one had told me, so I'm certain I looked rather shell shocked to be taking a solo bow. The audience called me back a couple of times, which was nice. I heard a recording of the performance the next day and the pause before the last note was so tiny that it was not detectable. Things on stage are not always as they feel, or off stage for that matter. Another good lesson.

Then I learned that the management had been having a fight with their star basso—who should have been playing Gremin that night—and they had hired me to give him a good scare. He had been at the performance and apparently, when he realized that he was about to be replaced, resolved his contract difficulty immediately. So, there had never been an opening for me in the first place.

I was out of money and out of gas. I had an epiphany. If I was working this hard and being this unhappy, why not stop working so hard and just be unhappy at home? I also realized that having sung with a European Opera company had cured me of my fixation with opera. I should go home and be in the musical theater and be at peace with my decision. I felt like a giant rubber band that had been pulled too tight and then suddenly released. SNAP! I had learned that America was a bearable place after all. I had learned that there is no perfect world of art OUT THERE somewhere. And I had learned that Graz, Austria was rather like Ponca City, Oklahoma in the 1950s. Good to know.

TWENTY-EIGHT

Goodbye to Germany

(Circa 1981)

RECALLING ALL THIS, I CAN'T imagine what I was living on all this time. I didn't have any money—but I was used to that—so I just muddled along somehow. In that blissfully blasé state, instead of racing back to the States to get a job, I decided to stop off in Trieste to see Roberta Knie in one of her most famous roles, *Fidelio*. The social climate of German and Austria had so possessed me that I could actually feel it fall away as I left the country. (I recalled the first day I arrived in Graz, when my cab was held up in the street by a large group of Neo-Nazi youths. It was 1980 and there was a group of young Nazis large enough to stop traffic.) When the train cleared Austria and crossed over into Italy, the very air seemed to change. And as we pulled into Trieste, an old baggage handler was singing, "O Sole Mio," for all he was worth, as if he was an extra in a Coppola movie.

I checked into a glorious old world hotel right on the bay of Trieste called La Grande Albergo Di Trieste and it lived up to its name. On a gorgeous Italian afternoon, Roberta asked me to go out on the pier with her. She said she had something important to do and she didn't want to do it alone. Now, I didn't know Roberta that well, so I was fairly surprised at this request. When we got out on the water, she confessed to me that she had left her lover and coach of twenty years, for someone else. The coach, who had built Roberta's opera career brick-by-brick for all those years, was slightly miffed. Her former coach/lover had, in fact—cursed her—a real opera-style "Ti Maledico" type curse. Her lover told her that she would never be able to continue her career without their union and that without constant coaching she would lose her voice and come to ruin. Roberta had heard a legend that if you threw a piece of jewelry into the bay of Trieste you could break a curse. So there I stood, at the end of the pier on the Bay of Trieste, while this famous soprano threw a ring—that had been given to her by her former lover and coach—into the water—to break a curse.

The little jewel box of an opera house in the center of Trieste is the location where Maria Callas sang her first *Norma*. Now I was going to hear a woman I knew sing *Fidelio*, an opera I had never seen before. I was a bit taken aback by Roberta's first entrance. *Fidelio* has some spoken lines and when she was supposed to say, "Was wilst du denn?" (What do you want?) What she actually said was, "Waws weelst deeu deuhn?" with a thick Oklahoma accent—after living in Germany for twenty years. She sang quite beautifully though, with a big even glowing sound. And I was very happy to have seen Beethoven's only opera. The following year Roberta lost her voice on stage at the Metropolitan Opera—I was there—and her career ended. I hear she has her own explanation for it. I'm going with the curse.

For my farewell to Italy, I met a handsome Italian in front of my hotel who drove me to a local parking spot. He didn't speak a word of English and my Italian was terrible, but we managed a backseat-of-his-Volvo date. He had seen the American Fleet moored in front of my hotel and asked me if I was with the Navy. I thought that it sounded sexier to be with the American Fleet than an audience member at *Fidelio*, so I lied—in very bad Italian. This caused him to ask me many questions about life at sea and I lied my stupid head off in a language I could barely fake—never a good idea. When our "date" was finished, he drove me back to my hotel on the pier where the gigantic American ships HAD SAILED. He looked extremely confused and I ran into the hotel laughing—some things just can't be explained in bad Italian. With this silly experience in this lovely location, I said goodbye to my ex-patriotism and came back to America to restart my life and my career.

TWENTY-NINE

Starting Over

(Circa 1982)

I CAME HOME KNOWING WHAT I didn't want to do. But what did I WANT to do? I started teaching again and developed a very large studio of students. I worked all day every day—except Sunday—seeing every kind of singing student imaginable. But felt that I was not realizing my potential as a person or as an artist. I was no longer a "young" man. I was 30-years old. I was not yet a character man. What was I to do?

I went back to studying at a school called The Actors Institute. I found a lot of like-minded people there who were looking to reinvent themselves. They encouraged me to take a marketing course for actors called "Samurai" that met twice a week at eight in the morning. I have NEVER been a morning person. If you missed or were late, you were thrown out of the group. They were serious. You were assigned a partner and a support group. You would share with them your goals and your blocks and they would encourage you to move forward—strongly.

One day, I shared with the group my frustration that I was not performing and how I wanted to jumpstart my career somehow. When asked what I would be willing to do in that regard, I answered that I would take the next performing job that was offered to me no matter what it was. The man to my left turned and said, "I've written a review that is a celebration of the Jewish holidays. Will you do it?" It turned out that I was sitting next to someone who actually knew my work. The roomful of people all turned and stared at me. Of course I said, "Yes." The man was Hank Levy, a very talented composer and

110

pianist and the work he had written was called *The Lord Loves Music*. It was booked into Mickey's—a very successful cabaret in the East Fifties. I had never thought of playing a cabaret. Now, I was headlining in one.

Mickey's was a wonderful "old world" kind of place with a bar and restaurant on the ground floor, and a cabaret room up a steep flight of stairs that had been the launching pad for Cissy Houston, Karen Akers, Bobby Short and a host of others. I knew nothing about the Jewish holidays—the only one I could name was Chanukah. I figured nobody would notice the little three person review and that I would do it for a couple of weekends and continue my search for musical employment. However, *The Lord Loves Music* caught on with Hadassah groups and ran for a YEAR. So, here was a nice Irish boy singing and dancing about the Jewish holidays and being the toast of the Hadassah set—many of whom had seen *King of the Schonorrers*. What next, *Fiddler on the Roof*?

I had been celebrating the Jewish holidays for a couple of months when Mickey, the extremely colorful owner of the establishment, cornered me. Mickey was Israeli with the most fabulous personality and an equally fabulous accent:
"So, venn are you doink your echt?"
"I don't have an 'echt.'"
"So, venn are you doink it?"
He continued in this vein every time he saw me. So it was that I reluctantly gave him a date for an act that I did not have. I began to try and prepare one before the big night arrived.

I went through my files of music and pulled out all my favorite songs. I laid them all out on the floor to get an overview. I began to think, "This one is an up tempo and seems like an opening number; this one is introspective and seems like the closing number; this one is rousing and seems like an encore." As this continued, I began to come up with a concept for something that might be considered sort of an act.

Then, I noticed it. All the music on my floor was from the 1930s. There were, perhaps, one or two exceptions. So I removed those and refined my choices. I called the act *Mostly Thirties*. I bought my first Armani suit—grey, double-breasted with very wide lapels. I had a logo drawn of myself as a 1930s crooner by the wonderful caricaturist, Ken Fallin. *Mostly Thirties* opened at Mickey's, the fabulous East Side boite with the fabulous Hank Levy accompanying me fabulously. We got a spectacular review from The New York Post and voila, I was a cabaret artiste. We also recorded my first solo LP. Unfortunately, about 5-minutes later, LPs were out and CDs were in. Oops.

I had been performing for many years and had never gone on stage without stage make-up. I had been given classes by an expert from *No, No, Nanette.* It never crossed my mind to do anything else. Mickey said to me one day, "You know, cabaret is a very intimate form; you really don't have to wear make-up." I had never worked without it and it was part of my ritual. I told Mickey that I didn't feel comfortable working "naked." He said, "All right," and I never thought about it again.

Then, one night, I got a call that Karen Akers had to cancel a sold-out show for the Yale Club and I was asked to fill in. I arrived early and did my usual preparation. I was in very good voice and was looking forward to the evening. But when I walked out and began, I felt something strange in the air. There was a big, fat, bald, middle-aged, American businessman at the front table with four diminutive Asian clients.

I was about one number into my set when the fat man blurted out in a stage whisper to the Asians, "My God, he's wearing makeup! That guy's a fag!" And it didn't stop there. He kept on and on, punctuating every silence with another sexual expletive. I just didn't know what to do. It wasn't an act about snappy one-liners. It was a collection of the most beautiful songs I could find, all of which were my personal favorites. Including "All the Things You Are," which had been with me since my first job.

I once saw Gretta Keller, the famous old German chanteuse, in a Chicago dive, towards the end of her career. (She sang the song "Heirat" in the movie of *Cabaret* as Liza Minelli and Michael York made out.) She was in her 80s and had been performing all her life. She had a drunken heckler at the back of the house who kept screaming that she was a stupid old bat; that she couldn't sing and that she should get off the stage. She sang wearily, through the whole set. At the end, she slowly raised her hand and whispered into the microphone, "No encores tonight."

I wish I could have been so poised. I stumbled through my entire set and walked off the stage without acknowledging the applause and did not come back for an encore. I wish I could say I just shrugged it off, but I was never the same again. I wish I could say I no longer wish that man ill. I played the rest of the year at Mickey's—minus my stage make-up. Some lessons are harder than others.

THIRTY

Other Cabarets

(Circa 1983)

I WANTED TO WRITE AN original act from scratch. I began composing a cabaret work for myself in which the opening, closing, and climactic numbers were written specifically for that purpose. I wrote it in French, German, Spanish and English and based it on the idea of all kinds of love songs: unrequited; remembered; wished for; consummated; unexpected; etc., and called it *Nightsong*.

I would have debuted it at Mickey's, but dear old Mickey tired of the New York rat race, closed the club and moved to New Orleans. I opened my new act at "Caroline's," played there for months and then moved the act to "Don't Tell Mama's" on Restaurant Row. While I was doing that, I began writing a little show that went into "The Silver Lining" also on Restaurant Row. I called it *Hotel Broadway;* it was about a broken down residence for aspiring actors in the 1930s and had a cast of four, one of whom was myself. It also had a specialty spot for a guest star who would "check into" the hotel so that we could plug in a famous person every week. The first person to do this guest spot was George Rose. I supplied the vehicle for George Rose's cabaret debut.

George approached me to teach him how to sing. Imagine getting a phone call one day, from the person in your profession you most admire and having him tell you he wants to study with you? It was an amazing situation. George had been hired by Alan Jay Lerner (who wrote *My Fair Lady*) to star in his new—and final—musical on Broadway, *Dance a Little Closer*. George had an idea that his character should sing like a lieder singer—Hermann Prey, in particular. He wanted me to help him achieve this effect.

I was teaching up a storm at this point. I was still coaching the entire Broadway cast of *A Chorus Line* and guided at least half a dozen Cassies through that treacherous number. I even got to do Alyson Reed's vocal preparation for Cassie in the movie. Alyson did something that mirrored George exactly. They both walked in the door like total beginners and stood there saying, "Tell me what to do." Models of professionalism.

George joked with me at his first session, "Who could have dreamed that the mantle of American musical theater would fall to me?" At this point he was perhaps the most successful star of musicals on Broadway. He never expected to be anything other than a classical actor. Some really do have greatness thrust upon them.

George never succeeded in sounding like Hermann Prey—even Dietrich Fischer-Dieskau never did that—but he did sound better than he ever had and I was thrilled to have participated. But *Hotel Broadway, Dance a Little Closer* and the movie of *A Chorus Line* all met a similar fate—oblivion.

The offshoot of all this teaching and cabaret performing was that I got a new wardrobe from the teaching and I got my face plastered all over town, in every magazine and periodical from the cabaret work, for a two-year stretch. This changed my level of recognition and changed the way I perceived myself as well. I parlayed this into the next step of my career, my second act.

THIRTY-ONE

The Three Musketeers

(Circa 1984)

I WAS SUBMITTED FOR A Broadway reworking of Rudolf Friml's operetta, *The Three Musketeers*. What was surprising about this was that I was, for the first time in my life, being considered for a big starring character role in a Broadway show. I had never been in this league before, the kind of role that a George Rose would play. I had no idea if I could pull it off. What was particularly interesting about this part was that it was the role of Cardinal Richelieu. I felt that my religious upbringing made me particularly ripe to bring something interesting to the assignment. I went in and met the great Tom O'Horgan—creator and director of *Hair, Lenny* and *Jesus Christ Superstar*. As it turned out, he was an extremely nice man, an old hippie, in fact, and we hit it off right away. Although I felt that I knew something about the lines that I read at the audition that no one else could possibly know, the feedback afterwards was that I needed a song for the callback that was more "evil." Cardinal Richelieu—for those of you who slept through history class—was a very bad man.

Now, if you've ever tried to come up with a scary or evil song for an audition, you'll be with me on this. It's very hard to find a scary/evil song. I felt I had a really good shot at this part and I was not about to let it slip through my fingers because of a song shortage. So, I wrote a scary/evil song, took it to a music copyist and memorized it in two-days for the call-back. It seems normal enough to me now, because it's something I have done many times since then; created a specific song for a specific audition, but at the time, it seemed very radical and very risky.

The song was titled "A Villain's Work Is Never Done." It was quite long, had an intro, a patter section, a sustained section and an up-tempo section that went from a low G to a high C. This was one of those call backs where virtually all the staff members involved in the production were seated behind long tables—it was like doing a performance for a small auditorium of people. After my scene and song, Tom O'Horgan asked me if I would vocalize for them, a very unusual request for an audition. I don't know what possessed me, but I felt I had to say something. I mean, I had just sung from a low G to a high C; what the hell else could they want? So I drolly said, "You know, whenever someone asks me to vocalize at an audition, I always feel like I'm having my pants pulled down." I thought this would get some kind of reaction from the large crowd, but they all stared at me like mannequins in a store window. So I went on, "Not that I mind." At this, Tom O'Horgan burst out laughing and the rest of the room followed suit. Auditioning is a very dicey art form, even for the very experienced.

I got the part of Cardinal Richelieu. I was no longer just a guy singer. I had made the transition to character man in a great big multi-million dollar Broadway show. Some life hurdles go unnoticed in the march of time, this one did not. I knew something important had happened.

Everything about *The Three Musketeers* was thrilling for me. We rehearsed at 890 Studios, the work space created by Michael Bennett, with his money from *A Chorus Line*. It was the most state-of-the-art rehearsal studio in the city, including an "in-house" theater space. Irvin Feld—who ran Ringling Brothers Circus—was producing the show and swore to us that he was committed to us completely and that no matter what the critics said, we were going to run forever.

Freddy Wittop, the legendary costume designer of *Hello Dolly, I Do, I Do* and *On a Clear Day You Can See Forever*, came out of retirement to do the absolutely spectacular clothes. We were booked into the gigantic Broadway Theatre. I had the dressing room on the stage level, just off stage right. It was my first private dressing room, and no stairs. Arrival!

However, from the beginning, things did not go well. If you know the book of *The Three Musketeers*, it's basically the same story twice. In the first act, the Musketeers are desperately trying to save the queen by getting back a love letter that she wrote to the Duke of Buckingham, which will surely lead to her doom. In the second act, the Musketeers are desperately trying to get back the jewel that she gave to the Duke of Buckingham, which will surely lead to her doom. Not good dramaturgy. We were assured that this problem would be addressed during rehearsals, but as per usual with such rehearsal promises, it was not.

Dear Mr. O'Horgan, who really liked the 1960s way of letting shows develop in an organic manner, seemed to get run over by the massive number of cast members and enormity of the production. We were WAY behind schedule as the first preview approached. We had spent weeks playing theater games and tossing around a giant medicine ball. A medicine ball?

The Three Musketeers was my first encounter with Michael Stewart, the historic book writer, lyricist or both for *Bye Bye Birdie, Carnival, Hello Dolly, George M, Barnum* and *42nd Street*, among many others. He reminded me of David Merrick and the ilk of show business dinosaurs that had mostly died out by 1984. He was by turns mean; cantankerous; insulting; scary; belligerent; intimidating; threatening; condescending; snooty; snide and unpleasant. I heard later that he was not in good health; he died two years later. But at this point, he seemed to be on some kind of amphetamine bender.

No one knew exactly what he was doing there. The show had been written by his protégé, the estimable Mark Bramble—with whom I would become fast friends—but there was Michael Stewart, acting like the book writer. The show was being directed by Tom O'Horgan, but there was Michael Stewart, acting like the director. I once saw him kick open the door to the rehearsal space where the musical director was coaching us and enter screaming, "No, no, no, no, no!" when he hadn't even heard what was going on in the room before he entered.

One day, while rehearsing in the theater, he was going around insulting everyone. I managed to avoid him most of the day, but eventually, I ran into him in the hallway. He snarled, "And YOU! You're...(*long pause*) impeccable!" He said that last word as if it was the worst insult ever delivered and stormed away.

Roy Brocksmith was playing King Louis VIII. Roy was hilarious and destined to get the best reviews in the show. He also looked like a fat pear that had fallen off a tree and rotted. Roy was a sight gag who could not be ignored. One day Michael Stewart decided, for some reason, that Roy deserved a reaming out in front of the whole company. But Roy, to everyone's astonishment, pulled himself up to his full height—about 5-feet, same as his width—shoved his fat finger in Michael's face and screamed at the top of his lungs, "OH YEAH? WELL, FUCK YOU, MICHAEL! FUCK YOU! FUCK YOU! FUCK YOU!" At the height of Roy's fury, he seemed to levitate off the floor.

In the dead silence that followed this amazing display, the entire company held its breath. Then Michael Stewart turned away without a word and left the stage. Nothing more was ever said of it. There's a lesson in there somewhere.

On the other side of things, the very likeable and multi-talented Brent Spiner—now famous as Data on *Star Trek: The Next Generation*—was Aramis. You'd never know it from *Star Trek*, but he has GREAT high notes. Liz Calloway sang gloriously as Constance. Michael Praed, fresh from a big success with *Robin Hood* on the BBC, had come over to play D'Artagnan. He was absolutely delightful, both on and off stage. But there was a big brouhaha by American actors about why a "Brit" had been brought over to take one of our jobs. Michael started a game of "dirty limericks" with us during rehearsals. We were all engaged in a contest to see who could come up with the most revolting limericks on a daily basis. This would come back to bite me in the ass later.

About seven days before our first preview, we walked in to discover that Tom O'Horgan had been unceremoniously sacked and replaced with Joe Layton, who had almost countless Broadway credits. Joe had often worked with Michael Stewart...hmm. Beside the fact that this was very upsetting to the company, the two men could not possibly have been more different in their directing styles. Joe Layton seemed to be trying to emulate General Patton in his last campaign. No one was allowed to speak in his presence. No questions were allowed. No responses were required. "Go there and do what I tell you," was the order of the day. He always had a cigarette in one hand and a giant pewter mug of vodka in the other. I was not privy to what else was being consumed, but rumors were rife. He did get the show up and running in seven days, but it was neither this nor that. Not what we had started out to do and not yet something else either.

The tech rehearsals were terrifying with giant scenery moving around on all sides and seemingly countless soldiers with swords just inches from your face at all times. I had a 15-foot train of seamless red satin designed by Freddy Whitop. During tech, a soldier stepped on it and ripped it in half. It was very expensive. They replaced it and the same soldier ripped it in half again. Mr. Wittop was not amused. I had to cross a catwalk 35-feet above the stage in that train. It may have been grand, but it was damned challenging.

And then there was the horse. I can't recall whose idea it was to bring a live horse down the aisle of the Broadway Theater and try to lead it up a narrow ramp onto the stage. Aside from the fact that the poor beast was terrified and only lasted a few days, I can testify to the fact that once a horse has relieved himself in the middle of the orchestra section of a theater—next to a critic and a producer—nothing will get the smell out. And nothing will get those luminaries back into their seats.

In spite of all this, I was so happy to be there in that wonderful role, in those wonderful Freddy Wittop costumes, that I was basically oblivious to all the signs of disaster. Brent Spiner, who was much more savvy than I, was the voice of Cassandra. His message was quite clear; "WE ARE DOOMED." I, in a state of complete denial, went around on opening night giving out lots of presents. I gave everyone an LP of *Mostly Thirties*, a bottle of my favorite champagne and a personal gift; I wrote a filthy limerick for every single member of the cast and crew. It was A LOT of limericks—and this was before computers. They were prepared on an ancient Smith-Corona typewriter and Xeroxed.

We had a sold-out opening night that received a rousing standing ovation. We went to a lavish party at Tavern on the Green. Then, the reviews came out—disastrous! You've never seen a room clear so quickly, and Tavern on the Green is LARGE. Snap—empty. Suddenly, my filthy limericks, based on all that joking around during rehearsals, became just that, filthy.

Irvin Feld, our producer, who had sworn to stand by us until death, did just that. The poor man died during the final rehearsals. The show was taken over by his son who had no interest in keeping a sinking ship afloat. We closed shortly afterward, but before we did, one of the arrangers—who had not been in on all the limerick hijinks during rehearsals—sent me a scathing letter. It was in the form of a limerick. He said how tasteless and crude I was and how I had "screwed" everyone with my poison pen—second poison pen reference of my career. I thought about going to him and explaining the whole back story, but I just didn't feel up to it. Besides, he didn't send a record and a bottle of champagne along with his limerick, so blank him and his blanking man from Nantucket.

I know this all sounds like a rather terrible time, but the truth is, it wasn't. To this day, *The Three Musketeers* is one of my favorite memories. I liked so many of the people in that show. I liked my part. It was the beginning of my life as a character actor. I was also madly in love with someone in the company and we often carried on in my dressing room with me in full Cardinal Richelieu Regalia. I will always remember those divine Freddy Wittop costumes and the star dressing room of the Broadway Theatre off stage right.

THIRTY-TWO

13 Days to Broadway

(Circa 1985)

WHEN THE DUST CLEARED FROM *The Three Musketeers*, I went into a kind of mini-depression. "How would I ever get another part as great as Cardinal Richelieu?" The answer was very swift in arriving. I was cast in a workshop of a brand new musical by Cy Coleman called *13 Days to Broadway*. Well, actually, I think it was originally called *Seven Days to Broadway* or some other number, but THIRTEEN was the final decision.

The part I was to play was the insane director of a doomed musical on the road, a fantastic role. Cy wrote it with Russell Baker—The New York Times columnist who had just won the Pulitzer Prize for his autobiography, *Growing Up*. Cy and Russell had written a musical together before with lyricist, Barbara Fried, that had been a disaster, a famous one.

The disaster was called *Home Again, Home Again*. It closed on the road without ever arriving at its intended Broadway destination. Russell Baker kept a journal about that debacle—a hilarious record of *Home Again, Home Again's* demise, complete with thieving producers, misbehaving stars and attempts to raise missing money on the High Holy Days. This was to be the basis of *13 Days to Broadway*. Russell had kept a journal because he had never before been involved in a musical or anything to do with Broadway and his "outsider" viewpoint was hysterical.

The cast included Rob Marshall, now an Oscar-winning movie director (*Chicago, Diary of a Geisha, Nine*); Bebe Neuwirth, before becoming Lillith on

Cheers and winning multiple Tonys; and several of the best character men in the business: Evan Pappas, John Christopher Jones and Jonathan Freeman. My role of The Director was a dynamic and hilarious portrait of a kind of megalomaniac that I had encountered several times, and it was a blast to play. I couldn't believe I was going to get to be this amazing character on Broadway, yet that's clearly where the workshop was headed.

Another major perk was getting to work so intimately with Cy Coleman—a particular joy for me—since he was the composer of *Sweet Charity*, the very first show I saw on Broadway. Not all composers are good pianists. Some, like Richard Adler, (*The Pajama Game* and *Damn Yankees*) can't play at all; and some like Harvey Schmidt, (*The Fantasticks* and *110 in the Shade*) can play fantastically, but they can't read music. But Cy could do it all, in all styles and all modes and he could do it at the drop of a hat or after six cocktails—I've seen him do that last trick while liquoring up investors at a backer's audition.

It was a joy to be around such a famous columnist as Russell Baker. I mean, he HAD just won the Pulitzer. But the person I liked the most and became closest with was Barbara Fried, the lyricist. She looked like your favorite Jewish grandmother—even if you weren't Jewish—but man, could she pack a punch! During our very first conversation, I asked her what a particular aging starlet was like since I knew Barbara had worked with her on *Home Again, Home Again*. Without mulling it over for a tenth of a second, she quipped, "A real dumb cunt." She said it so matter-of-fact, the way one might say, "She had brown hair." that it just slayed me. I suggested we become best friends forever. And so we did.

The piece came together beautifully and I got more and more excited about being the person who was going to launch this fantastic part in New York. Then I started to hear the guest list for our presentations. I was going to be performing for Liza Minelli, Chita Rivera, Lauren Bacall, Shirley MacLaine, Warren Beatty, Dustin Hoffman and Bob Fosse—you get the picture. We only did a few performances at 890 Studios, but man, they were "cherce."

I remember the first time Bob Fosse laid eyes on Bebe Neuwirth. She appeared in a French cut leotard with a cigarette hanging out of her mouth and cut a swath across the center of the rehearsal studio. And it was obvious that for him, there was no one else in the room. Within minutes, it seemed, he cast her in his revival of *Sweet Charity*. She won the Tony, moved to Los Angeles, got on *Cheers* and the rest is history.

13 Days to Broadway was very strong. It was very funny. It was very inexpensive to produce. But the subject matter, a "Broadway Flop," did not inspire investors. We thought we were moving directly to the Great White Way, but that turned out not to be the case. What did happen was that we began a series of backer's auditions the likes of which I have never experienced before or since. We performed for rich people in their homes on Fifth Avenue; we took it to their summer residences on Long Island; we took it to their mansions in the Carolinas; we performed for millionaires in our designer, Robin Wagner's studio; we performed in the producer's home on Park Avenue; we did it, many, many times in Cy Coleman's beautiful Eastside townhouse. In the year that followed—I didn't know this until I got my tax form from Cy—we had done FIFTY backers auditions for *13 Days to Broadway*. It is now 20 years since that first performance and it has yet to be produced, and THAT, as they say, is show business.

THIRTY-THREE

Pippin

(Circa 1985)

PIPPIN WAS PLAYING NEXT DOOR to *No, No, Nanette* while we were at the 46th Street Theatre; they were at the Imperial. We shared the same rear wall at the back of the stage and you could hear them rocking out next door in the middle of our show. That initial production of *Pippin* was so glittering and so innovative that it always seemed an impossible prize. All those fabulously gorgeous dancers running around in leotards; it just never seemed like something that I would ever be a part of. I was certainly not a Fosse dancer, and since I was only 35, it had never occurred to me that I could play Charlemagne, the very funny character lead.

Nevertheless, I heard from my agent that I was going to be seen for that part, in what was being billed as "The Last *Pippin* Tour." The audition was at Radio City Music Hall, a very odd location for an audition; in fact, I had never set foot in the place. When I arrived, I found the illustrious Ben Vereen, who was not only starring in, but in charge of the entire production, seated behind a long table in a Hawaiian shirt. He was sporting green contact lenses so intense that they showed through his sunglasses, which he never removed. The contact lenses were much larger than the irises of his eyes, so their green glow spread eerily across the whites of his eyes. Oh, yes, and he called everyone "baby" in virtually every sentence. It was like he had wandered in off the set of a Hollywood movie parody.

To my great surprise, he cast me in the role of Charlemagne, who, to the best of my knowledge, had only been played by one actor previously, Eric

Berry. Eric was twice my age and different from me in every way imaginable from hair color (mine was still brown) to nationality (he was English) to body structure (I was still rather fit). Nevertheless, I was going on the road with *Pippin* opposite its original star. The theory was that Ben was directing the show as well, but most of the work was actually done by Fosse's longtime assistant, Kathy Doby. Ms. Doby had the personality and demeanor of a storm trooper in the Nazi army. Oh, yes, and the accent to go with it. "You vill shtand here! You vill do it like zis!"

I would say a line and Kathy would say, "You must separate ze little finger from ze rest of ze hand venn you say zat line!" I would point out that the choice she was referring to was made by another actor twenty years before and had nothing to do with my performance. She would then open her gigantic workbook from the original production, produce a letter in Fosse's own hand and quote, "Bobby says you must separate ze little finger from ze rest of the hand!" This was not fun.

Another difficulty was that Ben—who continued to wear sunglasses and, for some reason, dozens of wrist watches on both arms—refused to participate in the scene work. I would do a scene, supposedly with his character, but he would sit behind the table watching and would not say the lines with me. Nor would anyone else stand in for the missing part, since Ben was right there. So I would say my line, there would be a hole where his line should have been, and then I would say my next line. This, as you might imagine, is not a very productive way to work.

In spite of this, I felt that I was creating some interesting ideas in the other scenes with my wife, the hilarious Ginger Prince. I decided that Charlemage had secondary syphilis from his many dalliances; bad knees from too many campaigns; and was a raging alcoholic. To my mind, the original version had simply been "kingly." I thought my version was not only funnier, but much more me. The rest of the cast seemed to agree since they roared with laughter at everything I did. I noticed that Mr. Vereen did not. But since he was not really participating in the process, I didn't think much of it. My biggest fear was that the final run-through for Bob Fosse was approaching and I had never actually done the scenes with Ben.

The day of the run-through arrived and Ben finally roused himself from behind the table and sauntered slowly across the room toward me. I was expecting some kind of complement about my interpretation, since I was so proud of my originality. What he said was, "I think I have the secret to what you are missing in your part. Come with me." I followed dubiously behind him as he took me out in the hall and walked me silently all the way down to the end of the corridor. He opened the door to a vacant rehearsal studio—the largest one at 890 Studios. It was lit only by sunlight coming in through the air shaft, so it had a sort of creepy deserted feel to it.

We walked silently to the middle of the floor. He put his hand on my shoulder and said deliberately while staring into my eyes with the green of his contact lenses veering wildly outside his irises, "Now I'm gonna explain to ya da secret of this part. Ya see, you da King, and Pippin is yo son. Ya see." I stood there waiting for the rest of the pronouncement. But after a few moments it dawned on me that it was over. That was his information to me. I was the King and Pippin was my son. I started to laugh. I laughed so hard that I bent over double. All the while Ben kept asking, "What? What?" I finally stopped laughing. We left the rehearsal room and walked silently back to rehearsal. That was the end of my lesson.

After the run-through—which went fine in spite of all—I got to sit down with the great Bob Fosse for the first time in my life and discuss the play. Here's what surprised me more than anything else could have, about him. He was quite soft. I expected that he would be angular, sharp, hard, and all the other Fosse trademarks; but he was soft and quiet and kind of gray. Oh, he wore his signature black shirt and pants, as always, but they were covered with old cigarette ash. His hair and complexion were gray and his face was rather indistinct and well—soft. I couldn't have been more surprised. Fosse made some generic remarks about the piece. He was very complimentary. Then he was gone and we were back in the claws of Kathy Doby.

The sets and costumes from the last bus and truck of *Pippin* arrived. We began to work with those tatty worn out items. The original production had been such a glittering glory. However, the miserable wreckage—stored away for years in trunks—of Tony Walton's fabulous design was something quite other. It was hard to look Kingly in what was left of Charlemagne's attire. The ermine and velvet tunic looked like an old terrycloth bathrobe. The once fabulous macramé palace was little more than old rope.

I was supposed to make my entrance through a portal on stage right behind a black screen. The black screen would then be flown out and I would appear as if by magic. However, Ms. Doby informed me that would not be the case in this version. I was to walk on holding a black cloth in front of myself that I would then drop, revealing myself still holding my arms up in the air where they had been while holding the cloth. "You've got to be kidding," I insisted. "Nein," she insisted, "Zis is how ve do it on ze tour." I asked if I couldn't just walk on and make a proper entrance without the cloth. "Absolutely not!"

I picked up the moldy cloth from the bin where it had been stored for years. It was covered with dust and cobwebs. I shook it out and then held it in front of my face. I noticed a peculiar smell. It was cat piss. I dropped the cloth and stepped back, aghast. Kathy Doby insisted that I pick it back up. I refused and suggested that perhaps she should hold it in front of her own face. This went on for a while. In the end, we went on the road and I held the cat piss black cloth in front of my face for the next year. My favorite gift on the road was a lapel button that someone found for me as an opening night present. It said, "Please ignore the urine smell."

We arrived in Buffalo in the middle of a gigantic snow storm and the crew hung the show a bit too hastily. When my macramé palace flew in on opening night, it was an unrecognizable wad of twisted rope hanging above my head. Everyone else seemed to be ignoring the elephant in the room, going on as if nothing was wrong. I looked up at the mess and mused, "I have to have this palace redecorated!"

Not only did the audience find this hilarious, Mr. Vereen lost it completely and laughed so long and hard that he walked off the stage. This sent the audience into another round of howling. He came back on and tried to start again, but wasn't able, so he left the stage for a second time. By now, the audience was screaming and stamping their feet. Finally, the laughter subsided and he came out a third time and we were able to go on with the scene. It was my favorite moment with Ben and my favorite moment on the tour. Truthfully, my favorite moment on the tour involved the visiting brother of one of the cast members. But I'm not talking about that since he still hasn't come out to his sibling. But it was a memorable enough encounter that I almost missed the show the next day.

When we arrived in Dallas, my high school drama and chorus teachers both arrived from Oklahoma. It was a treat to be able to bring them to an opening night party. Mabel Ritzman, the drama teacher, was in heaven being around show biz; but Lucille White, the chorus teacher, seemed to find everything displeasing in one way or other. When Ben arrived at the party with his very blond wife, Lucille literally grabbed her pearls, let out a sharp expulsion of air and whispered to no one in particular, "Salt and pepper!" Sometimes, I forget where I came from.

Another reminder came a few days later when I was in my dressing room making up for the evening show. A call came over the intercom saying that I should come to the stage door. I pulled on a bathrobe and went down with half my face made up; my shoulder length graying hair sticking out in every direction and my robe only partially closed. When I opened the door to the outside, there stood my mother's passive-aggressive brother Gene, and his shrew of a wife Mary.

In the intervening years, I had forgotten how uptight, small and mean my family could be. It all came flooding back. There stood Gene, a deacon in his local hell-fire-and-damnation church, in a clip-on tie. And Mary, a parody of a church lady, with hands clasped in front of her groin and a brown Dynel wig crammed on the top of her head.

At the previous matinee, TWO-HUNDRED-AND-FIFTY Dallas Bible-belt patrons demanded their money back because they thought *Pippin* was obscene. *Pippin* was twenty years old at this point and the naughtiest thing in it was some girls dancing around in bikinis. Oh yeah, and my character said "asshole." Horrors.

So, my Aunt and Uncle from Tyler, Texas *(they pronounced it "Taaaaaaaaaaylrr")* sat through *Pippin*. The show ended and I went to the stage door. They were standing back a few feet looking at their shoes. I tried to start a conversation, several times, but they were unable to speak since *Pippin* had so filled them with revulsion. We drove silently to a cheap restaurant. After we had been seated for a few minutes, my Aunt finally raised her eyes like burning coals to mine and hissed with inexpressible hatred, "In Taaaaaaaaaaaylrr, where we live, there used to be a dinner theater, and when we went to see those shows...THEY were delightful!" *(pronounced "delaaaaaaaahtful.")*

It was a long evening. When I was finally dropped off at my hotel— actually a motel on a highway—I woke up everyone in the place and forced them to come down to the bar and get very drunk with me. For some time I had actually thought I made up my childhood. I hadn't.

Eventually, the tour petered out. At the closing party, Ben kissed me right on the lips and said, "When we get back to town, we gonna have LUNCH!" I was too stunned to reply. To this day it's the only time in my life anyone's actually given me the ultimate Hollywood kiss of death, "We must have lunch."

THIRTY-FOUR

The York Theatre

(Circa 1986)

SOMEHOW, I SKIPPED MY INITIATION into the York Theatre. The delightful Janet Hayes Walker, who had begun as a chorus girl on Broadway in *Lute Song* with Nancy Reagan (then Nancy Davis) founded the tiny York Theater to create new musical works and revive forgotten ones. It operated out of the basement of The Church of the Heavenly Rest on Upper Fifth Avenue. They got quite a reputation, largely due to their fondness for reviving Sondheim works. They paid virtually no money so it was with great trepidation that I auditioned for their new production of *Moby Dick,* penned by the very talented team of Doug Katsaros and Mark St. Germain. However, when they offered me Captain Ahab, one of the great literary characters of all time—*Moby Dick* is truly one of the greatest books ever written—I wasn't about to turn it down, even for minimum wage.

It was the biggest role I had ever played, certainly in New York, and probably anywhere. It took Ahab a while to come on, but once he did, he never shut up, and the singing was spread out over more than two octaves. I thought the music and the adaptation were wonderful and so was the cast, which included Dennis Parlato, Steve Blanchard, and Victor Cook.

Rehearsals were very exciting. The prospect of opening this dynamic work in New York was very exciting to us all. My first problem—other than learning the massive part—was deciding what to do with my leg. If you are a stranger to English literature, Captain Ahab lost one of his appendages to a giant white whale.

After trying the age old practice of tying up one leg behind and walking on a stump, I opted for inserting my leg into a plaster prosthesis while pointing my foot and wearing a built-up shoe on the other foot to match the length of the "peg leg." This was before I learned that the set, which was the deck of a ship, was all stairs. The plaster cast surrounding my pointed foot was heavy and the pain it caused was almost unendurable. Walking with it meant hiking up one hip for every step, and of course, each tread on the endless flights of stairs was both death defying and painful. It took a year for my hip and spine to realign.

A larger problem than my discomfort however, was the rewriting that took place during the rehearsal process. Rewrites are always hard when you have a very large part, but let's just say, some of the changes were harder than others. One such example was the gorgeous little song constructed for poor Pip, played by the extraordinary Victor Cook—now famous for *Three Mo' Tenors*. Pip was supposed to be a pitiful little cabin boy who goes mad after being lost at sea during the height of a whale hunt. The original haunting refrain was heart breaking and true to the situation. However, when it became clear that Victor could sing like Aretha Franklin—YOUNG Aretha Franklin—the number began to take a tragic turn. Suddenly, the "pitiful" waif became the most dynamic person in the play with the most show stopping number. It built and built to such monumental heights that the entire musical turned on its side and went belly up. It was impossible to think about the show without thinking of that earth shattering moment. What could I say to the creative team? It would sound like sour grapes, as if I was jealous of Victor's blow-out number—which I was, but that's beside the point. So, I kept my mouth shut and went down with the ship.

I was in the middle of a tragic relationship of my own at this time, perhaps the worst of my life, which is really saying something. Somehow, this fed into my whole characterization, along with the physical pain of my peg leg and the rigorous physical, emotional and vocal demands of the role. By opening night, there was virtually no split between me and Captain Ahab. By the time I threw that last harpoon at the end of the show and was dragged to the briny depths, I truly was that crazed person in that crazed condition.

Tears were leaking from my unfocused eyes as I scoured the horizon seeking my baleen destiny. I had tremors of pain and exhaustion. I didn't understand why I couldn't find what I was looking for in my life; why I wasn't being paid properly when I was working so hard; and why I had so little to say about my destiny. In short, I was Captain Ahab.

At the opening night party some very scary woman literally threw herself at me in front of the hors d'oeuvres table. All I could think was, "Damn, woman, if you think what you just saw on stage is desirable, you're as crazy as Ahab." Then the reviews came out. The show was crucified, but everyone seemed to like the Aretha Franklin number. This was very hard to endure.

Endure it we did and the run came off very successfully because people loved the show and came in spite of it all. During the run, a terrible cold went through the company and since I was exhausted, I came down with it big time. In the end, I had almost complete laryngitis. But I had no understudy, so it was either try to go on or cancel the performance. The theater was sold out. I went on. I had sung with laryngitis before, so I thought I knew what to expect. This was a faulty assumption. I walked out, opened my mouth and aimed for one pitch and a completely different pitch came out. The pitch that came out was not slightly off, it was about a third away from the correct one, maybe a fourth. This kept up all evening.

Two interesting things happened that night. First, I found out that if you really know who a character is and what he is made of, you don't need correct pitches to make it happen. The second thing that happened, a casting director for television was there and hired me on the spot to do a Captain Black Pipe Tobacco commercial based on that performance. It was a national spot and ran for a year. Sometimes, just showing up is enough.

In spite of the leg pain, bad pay, laryngitis and all the rest, it was a great experience to play that amazing character in that compelling little musical. It never ceases to amaze me how critics can go out of their way to destroy a little show in an out-of-the-way venue that costs a few thousand dollars, as if some bloated Broadway producer was trying to shove some overblown monstrosity down their throats. This was a little art piece; by very talented writers; that had some problems amid some gorgeous writing. The reviews guaranteed that it would never have a life. Critics can be extremely annoying.

Another perk from this period at the York was that I got to reconnect with Cy Coleman. Cy wanted to rework *On the Twentieth Century* at the York and turn it into a smaller musical so that it could have wider distribution. I had the fantastic experience of doing fund raisers with Comden & Green and Cy on numerous occasions, where the four of us would do all the numbers from that marvelous score. Comden & Green were really getting up there in age—I never had the feeling that they knew or cared who I was. Cy on the other hand, was a terrific friend to me and I enjoyed our interaction enormously. Also, I had just completed writing a new work and had the opportunity to present it to Janet

Hayes Walker and the staff of the York Theater, since I was practically living with them at this point.

During the run of *The Three Musketeers* we briefly had a supervising fight director from The Royal Shakespeare Company in London. One day after watching a scene of the extremely sinister Cardinal Richelieu, he pulled me into the wings and said, "You know, you should play Shylock!" I had only a cursory knowledge of *The Merchant of Venice*, but his words impacted me, given his status, and I began to study the play. The words of Shylock spoke to me in a way that no play ever had before. His sense of alienation, frustration and degradation matched almost perfectly the secret inner dimensions of my heart at that juncture in my life.

I became fixated on it, particularly the "Signor Antonio, many a time and oft on the rialto" speech. I memorized it and began endlessly reciting it. "But, who in their right mind," I thought, "is going to cast an actor with nothing but musicals on his resume in the role of Shylock?" So, I began composing an opera of *The Merchant of Venice*. I wrote it in a frenzy—it was completed in mere months. I called it *Shylock* because I told the story completely from his point of view.

I called Janet and told her I had the score of a new work that I wanted to show her. She paused only a moment and then told me to come to her apartment a week later and show it to her. When I arrived with the score under my arm, there sat the entire board of The York Theater. I sat down at the piano, played and sang through the entire score, all the roles, from the beginning to the end, including the duets and ensembles. When I finished, I closed the score and Janet said, "We'll do it." We never signed a paper or contract. She simply told me that it would be done the following season.

When I went out on the road with *Pippin*, I almost felt that I had dreamed the entire episode. But just before the tour ended, I got a large package of mail from home. One of the pieces in that envelope was a flyer from The York Theater announcing the debut of a new musical by Ed Dixon, *Shylock*. Janet Hayes Walker was good for her word.

THIRTY-FIVE

Shylock

(Circa 1987)

I ASKED MY OLD FRIEND, Lloyd Battista, to direct *Shylock*. He had directed me in *Oliver Quade* and *Hotel Broadway*. I couldn't imagine doing it without him. If I was going to be starring in a musical—actually an opera—of my own composition in New York, I needed someone I could trust to guide me through it.

My first hurdle was finding a Portia. I had written a very difficult role for a soprano, who had to have a sparkling high register and then come on disguised as the judge in the courtroom scene while singing in a low character voice. Who on earth would I find? Several people told me, "You have to hear Lisa Vroman." I didn't know her and I thought I knew EVERYBODY. I called her and she agreed to come to my apartment and look at the score.

She arrived in jeans and a t-shirt with her hair tied up in a schmata. Her personality was ebullient and easy at the same time and utterly charming. She proceeded to stand over my shoulder at the piano and perfectly sight read the entire score. And her voice! It was simply and utterly sublime. I cast her in my mind right then and there, but she had to go through the formality of meeting the rest of the staff at the official audition.

At her audition, her version of "Steal Me Sweet Thief" from Menotti's, *The Old Maid and the Thief* was incandescently beautiful and in a completely different world from all the other singers who auditioned for us that day. I tried to recount this story many years later while announcing Lisa at an evening of my songs at Dillon's, in midtown. I got halfway through a description of the beauty of her singing at that audition and burst into tears. I think everyone got the picture.

It's worth mentioning that, though Lisa was obviously a great talent and pretty and sexy at the same time; she was not pretty and sexy in the way that was popular at that moment in theater. And she was not having much of a career. Since then, she has broken the mold and become quite famous in her own right. She may have made more money out of *Phantom of the Opera* than any other Christine to date, and the word is that she was Hal Prince's favorite. I am very proud that Portia was her breakout role in New York. Dennis Parlato, who had been my Starbuck in *Moby Dick,* was cast as the Merchant and Charles Pistone, who would soon be nominated for a Tony for *The Most Happy Fella*, was a swarthy Bassanio. It was a great group and rehearsals were a joy—at first.

The Rector of The Church of the Heavenly Rest came to me. He had received a piece of hate-mail from the Jewish Defense League regarding my work. Of course, the JDL had not seen my work and had no idea what tack I was taking with it, but they let the Rector know, in no uncertain terms, that they were appalled that his church was presenting such a terrible thing as an opera of the "anti-Semetic" *Merchant of Venice.* He told me that I had to write a reply to them. I didn't want to, but he insisted. So I wrote a very terse letter to the JDL, saying that I was telling the story from Shylock's point of view and it was an utterly positive depiction of him. My friend, Judd Woldin, who had written *The King of Schonorrers* heard my score and told me that, "The Jews have waited 400 years for someone to do this to *The Merchant of Venice*." I didn't feel that I had the right to quote him to the Jewish Defense League. So in my letter I said that I had been told this by a famous Jewish composer. The whole tenor of my letter was petulant and annoyed, because I was—petulant and annoyed.

A week later, the Rector told me that he heard back from the JDL. They were so happy with my letter that they wanted it printed in its entirety in the program. I explained to the Rector that I hadn't been careful with my words; that the letter could not be put in the program and that if it was, it would be quoted by the critics in an unfavorable light. He then informed me that he had promised the JDL that my letter would appear in the program and that if it did not, he would prevent *Shylock* from being performed at all.

Now, I distrust all so-called "religious" persons, but this bloated sack of contempt was a bad example even of his revolting ilk. He had me over a barrel and knew it. Even today, I wince when thinking of his face during that ultimatum. A piece had been put into play that would come back to bite me firmly in the ass.

I knew that there would be backlash from starring in my own adaptation of Shakespeare in New York, but I was not prepared for the firestorm that came down on my head when we opened. Even normally mild-mannered critics went out of their way to hurl epithets of displeasure at me. No one mentioned Lisa Vroman's sublime performance in two impossible roles, or Dennis Parlato's high-flying Antonio, or Charles Pistone's black voiced Bassanio. They all just wanted to ask who the hell I thought I was starring in my own version of a Shakespeare classic. They didn't even knock my performance, just the nerve!

Clive Barnes was the worst of them all. Of course, he used the letter in the program to the most hideous effect possible. He quoted the line from Judd Woldin—still anonymously, thank God—and then quipped, "I'm only half-Jewish, but I would have been willing to wait another 200 years." Not a year later he would give me one of the greatest reviews of my life, but I would never forgive him for pummeling *Shylock*.

That's how it went, except for Howard Kissel from The Daily News. I know it sounds disingenuous, but he had always been my favorite. He championed me and my work in every imaginable way. So in the middle of all that upset, I had this glowing review talking about the beauty of the score and the choral writing and the majesty of my performance—this helped keep me from jumping out a window. It's worth mentioning that *Shylock* was then, and perhaps still is my favorite composition. So the entire experience of opening it to the press was a bit like sending your favorite child off to school and having her kicked senseless by the football team.

Then came the cruelest blow of all. I came to the theater and was met by Janet Hayes Walker who told me that someone on her board had accused me of plagiarism. They were positive that they had heard my setting of "Tell Me Where is Fancy Bred" somewhere before. "Somewhere," I queried. "Where, tell me where they have heard it, since it and the other five thousand original themes in the piece are all mine." No matter what I said, she continued to look at me with a jaundiced eye.

So now, I was being told that I was not even the real father of my favorite child. It was really too much. I never confronted her about this awful accusation, but I never forgave her either. That's not quite true. I forgave her when she died. Her obituary in The New York Times mentioned only three people from her history with the York Theater: George Abbott; Stephen Sondheim and Ed Dixon. I had never made it into anyone's "obit" before, nor had I been mentioned in the same breath with those two giants under any circumstance. Forgiveness was required.

Shortly after *Shylock* closed, I returned to my Greenwich Village apartment to find the most amazing message on my answer machine—yes, people still had answer machines in 1987. The press representative from the York Theater explained that I had been nominated for a Drama Desk Award for Best Actor in a Musical for my performance in *Shylock*. The other nominees were Colm Wilkinson for *Les Miserables*; Robert Lindsay for *Me and My Girl* and Mandy Patinkin for *The Knife*.

I thought he was putting me on. I didn't even know that I was eligible. Then I went downstairs and got the paper and there it was in black and white. I was nominated for a Drama Desk Award as "Best Actor in A Musical" for my musical adaptation of a Shakespeare play.

The two finest performances I had ever seen on Broadway, by men, were Robert Lindsay in *Me and My Girl* and Mandy Patinkin in *Sunday in the Park with George*. As for Colm Wilkinson, *Les Miserables* was the hottest ticket on Broadway and cost mega-millions of dollars to produce. And here was my little *Shylock* musical, which cost maybe $10,000 mentioned in the same category. It was completely overwhelming. That night I woke up in the middle of the night, sat bolt upright in bed, and said out loud, "No matter what happens for the rest of my life, I have been nominated for Best Actor in a Musical in a show I wrote myself!"

THIRTY-SIX

Pittsburgh and the Dominican Republic

(Circa 1987)

IT'S HARD TO IMAGINE THAT at this point in my life I was still penniless, but that's the way it was. All of the work I had done at the York paid not even enough to cover my cab fare. I had become phobic about subways and busses—still am today. My taxis to and from the York, cost more than I was making. I was still living mostly on my teaching and that was killing me. Oh, yes, and I was drinking heavily.

One of my best friends of many years had recently become a very small time drug dealer and was constantly offering me uppers, downers, marijuana, speed, acid and just about anything else imaginable. I say all this quite glibly, but it was the 1980s in New York and everyone, as they say, was doing it. At least everyone I knew. I did not become addicted at this point, but a very bad thing happened, I stopped being afraid of drugs. This was a very bad thing. Familiarity breeds a great deal more than contempt. It breeds, among other things, a blitheness of spirit that can be very deceptive.

So, in my slightly woozy and cash-deprived state, I got an offer to go to Carnegie-Mellon University in Pittsburg and mount a new musical of mine plus teach on the faculty there for a semester. Now, I didn't have a degree from anywhere, so I found the idea of teaching at a prestigious university very appealing, and amusing. Besides, my life was spinning out-of-control and I thought this would be a good vacation from it. But, you know what they say, "Wherever you go, there you are." I and my troubles accompanied me to Pittsburgh.

The musical that they had requested of me was an adaptation of Oscar Wilde's *The Picture of Dorian Gray* that I titled *Portrait*. The work was unfinished when they invited me, we all knew this. I was to finish it on campus, but this was a pretty safe undertaking since the work was to be performed in-house and was not going to be reviewed.

The problems started as soon as I arrived. At the auditions, I was absolutely stunned by the condition of the senior class. They were—to put it succinctly—not talented. Now, the juniors were wonderful, the sophomores were terrific, and the freshmen were spectacular! The freshman class included such wonders as Billy Porter, Natascia Diaz and Michael McElroy, but I was not allowed to use them. The powers that be informed me that I was to cast *Portrait* only from the senior class. I told them that I would be better off with an open casting call outside the school. They did not take kindly to this suggestion. The seniors were cast. One of them, the main female—a great favorite of the staff for some truly mysterious reason—was an albatross around the neck of the production from beginning to end. The day she was cast, you could hear my screams in the next county.

I will say the production was beautifully designed and lit and had a wonderful graphic design. The conductor—who also did the wonderful orchestrations—was a young man who showed great skill and even greater promise, Keith Lockhart. He is now the conductor of the Boston Pops. The performances though, were awful and my work was very, very sloppy. It was never really finished. There were a couple of things in it that were bearable. I inserted that lovely song from *Identity and Other Crises* I had written about my Jacques Brel fling and the opening number was rather good. But, all in all the show was pretty awful. Oh, yes, and in the end, in spite of what I had been promised, they invited the press.

Unlike the previous experience, I got great reviews. Oh, yeah, I was in the piece as well. This was just stupid. But like I said, I was drinking too much and not making good decisions. I also had a fling with one of my students. This, of course, is a REALLY stupid decision and a mistake one could only make while inebriated. The student was 23 and I was 38, not illegal, but really, really stupid. Anyway, I got good personal notices and the piece and the students were soundly slammed. This did not go down well.

I limped out of Pittsburgh and got a remarkable phone call from George Rose. He invited me to visit him in his new villa in the Dominican Republic. I felt a bit like someone who had just received an invitation from Noel Coward to come to Firefly, Coward's home in Jamaica. It would cost nothing but the airfare. I jumped on a plane and disappeared into the Caribbean. However, when George picked me up at the airport in a little red Toyota, there was someone in the back seat. Now, George had told me that he was involved with someone in the Dominican Republic, but there, in the back of the Toyota, was a boy, maybe junior high school age. To say that I was speechless would be to put a positive spin on an unspinable situation. I was apoplectic.

Here was the man I respected more than anyone in the world, and had for many years, in the company of someone who was maybe 14-years old. George was 67 at the time. My internal landscape tore down the middle like a tattered sail in a high wind. We drove to his newly purchased villa on the ocean. It was a big adobe hacienda with servant quarters and a pool surrounded by a high wall. In order to get there, you had to drive down a long deserted road that was really just two ruts through wild tropical vegetation. I was terrified.

The next day we drove into town as I was desperately trying to think what I was supposed to do. On the way back, another little Toyota came up behind us and began wildly honking. We finally decided to pull over, in the middle of nowhere. There were at least ten people crammed in their little car. The front window was broken out and I could tell by the pattern around the edge that it was a heat fracture, something that happens to car windows in tropical countries. A very agitated man was explaining or rather, yelling at George in Spanish, that a rock from our back tire had broken their windshield and they wanted us to pay them $200. George wasn't getting the gist of the Spanish, but I was, and I cautiously whispered to him, "Gun it, we've got to get out of here!" So we took off on two ruts between 14-foot high growths of sugar cane as fast as the little Toyota would go, which was pretty fast—with a car full of angry men directly behind us, a 67-year old man at the wheel of our shaky Toyota and a sullen 14-year old boy in the back seat.

We saw a military installment with a soldier standing at attention in front of a kiosk coming up. We swerved off the road in front of him. Before we could explain our situation, we were overtaken by the carload of locals who were pouring out their side of it to the soldier. The soldier decided that rather than try to discern the veracity of either side, he would escort us to the closest police station—a little cement block barracks a couple of miles away. The men and the soldier seemed very well acquainted with each other. Everyone in the Dominican Republic seems to be everyone else's brother, or at least cousin.

When we arrived at the little police station on a dirt road, the entire town, maybe a hundred people came out to see what was going on and surrounded the police station in a big circle. Soon, we learned that the police station had no phone! The captain took George's driver's license and passport. He was a prisoner, but I was not being held. The 14-year old sat silently in the back seat. A man standing next to me asked me in Spanish what was going on and I replied in Spanish that the man making the accusation was crazy. The stranger angrily replied, "Mi hermano!" (My brother!)

I walked out of the town to the main road and hitchhiked back to Sosua—the sleepy little town where George had rented the car. The woman who ran the place was an ex-patriot American who had married a Dominican, so she spoke beautiful English and Spanish. She drove me back to the town with no name and we rescued George. The next day, the police matter was continued at the Sosua Branch, which was a proper police station. However, everyone in charge was pretending not to speak a word of English and insisting that we pay the $200 for the window broken by the heat. George turned to me in frustration and whispered "This could never happen in America." The police chief very clearly hissed in English, "You no in America, now!" Eventually we paid the money and left.

I told George that I was terrified and expected a torch to come through the window of his villa at any second. (Unspoken subtext, "What the hell are you, the greatest living character actor, doing in the Dominican Republic with a 14-YEAR OLD BOY?") George simply replied, "Oh, no, dear boy! It's perfectly fine. It's part of the culture here."

I couldn't take it. I got on a bus and set off for Santo Domingo the capitol city, on the other side of the island. I no sooner got on the bus when I realized, "Oh, my God, this isn't like Puerto Rico where everyone speaks English. No one speaks English in the Dominican Republic and I'm all by myself." Still, it was better than staying in Sosua with the unbearable situation. What do you do when the person you admire most reveals such a terrible secret? I don't know about you, I simply ran away.

George did follow me across the island a couple of days later and took me to dinner. We did not speak of what was going on back in Sosua. I just couldn't. It would all have a very bad end, but then, I knew that. We made inane small talk with deafening subtext and had one last meal together.

THIRTY-SEVEN

Les Miz at Last

(Circa 1988)

I RETURNED TO NEW YORK to find that I had a replacement audition for *Les Miserables* on Broadway. This wasn't my first *Les Miz* audition. I had auditioned for the original company. In preparation for THAT audition, I read the book—all twelve hundred pages. I decided that the part for me was Javert.

Now, in the old Hollywood movie, Javert was played by Charles Laughton. And since my youth was fading and my weight was rising, I thought that would be the part for me. So, I yellowed in every line of Javert's in the entire book and blued in every reference to him. I then typed this into a work script and memorized it. I wrote a song that I felt captured these qualities and bought an outfit that seemed in the ballpark of the character without being ostentatious.

The song I wrote was called "I Cannot Be Swayed" which pretty much summed up Javert's dilemma in my estimation. I did it for Trevor Nunn and John Caird at 890 Studios. They did that ever-so-English thing of coming out from behind the table and talking to me so closely that I could feel their breath on my skin. It made me VERY anxious. Now, I know that's just English style, but I still blanched. John Caird asked if I ever did other people's material at auditions and I replied, "If required." I then did a Maury Yeston song and felt I would hear something from them soon. I did not.

I found out that in their envisioning of the show, Javert was to be young and dashing and look fantastic in a tight blue policeman's uniform with gold buttons. In fact, they were planning on using Terence Mann, who had previously been the sexy Rum Tum Tugger in their production of *Cats*. Not exactly the Charles Laughton take I had been going for.

So, it was with no little trepidation that I went to a replacement call after the show opened and had become arguably, the biggest blockbuster in Broadway history. By that time, I had rethought my position and went in for Jean Valjean. The audition was on the stage of the gigantic Broadway Theater and on the gorgeous set of *Les Miz*. I opened with "Bring Him Home" and felt that it went quite well. They asked me for the big soliloquy and I did it with the many B flats at the end in a mixed sound. A voice from the back of the auditorium asked me to go back and take the B flats in full chest sound. It was the voice of the musical director Bob Billig, who had been the musical director on *King of Schnorrers* with me.

Now, I did not then and never have had a B flat in full chest. A mixed sound, yes—in full chest, no. But there I was standing on the stage of the Broadway Theatre being asked for it and I thought, what the hell! So, I went for it and let out a screeching yodel that could call in the pigs on a farm. I stood there for a moment reliving my first audition at Casa Mañana and then Bob said from twenty rows back, "You wanna go off and get some water?" "Sure," I said, knowing full well, that water was not going to make me have a B flat in full chest.

When I came back onto the stage, another voice addressed me, a voice I did not know. It was Richard Jay Alexander, who unbeknownst to me had taken over complete charge of the company after John Caird and Trevor Nunn left the country. He said, "Do you have something funny?" I knew at that moment that the Jean Valjean audition was over, but that a whole new avenue had just opened up for me.

I handed a song of mine that I often used for auditions to the accompanist, or rather I handed it to the disembodied hand that silently extended from the pit. The song was "Fairplay" a number that I had written several years before for a show called *Captain America* which never materialized. It ended up being so apt for me that I've used it more often than any other song. It was also useful because it had a quality that could be skewered in any number of directions to make it applicable for almost any situation. I did "Fairplay" conjuring up, as best I could, the vulgar quality of Thénardier, since I knew that's what they were after.

When I finished it, Richard asked me if I would sing "Master of the House" for them. I said that I didn't know it. He asked me to go down into the pit and read it off the piano score with the accompanist. It was only when I got down into the pit that I realized the pianist was Sande Campbell, who I had known since I first came to New York. She had played countless auditions for me. I had an old friend in the pit. I sat down next to her on the piano bench, put my arm around her, swayed back and forth and sang through "Master of the House" for the first time in my life.

I finished the last note, my arm still around Sande's shoulder and Richard's voice rang out from the back of the auditorium:
"So, will you do it?"
"What?"
"Will you do it?"
"Don't you think you should call my agent or something?"
"What, do you have another job lined up?"
"Just some summer stock."
"Well, wouldn't you rather do this on Broadway?"
That's word-for-word how it went. He did call my agent and about a week later I was rehearsing to be one of the very first replacements in the hottest show on Broadway.

When the deal was completed, I realized that we inked the contract almost twenty years to the day since I had begun my show business journey at Surflight. Finally, after two decades, I was playing the right part in the right venue for the right salary. It had taken me TWENTY YEARS to accomplish this miracle. As I pondered my situation, I thought that I could have become a doctor, a lawyer and a nuclear physicist in that length of time. However difficult and however unpleasant parts of it had been, I had achieved my goal.

This realization was not completely pleasant. I had been fighting for so long that I didn't actually know how to be happy. Don't get me wrong, I was very pleased to be in *Les Miserables* on Broadway. But deep down inside, I had this realization dawning that if one isn't happy being nominated for Best Actor in a show one wrote one's self, and isn't happy being in the biggest hit on Broadway, something is askew. Now, this wasn't a full blown "aha!" it was only a niggling suspicion in a dark corner of my consciousness.

They put my picture up out front; gave me a private dressing room on the top floor—and a good salary. The crowds were hysterical and waited for us outside for autographs and sent us fan mail. The management however, wanted me to play the part exactly as Leo Burmester had played it—I am nothing like Leo Burmester. Little by little I weaned the part over toward my personality, and eventually, they were telling the guys in the other productions—at one point there were over thirty—to do it my way. I should have been happy, but something was brewing, something big.

THIRTY-EIGHT

Disaster (From the Greek: Bad-Star)

(Circa 1989)

HOW DO THINGS START? SOMEHOW they just do. In spite of everything, they just do. I could give many explanations for the cataclysm which came into my life in 1988. I could say that I had a nervous breakdown from decades of unrelenting stress. I could say that one of my best friends died horribly of AIDS. I could say that my beloved mentor, George Rose, revealed to me his tragic flaw and was viciously murdered because of it. I could say that my beloved *Shylock* was damned by the press and disappeared into obscurity. I could say that I was in the single worst (and longest) relationship of my life. And although those dominos did fall against one another and move my life in an inexorable direction, it would be disingenuous to claim that what I did and what happened to me during my time at *Les Miz* was the result of any or all of those things. It was my destiny and it was my doing.

Yes, my psyche was a minefield waiting to explode. Yes, it was horrible to see my old friend James, be corroded away inside his own body from the scourge of the 1980s. And yes, most horrible of all, was to have my idol fall from his pedestal and then be murdered by the family of the boy whom he had adopted in the Dominican Republic.

It is worth noting that the family did not kill George because he was doing something terribly wrong with their young relative. They killed him because George had adopted the boy and was about to bring him to America. His family thought that George was very rich and that if they killed him they would get his money. They did NOT understand who he was, what he did for

144

a living, or that his death would make the front page of every paper in New York. They were tracked down and imprisoned, but they did not stay incarcerated for long. Everyone is related to everyone in the Dominican Republic. "Mi Hermano." George's death devastated me, but it did not push my life off the cliff. That happened quite by chance on a Monday afternoon.

I was friends with a group of guys who were not bad sorts. They were a bit naughty, perhaps, but not bad boys. We hung out together, we went to clubs and restaurants together and we sometimes did the odd recreational drug together—as a social event—the way so many did in New York City during the 1980s. I can't really recall how this silly game started, but we all had animal names for each other. One was "the bird," because he was so flighty; one was "the pig," because he was so over indulgent; and one was "the dog," because he would chase after anything that moved. There was one other character on the outskirts of this little group. I don't think anyone knew exactly whose friend he was, but he didn't have a job or any visible means of support and he was clearly unsavory in some indescribable way. We called him "the lizard." I was sitting in my apartment on Washington Place, resting from an exhausting week at *Les Miserables*. My doorbell rang. When I answered the intercom, a voice on the other end said, "It's the lizard."

As I waited for him to climb up the four flights, I thought, "What on earth does he want? I hardly know him. No one just drops in on anyone in New York." When I let him into my apartment, we sat in the living room talking—about nothing in particular—and then he had out with it. He had some drugs with him and he wanted to know if he could do them with me. This was a very odd request. No one just shows up at your door and offers you drugs. But the funny thing is, I wasn't afraid. No red flags went off. No warning shots fired across the sky. I just realized I had nothing on my schedule that day and said, "Sure, why not?"

If I had known then what I know now, I would have realized that the lizard had nowhere to go. He was already homeless by the time he rang my bell. Could I really be so stupid as to step off a cliff simply because it appeared? What he had brought to my door was a very, very serious drug.

The moment I did it, I knew that I was in trouble. I had lost my fear of drugs by familiarity, so, I falsely believed that one drug was like another. I falsely believed that drug addiction and alcoholism were just excuses made up by people who weren't really trying. And I also falsely believed that I couldn't really get into any serious trouble, because I had no family and no support system to fall back on. I was autonomous. If I didn't keep the ship afloat, there would be no ship. This would protect me, I falsely believed. Wrong, wrong, wrong—wrong.

All my false beliefs aside, the moment I did this drug, it was as if a key had been put into a lock. A tumbler was turned, my world shifted and there was no going back. It was mythic and mystical in nature. I literally felt that I had lived all my life with a hole in my heart and that at the very moment that drug entered me, the hole was filled for the first time. I was complete. If you ever have this feeling about anything—and it's not God or your soul mate—you're in a heap of trouble. By the end of the week, I knew I was in big, big trouble. And by the end of the month, I knew with absolute certainty that I was going to die.

I had been on the same track for many years at this point, so my body and my spirit kept going in the direction that they had been programmed to go. On the surface, I went to work. I sang and danced, I laughed and joked. But inside, I was now a drug addict and I knew it. I began to spend all my disposable income on drugs. I was still teaching and all that money went to drugs; plus most of my Broadway salary, as well. I began to cancel students. I'd fall asleep sitting upright at the piano during lessons—those students didn't come back. And my apartment began to fall into disrepair. One day, a student sniffed the air and asked me if I had a cat. When I said that I did not, we both laughed, but it wasn't funny. Students would arrive for lessons and I would be sweating so profusely that I had to put a fan right next to my face. Finally, the students stopped coming.

At first, my performance went on of its own volition. I had literally been performing all my life, so I could operate totally on muscle memory. But there comes an end to that, as well. I had the brilliant idea that I should use alcohol to try and wean myself off drugs. This is when I learned how poisonous that perfectly legal substance can be. I actually had a worse reaction to the booze than to the dope.

During the worst of the drinking, I suddenly lost all the memory banks on which the show was stored. One night, I walked out to begin "Master of the House" and nothing came out; that is, nothing past the title. I sang "Master of the house—" and paused. One of my understudies was standing right next to me and realized that I was in trouble, so he chimed in with "Quick to catch your eye—" This freaked me out, so I missed the next line. By this time I had moved over to stage right—my body kept doing the blocking even without the words. My second cover sang the next line. This kept up until we got to the first choral response from the entire ensemble. They came chiming in with a response to a line that I had not sung. Eventually, Madame Thénardier sang her part and we limped to the finish. I had not sung a single word past the title. I jumped up on the chair to end the number. The lights came up full, the orchestra hit the last chord, I threw my arms out and the audience applauded as if they had heard the number.

I began to run my lines constantly when I wasn't on stage. It did not help. One night, I walked out into the ballroom scene and Hugh Panaro—who was playing Marius—sang his first line to me; I could not answer. He sang his next line; I did not answer. It would be very difficult to describe how embarrassing this was. The entire ensemble was on stage watching me miss an entire scene while standing at center stage with a sold-out house. Then things took a turn for the worse.

I was no longer able to save even one dime out of my paycheck, it all had to go for drugs and paraphernalia. I couldn't buy a sandwich or a cup of soup. I began to go through the giant Rolodex on my desk and pick any name at random that I thought might respond positively to a request for cash. Everyone knew I was in a Broadway hit, so I had to invent elaborate lies to get $50 or $100 "loans." Honestly, I thought at least half of the people knew that I was up to no good, but figured if I needed money that bad, what the hell. As I would go through the Rolodex, I would look at the name of some kind person and think to myself, "You can't call so-and-so, they deserve so much better than that!" It was as if I was looking at my own life through a keyhole. I could see it, but I couldn't do anything about it. I had become an observer of my own life. I previously had no idea there was any such condition.

One day the Rolodex fell off the desk and broke apart into a thousand loose cards. I put them in the drawer and continued making random calls for cash—sometimes in the middle of the night. While rummaging through that drawer one night, I came upon the reading that had been done for me by the Hawaiian psychic several years earlier. It said, "You need to be careful of drugs." Then later in the same document it said it again, and finally a third time. At that point she wrote, "When things come up three times in a reading; you need to pay careful attention." I was paying attention now.

What had once been a deviation; now became the constant. I could not stay sober for a single day. My phone service was turned off for lack of payment. I had it turned back on with my next check. But the second time it was turned off, I decided I could live without a phone and spent that money on drugs as well. Then, the lights were turned out. I don't know how many times I went through the rigmarole of having the lights turned back on by

Con Edison Utilities, but eventually I gave that up as well. I now had an apartment in complete disarray with no phone or electricity. That's how I was living. And I was starring in a Broadway show.

I sought out and went to an outpatient drug clinic on West 57th Street. I knew that I was in very bad shape. And they agreed with my assessment. They suggested that I go into full in-patient rehab and leave the show. I went to the management and asked for a leave-of-absence. They asked me what for. I said it was private. They denied my request.

I went to a new therapist. It did not encourage me when she gasped audibly as I told her the situation I was in. She wrote me a note saying that if I was not given a leave-of-absence I was going to die. The management still denied my request. "Anyone can get a note from a doctor" they said.

My apartment was broken into by some of my drug cronies. When I arrived at my door, the lock and door jamb had been smashed and the apartment door was ajar—they took everything that wasn't nailed down. In the hallway was my very dear neighbor Zabel, who observed my terrible state with nothing but loving kindness. She informed me that she was worried about me when she saw the broken door and had walked inside. What she did not say was that the vandalized apartment was in an unimaginable state, filled with nothing but drug paraphernalia and filth. All she said was, "Are you all right?" Of course, I was not.

One night, I came home to my darkened apartment, holding a fistful of drugs ready to get high and discovered a note from the Sherriff tacked to my still unrepaired door. A padlock was bolted securely across the jamb. I had been locked-out; for failure to pay my rent. It had been 6-months since I last paid! And all I could think was, "Where will I do my drugs?"

In that one moment I lost all my belongings; all my music and scores; all my clothes; all my poetry, compositions and plays; all my theater posters; and my signed music from Leonard Bernstein along with my precious personal letter from Birgit Nilsson—and still, all I could think was, "Where will I do my drugs?"

I found a place, of course. I shared my drugs with someone very much as the Lizard had done with me—now at last, I actually understood why he had come to my door. Fortunately, the person with whom I shared my drugs was already addicted so I did not have that crime on my head—a subtle distinction. The next day, I moved into my dressing room at the Broadway Theatre.

The Broadway Theatre is huge and has multiple exits so the doorman doesn't necessarily see you come and go. My room was on the top floor. The amazing thing about dealing with absolute disaster is that you come to accept any monstrous thing at face value. My life was destroyed. At least I had a dressing room to go to. Few people have ever been in a deserted theater in the middle of the night after everyone has gone—it's absolutely terrifying. There were also motion sensors everywhere, so I could not leave my room and would have been too frightened to try.

The next morning, a poor Lithuanian girl from the cleaning crew walked in on me asleep on the floor of my dressing room. She didn't speak English, but somehow I managed to calm her and explained that I had missed my commuter train—or some such cock and bull story. She left; and for some reason did not report me. This scenario became quite regular.

There were nights when I could not stay in the theater for one reason or another, usually because I was out finding drugs. I slept in the lobbies of hotels—the really large ones take no note of such things. I spent several nights sleeping in Central Park. There is a rocky promontory around 60th Street that seemed relatively safe to me. I was in a nightmare of unimaginable proportions and still I kept showing up for work on Broadway. One has resources that one cannot imagine until they are called forth.

THIRTY-NINE

Further Adventures in Hell

(Circa 1990)

THE UPSIDE OF THIS ENTIRE scenario—if one can be allowed to use such an expression—was that I learned things about myself and about the world during this period that no one could begin to understand who has not survived such a trial. All my life I had felt that I was something of a hothouse flower—artistic and delicate. Surviving my drug addiction and the world that surrounded it—dispelled that quaint notion for all time.

As I descended further and further into the lower rings of hell, I found myself going toe to toe with thieves, murderers, pimps, whores, drug dealers and hosts of supernumeraries who are not likely to show up at a church social. I learned all the places in Manhattan where drugs were dealt and went there with the other junkies. I remember quite well the first time someone referred to me as a junkie. At first I started to protest, but then realized that they were correct. I was a junkie. Now there's a sentence you never expect to say.

There is a great deal of wisdom that one would not expect to find on the underbelly of society. One of the first times I actually bought drugs on the street from a pusher, I was walking away from him with my purchase in my hands when he called after me, "In case you haven't figured it out yet, this is a very serious drug." I was so shocked at his admonishment that I asked him to repeat it, which he did. I must confess, I didn't fully understand the instruction he was offering.

I would often see the same cast of outsized characters at different drug locales around town. One such character was a tiny African-American woman who had the affectation of always having a cardboard guitar around her neck. I never asked why, it was just "her thing." She would make small talk with me when she saw me coming and going out of Clinton Park on 53rd and 11th in the middle of the night. One night, she saw me getting into a taxi and she yelled:

"You take CABS?"

"Of course."

"Ain't that sumpthin'!"

Many months later she saw me exiting the park on foot. She called out:

"Why ain't you takin' a cab?"

"No money."

"Oh...you graduated."

Clinton Park was a ballpark for kids during the day, but after midnight, an uptown gang took it over and dealt drugs like a supermarket. They posted a large gang member, with a baseball bat, at each exit so there was one on each corner of the block. At the rear of the park, past the darkened bleachers and pitch black restroom facilities; a line would form as many as a hundred people long. It was amazing to see—dimly—a hundred junkies standing in line, in an orderly fashion, each one waiting their turn as if they were at Macy's.

One night, walking past the bleachers in complete darkness, I heard a voice from someone lying on the ground say, "Well, if it idn't Donald Trump!" Another voice beside him said, "Is zat REALLY Donald Trump?" The first voice said, "No, he just spend money like him." It was the first I realized that these shadowy figures knew who I was. Disquieting.

The dealer there once took $200 from me and then refused to give me my drugs. When I demanded that he give me what I had paid for; he pulled a knife on me. I walked right into him until the blade was against my stomach and screamed, "You give me something for my money!" He ran away. Yeah— I was a junkie, all right.

There was a 24-hour porno house on 42nd Street where no one watched the movies. People only went there to buy drugs. The dealer sat in the fourth row from the front, on the left hand side, three seats in. For some reason, that theater had an even rougher clientele than the parks. You could never go in there without being hassled in the dark, by very disturbed people on drugs who you could not really see, except by the reflected light of naked bodies writhing on the screen.

Once I saw another Broadway actor in that porno house on a drug run. He was not handling his drugs well and looked like a really, really insane person—which made me wonder if that's how I looked to him. It has occurred to me that he may have looked a tad worse than I did, since he did not survive his addiction. But, without question, we were at the same tea party.

A drug dealer I knew from there, Flaco (which means "skinny" in Spanish) was murdered, cut up and left in the street in a cardboard box. I actually know TWO people who met that fate. If you know two people who have been cut up and left in boxes on the street, you're on the wrong road.

I often walked out of the theater on 42nd Street and right past policemen while carrying hundreds of dollars' worth of illegal drugs—enough to put me away for distribution. Even this did not stop me. One day, I passed a homeless man lying on the sidewalk outside that porno house as I exited with my drugs and he said, "Hey, ain't you that guy from that show?" I was famous.

One time, three squad cars pulled up over the curb on 42nd Street. All the police piled out, surrounded me and shoved my face into the plate glass window of a porn shop. They asked me what I was doing in that neighborhood and began riffling through my pockets. Obviously, they had been observing me for months. I told them that I worked in the neighborhood and that I was just going to the movies. I was on my way to buy drugs, so I had nothing on me. They asked me where I worked and I told them that I was in *Les Misérables*. They looked very confused and rightfully so. The head cop was amazed that they found no drugs or paraphernalia; so he ordered the other cops to search me further, which they did. When they realized that I had nothing on me, they piled back into their cars and took off as quickly as they had arrived. I acted very indignant and yelled at them as they drove away. Then I walked around the corner and bought drugs.

One morning, at about 3:00 AM, I was walking down a street in the drug area of the Lower East Side—it was a constant search to find the area of town where I could score—when I saw a group of unsavory youths coming toward me on the sidewalk. I moved out into the middle of the street; they moved out into the middle of the street. I knew I was in trouble. Then, the guy at the front of their pack broke into a run directly at me. So I turned and began to run, but it was futile. He—being half my age—quickly overtook me and slammed me across the hood of a car and began going through my pockets. I had my drug money tightly clenched in my fist.

This was one of many divine interventions—completely undeserved—that I received during this period. A calm little voice in my head said to me quite clearly, "Yell as loud as you can." I screamed out, "Help," at the top of my lungs! It was very loud and the sound echoed off the surrounding deserted buildings. To my utter amazement, the group of young men scattered as if they had been shot. A moment later, I found myself standing there, alone, unharmed and still clutching my drug money in my tight little fist. When my eyes focused, I saw that there was an old homeless woman sitting on the curb next to the car where I had been thrown. She said in an astonished tone, "He had a gun!" I walked down the street in a state of amazement. I started laughing out loud in spite of everything; or because of everything. Then, I walked around the corner and bought drugs.

I often bought and did drugs at the Carter Hotel. I can say without question that in the 1980s, the Carter Hotel was the scariest place in New York. There was an after-hours club on the ground floor called Saigon Rose. It was run by a genuine Dragon Lady from Viet Nam who stood at the center of the round bar and ran the place with an iron fist. Drugs were sold in the bathroom. A very famous TV actor once confessed to me that he had smoked crack in that very bathroom. At the bar was every representation of every walk of life on the planet; post-op transvestites were having cocktails with off-duty policemen and midget prostitutes were cozied up with certified public accountants—it reminded me of the bar in *Stars Wars*.

The story was that Rose—the lady at the center of the bar—had escaped from Saigon just before it fell, with a suitcase full of money, and swam across the river to freedom with her three children in tow. Her husband did not escape. She was an amazing character. A year or so later, I saw her after she had sold the after-hours club and used the money to buy three piano bars; one for each of her three children.

At one of those piano bars—the one on 46th street—she came out and sat next to me one night—very odd for her. She was barefoot and had on a gorgeous kimono. I told her that she looked beautiful. She covered her face and said, "Oh, no! Not anymore." In that moment and from that gesture, I intuited that among her many other attributes she had once been a beautiful prostitute. I told her that there was a musical coming to Broadway called *Miss Saigon*, but that her story was much more interesting. She looked at me quizzically as if I was speaking gibberish. Then, she leaned over and whispered in my ear, "I know what you doing. Stop before too late." I was often arrested by the amazing things people said to me while I was on this terrible path; but her casual remark knocked me for a loop.

Upstairs at the Carter Hotel was every sort of debauchery imaginable. I actually accomplished the impossible there—I got a drug dealer to sell to me on credit. He walked over to the theater with me, looked at my picture out front as I posed next to it and said, "Okay, if you have a job like that, I know you'll pay me."

I was just getting used to this version of hell when a further development happened. *Les Miserables* had to leave the Broadway Theatre to make way for *Miss Saigon*. We were transferred to the much smaller Imperial Theatre. All this time, I thought that I was putting one over on the management by living in my dressing room, but they called me into the office to tell me that there would be no such carrying on at the Imperial. They also said that I was to stop borrowing money from the other cast members. They also mentioned that I needed to shower more: not easy when you're living in a park. You would think a person would not be able to survive such degradation. You would be wrong.

There was a very kindly doorman at the Broadway named Wally. He had a speech impediment—he actually sounded like Elmer Fudd—and a plate in his head from the Second World War. He was like one of those doormen from an old Hollywood movie; kindly and utterly of the theater world. He brought candy for the children, met everyone with a smile and with a kindness. Over and over he loaned me the same $5 so that I could buy a sandwich; and over and over I paid him back before I spent all the rest of my paycheck on drugs.

When we transferred to the Imperial, Wally came with us briefly to fill in for the Imperial Theatre doorman, who was on vacation. The first night, I tried to stay in the dressing room of that theater. Wally waited for everyone to leave and then spoke to me over the loud speaker system. "Ed...Ed...I can't wet you thtay here! I'm thorry, Ed, but they're gonna fire me. I'm thorry, but you have to come downthtairs. They're gonna fire me." I slowly walked down the stairs and Wally sadly patted me on the shoulder and put me out on the street with one last Elmer Fudd-like, "I'm thorry, Ed." He was genuinely upset. Wally was a very, very nice man.

I started staying at crash hotels in the Midtown area, a dangerous and disheartening business. One night, I was in a squalid little dive on 45th Street with a large amount of drugs—plenty in fact—even by my bloated standards.

In that dirty little room was no phone; no clock; no radio; no TV and no air-conditioning; not even a fan. I sat down to do my drugs and realized that there was not one person or one thing left in my life. I had destroyed every relationship and every aspect of my world. There was not one person who would take my call. I had lied, cheated and stolen from every single person who had known and loved me. I was completely and utterly alone. It was profound. Once again, a quiet little voice spoke from inside my head, "I'm still me" it said. "Even here, even like this, I'm still me." I wonder how many people on this planet have managed to divest themselves of everything with which they identify and still remain alive. Few, I hope.

I was unable to stay in that room. I went over to the Carter Hotel and picked a floor at random from the elevator buttons. I walked down the hall looking for someone, anyone to share my utter devastation. At that moment appeared a pitiful bedraggled drag queen. I asked him if he wanted to do drugs with me. I didn't care who he was; I just couldn't be alone. He said he had a room on the floor above that he was sharing with a writer from The New York Times. The New York Times? Did I want to share my drug addiction with a writer from The New York Times? I simply didn't care. I could not be alone.

We got in the room and I had a brief moment of relief just being in the presence of other humans; when suddenly the door was broken down. In came several very large African-American men in some kind of odd uniforms. There was also a very large woman who would have been the scariest of them all; had there not been a man who was at least twice her size, with a gigantic scar going lengthwise across his face, like a mask in a horror movie. They all had guns. Everyone in our room was robbed. The huge scarred man took me out into the hall and ordered me into the stairwell.

"So, this is how you die," I thought. I had not slept in days and was hyperventilating like crazy. I knew that he was going to kill me. Instead, he took all my drugs, all my money and my jacket—it was the coldest night of the year. He then began whispering to me that he had been in prison for murder and that he had a room where he was going to take me and "do terrible things" to me.

I was 40-years old and quite experienced in virtually every avenue of life, but it had never occurred to me that at this late stage someone might think of RAPING me. In spite of myself, I began making strange little squeaking sounds. They were just leaking out of me like an old balloon. This seemed to make my attacker very angry, but I could not hold them in. I just kept making these very high, "ooh, ooh, ooh!" sounds. They may have saved my life, or

155

at least my "honor." Eventually he threw me out into the freezing night with no coat. I went right back into the hotel and talked a dealer into giving me drugs on credit. Drug addiction has NO boundaries.

Something happened during this period that even under these conditions was surprising. *Les Miz* was often involved in things having to do with the Make-A-Wish Foundation. I saw a lot of sick and challenged children pass through our doors during my first three years there. One day, I was approached with some reticence by the Stage Management. There was a little boy from the foundation who wanted to meet ME. Now, Thénardier is not a nice character; he's scary and drunken and cruel to children; not the kind of guy children would want to chat up. Then, of course, there was my own personal situation. But, here was a little boy with leukemia, Down syndrome and autism; whose fondest dream was to meet the Master of the House before he died. The Management—knowing full well my condition—asked me if I was up to it. I said that I would do what I could.

I had seen enough children with autism to know that they hate being put on the spot, so I was pretty upset when all these people began barraging the child with questions; asking if he enjoyed the show, what was his favorite part and the like. He just shut down completely and refused to say a word or look at anyone. I was in a white bathrobe, my face still smeared with garish make-up and just held back quietly. Eventually, the parents and foundation people gave up and started to leave. Suddenly the child spun around, looked up at me, and proceeded to sing "Master of the House" acapella in its entirety, directly into my face. I knelt down next to him and people took our picture. He went out smiling. And I felt how miraculous it was that I could be useful to someone in my wretched condition.

Then the parents ran back to me and offered me a ride home. Of course I didn't have a home, so I demurred. But they were insistent, so I got dressed and gave them a made-up address. I sat in the car with them and their desperately ill child as they drove me, a homeless person, to an imaginary address and left me standing on the curb waving goodbye. Even a ghost can be kind.

FORTY

Salvation

(Circa 1991)

EVENTUALLY A CAST MEMBER BROUGHT me up on charges. I don't know how it took so long. My addiction went on for three years and everyone in show business knew about it, either from personal experience or the perpetual rumor mill. Certainly everyone in *Les Miz* knew all the gory details—well, not the ones I've just told you—but more than enough.

I received my notice of termination in my mailbox at the theater. It was the first piece of mail I had received in years. I took it with the same resignation to which I had become so vastly accustomed. I was walking to the theater the next day when I ran into my dresser on 8th Avenue:

"Did you save any money out of your paycheck?"

"Of course not."

"Why on earth not? You're about to become homeless."

"If I had any control over what I'm doing, I wouldn't be in this mess."

"Well, you'd better do something. In two weeks you're going to be on the street."

I did not reply to this. But inside my head a little voice said, "Something will happen. Something has always happened."

When I arrived at work, the Stage Manager—who had been sick to death of my condition for a very long time—surprised the hell out of me by asking me if I had called Richard Jay Alexander. Of course I hadn't. I hadn't called anyone in a very long time and certainly not the head of our production. She said that I should explain my condition to him and throw myself on

157

his mercy. I couldn't imagine anyone being merciful to me at that particular moment, but she gave me a dime and I went to a payphone. I called Richard and explained my situation to him; something I had not done when I previously asked the management for a leave of absence. He asked me what drug I was doing. I told him that I didn't want to say. He said that I had to tell him if I wanted his help. So I told him what I was on. I will always remember his reply, "Well, it's the 80s."

Then he said, "I'm going to put you into treatment and then I'm going to give you your job back." I couldn't believe my ears. Actually, I still can't. It was a miracle. I just had to last a couple of more days until a replacement could be found. When I arrived at work the next day for the matinee, I reached out for the handle of the stage door and the Company Manager grabbed my hand. He said to me, "You won't be going to work today." I thought they were reneging on the deal, but he walked me around the corner to The Actors Fund and bought me a sandwich on the way. He took me to the head of drug treatment there. I found myself in the middle of a group of people who did nothing but expedite treatment for addicts. I had no idea there was any such organization or any such support system or that it had been waiting for me just around the corner.

It had taken me three years to be delivered. I had lost everything I ever owned. When I arrived at the Smithers Treatment Center on the Upper East Side—in the old Billy Rose Mansion—I had all my worldly goods in a small plastic bag. The head of treatment saw my bag and said that a person who has divested himself of everything is ready to leave the planet. I couldn't have lasted another day. If Mark Andrews, our Company Manager, had not taken me to treatment that day, I would be dead.

I slept on clean sheets that night for the first time in years. I had actual food; which was quite a shock. Basically, for the last year of my addiction I was only eating what I could steal from grocery stores without attracting attention—and that was very little. I got caught in the old Victoria Market in Hell's Kitchen and was literally thrown out with a boot to my rear end like in an old Charlie Chaplin movie.

There was a full length mirror in my bathroom at Smithers. The first time I saw myself naked I thought, "Wow, my face looks like my grandfather's, but my body looks GREAT!" I was thin as a rail. Humor can accompany one to the most terrible places. When I sat down on my bed for the first time, I saw that someone had signed the wall next to the bed. In very clear cursive script, it said, "Dwight Gooden." Your guess is as good as mine.

I was desperately ill. I needed to be in a hospital, but hospitals were too expensive, so I was in a treatment facility, doing cardio and endless group therapy. It's not that I didn't need cardio and group therapy, I most certainly did, but right at that moment I needed to be in a hospital bed. I had been abusing myself twenty-four/seven for three years and I was not a young person. I celebrated my 40th birthday at *Les Miz*. The cast and crew—who didn't yet know my condition—hung up streamers and filled my room with balloons. When I entered my dressing room, I thought it was the saddest thing I had ever seen, because I knew the condition of the person whose birth they were celebrating. For my 41st and 42nd birthdays, there were no balloons or streamers—they all knew by then.

The crowd at Smithers was very colorful. At one point, we were joined by a guy who had been in the Olympics, as he repeatedly told us. He was very handsome, very charming and clearly sociopathic. It was also clear that his drug addiction had turned him into a criminal. During his brief stay with us, he came on to every one of us; from the patients, to the staff, to the cleaning crew, just to see if he could get something out of it. He was thrown out before his first day ended.

There was a fellow whose family owned a very famous Irish bar on the West Side in New York. He had worked there all his life and was a raging alcoholic. He had been mandated by the court for treatment after several DUIs. For him, it was either Smithers or jail. He was also a sexaholic and was warned from the first day to stay away from a particular woman who had a similar problem. They kept at each other and were given a written warning—to no avail. They sneaked into one of the offices after midnight, hoping to use the desk for something other than its intended purpose, but when they closed the door behind them it locked and they had to call security to get out. She was thrown out of treatment and he went to jail.

A wealthy and elderly socialite was admitted by her family because of her alcoholism. She was very refined and genteel. It was hard to believe that her family found it necessary to have her committed against her will. Her problem didn't seem to be that serious. She got out very soon after my arrival and returned to her Park Avenue apartment. She also returned to her usual level of alcohol consumption and died that very night. Most of the people I went to treatment with are dead now; the doctors make no bones about it. Serious addicts do not tend to recover. It's just too hard.

It was during this time that a famous batch of China White heroin hit the streets of Manhattan. It was all over the news and in every paper. A heroin addict opined to me that he couldn't believe he was, "Locked up in a god-damned treatment facility when the best smack in history was out there on the streets." I said unbelievingly, "You mean that stuff that's killing all those people?" To which he replied, "They just don't know how to DO it." Ah, perspective.

Treatment doesn't last twenty-eight days because that's how much time it takes to recover. It lasts twenty-eight days because that's all that the insurance companies will pay for. At the end of my four weeks I was just starting to be able to stand upright. They asked me if I felt well enough to return to work. "No way," I croaked. They sent me to a halfway house in Minneapolis.

This halfway house was called "Progress Valley." Sounds nice; like someplace you'd go skiing outside of Taos. It was a crummy little apartment complex in a bad neighborhood in Minneapolis, run by a would-be army drill sergeant. I arrived in the middle of winter, desperately ill and worn out. I had no money and no winter clothes and it was February—in Minneapolis. I expected to sink down into a nice warm bed until group therapy, but the drill sergeant informed me that I was to go get a menial job and not to return until I had one.

I took some gloves, a hat and coat from a discard bin in the front closet and set out into the frozen tundra of the Minneapolis winter. I had only gone a couple of blocks when I spied a sign in the window of a little greasy spoon diner, "Dishwasher Wanted." I thought to myself, "Well, at least it's close to the house." So I went inside. I spoke with the genial owner and filled out the form he gave me. I didn't know if I could do a menial job in my condition. I didn't know if I could hold a regular job, period. When I got to the line on the application that asked for my last year's income; I decided to tell the truth. When the owner saw the figure, he said, "Oh! You're in treatment!" Minnesota is the land of treatment centers.

The owner then shared with me that he once had a dishwasher who was from Broadway. I assumed that he had some chorus boy from *Hello, Dolly* working for him. But no, he was referring to a former dishwasher of his who was a famous playwright, a VERY famous playwright—it wouldn't be fair for me to out him in this book, but he's a VERY famous playwright. I didn't get the job. Perhaps the owner was holding out for David Mamet.

I continued down the road until I saw a help wanted sign in the window of a Blimpie's sandwich shop. All the employees were half my age and very disinterested in my arrival. Their application form asked me to do complicated multiplication and division in my head. "What's 4,326 times 259?" I sat there realizing that I hadn't done figures without a calculator in many years and I simply could not do it in my head. Needless to say, I was passed over for employment—at Blimpie's.

At last, I discovered the Plexiglas skyways that connect all of the downtown buildings in Minneapolis and allow you to avoid the cold weather. I began to get clearer in my thinking. What kind of job would I be able to withstand for the next three months? Preferably something that would not have me elbow deep in hot soapy water or burning up in front of a grill. Then I saw it; Grandma Gephardt's Cookies. All they had was coffee and cookies. Surely, I could do that—if the math wasn't too hard.

The Manager of that store was very kind to me, but his wasn't the store with the opening. There was another branch way out at the dead-end of an office hallway that needed someone. That Manager, a young man of about 27-years old, asked me a few questions. He found out I had been on Broadway and hired me immediately. I raced back to the halfway house thinking I would fall into bed, but no, I helped make the dinner and then was put on clean-up duty.

Everyone at the halfway house was about 20-years old—except me. Most of the houseguests at Progress Valley were mandated for treatment by the court system, so I guess the court figured they needed to be taught "structure." There were hundreds of pedantic and ridiculous rules. And as an extra perk, there was no space for me, so I had to sleep in a cot in a hallway on the 3rd floor.

Most of my fellow houseguests never held a job or finished school, so they didn't even have basic skills, like how to get up in the morning. Alarm clocks were of no use, they would simply ring until they ran down. Anything would wake me up; so someone's untended alarm three doors down would end my slumber. Fortunately, I had one of the earliest work calls; 6:30 AM.

I was very pleased to learn that I was capable of doing menial labor. I put on a paper hat and an apron—they made me look like an imbecile—and made endless batches of cookies—which I don't even like—and bottomless pots of several kinds of coffee. I found that I quickly made friends with the secretaries; the majority of my clientele. They told me about their bosses and showed me pictures of their children.

My boss was another story. It turned out that he was a failed musician. He was mean spirited toward me about my addiction and envious of my career. He was also a full blown alcoholic. Most mornings he would lie on the floor in the back room nursing a hangover while I did all the work. He humiliated me in front of the customers and treated me like a dull-witted high school student; badgering me about the "proper way" to fill a cup of coffee or the "best technique" of putting a cookie in a paper sleeve. It was hard.

I had to suck it up because if I was fired from my job, I would be thrown out of the halfway house. If I was thrown out of the halfway house, the deal that I had made with my union and with *Les Miz* would become null and void. I had to take whatever my boss would dish out. Plus, all the minimum wage money I made had to be turned back into Progress Valley to further subsidize my so-called room and board.

After work, when I returned to the halfway house, I would have to begin my second job; cleaning the house, preparing the food and doing the clean-up afterward. I felt like Cinderella, with twenty-five evil stepsisters. At group therapy, the underage offenders would rail on about how they felt violated having to share a house with an old homosexual. Of course, most of them had sold themselves for drugs before coming to Progress Valley—all young drug addicts do—but it seemed to have slipped their collective minds. There was a mode of therapy called "housing" in which all if the houseguests told you exactly what they thought of you while you had to remain passively sitting in a chair with your mouth shut. This was the brainchild of our drill sergeant overseer. It was almost unbearable; and I could bear quite a lot.

It really is amazing how much abuse a person can take and still continue to function in some way or other. Just before I was to receive my AA chip for 90 days of sobriety, I snapped. Somehow I got some kind of insurance check for over $100—there's no way any such check should have come to me, but it did. Suddenly, I had over a $100 worth of disposable income. I had accrued a couple of hours' worth of free time from the house, so I set off with one of the other guys to see a movie. It was to have been *La Femme Nikita*—a film I still have not seen to this day. Somehow en route, we decided to go get drugs instead. We both knew full well that it would be impossible to cover this up and that we would be thrown out of the halfway house. If that happened, he would go to jail and I would become a homeless person—and yet, we did it anyway. Addiction is amazing.

After a truly terrible night, on the wrong side of Minneapolis, we came crawling back to Progress Valley via the back alley. By a bizarre twist of fate, the door guard had fallen asleep. So we faked our names and arrival times into the sign-in book and went to our beds. Two hours later, I was up and on my way back to Grandma Gephardt's Cookies—one of the five-million miracles that saved my undeserving ass during this period.

I creaked through this exhausting abuse and unrelenting humiliation for three months until it was almost time for me to return to my life in New York and my job in *Les Miz*. I knew very well how lucky I was to have survived my innumerable mistakes and to have a good job to return to, when most of the others in the house were going back to lives of poverty and menial labor. Then, suddenly it dawned on me. I didn't have a penny to my name and no one I could call for help. I had exhausted every possible avenue of assistance before I entered treatment. When I returned to my job on Broadway, I would have no place to stay, nothing to eat and would not be paid until I had worked my first week. What would I do, sleep in the park again? That really didn't seem feasible at this point. Then, another miracle happened.

Normally, one was not allowed any visitors or phone calls at Progress Valley. I was expecting a call from my case worker at the Actors Fund about my readiness to rejoin society, so when a call for me came during group therapy, I was excused to take it. When I picked up the phone, it was not Roz— my wonderful coordinator from the Actors Fund—it was my old friend, Tracy Smith (now Smith-Trevett); from Surflight, so many years before.

In a life that was quite full of surprises, what she said to me then utterly knocked me out. She and her husband, Austin—a stoic New Zealander—had a large loft on 36th Street in Midtown Manhattan. They had a private apartment in the back and had lost their tenant. She wanted to know if I would like to take that apartment for my return to society. So once again, I was pulled from the fire by unseen hands, having done nothing to deserve the favor.

I graduated from Progress Valley and got on a plane to return to Broadway. I was still in pretty bad health—shaking, actually. I had only a couple of weeks sobriety and was carrying the terrible secret of my relapse; anathema for an addict. What on earth was going to happen to me?

With the incredible Christine Ebersole on her opening night at The Carlyle.

As Charlemagne in the Papermill production of *Pippin,* wearing the fabulous Gregg Barnes costumes, so unlike the ratty ones we had on the national tour.

With my dear friend, Kathie Lee Gifford at the New York opening of my *Fanny Hill.*

With Bebe Neuwirth and Shawn Emamjomeh in *Here Lies Jenny* off-Broadway.

Starring as Armand in Kathie Lee Gifford's off-Broadway production of *Under the Bridge*.

After a performance of *Under the Bridge* with my pal, Tony Danza.

With the delightful Lynne Wintersteller in my two-hander, *Scenery.*

One of my favorite experiences ever, The Modern Major General in *Pirates!*

At Rainbow and Stars with the great composer, Cy Coleman.

Rehearsing *Mame* with composer, Jerry Herman, who also wrote
Hello Dolly, Mack and Mabel and La Cage au Folles.

Celebrating my 60th birthday at Joe Allen's with the great Christine Baranski.

Backstage at the St. James Theatre as Old Max in *How the Grinch Stole Christmas*.

Backstage with John Kander of Kander and Ebb, the duo that wrote *Chicago, Cabaret, Kiss of the Spider Woman* and *Curtains*. I had a blast playing the Director in *Curtains*.

Rehearsing with Zoe Caldwell, one of the greatest stage actresses of all time.

Backstage at the Broadway revival of *Sunday in the Park with George* with the great man himself, Stephen Sondheim.

A portrait by photographer, Chris Mueller, of my Max Von Meyerling in *Sunset Boulevard,* for which I won the Helen Hayes Award.

FORTY-ONE

Re-entry

(Circa 1991)

I ARRIVED BACK IN NEW York and went to the Smith-Trevett loft on 36th Street. You had to have a key to get onto the floor (the 16th and top floor) and once you were there, you were in a secluded palace in the sky with beautiful views and the entire roof available for sunning or observation. You could see the Chrysler Building, the Empire State Building and Times Square from the deck. In my beautiful but tiny apartment in the back, there were already clean sheets on the bed and fresh towels in the large white tiled bathroom. I will never again take clean sheets and fresh towels for granted.

The Smith-Trevett's left the door to their apartment open that first night because somehow they intuited that I had the constitution of a frightened 6-year old. Now, mind you, they had a 2-year old daughter in the house. It was unimaginable, the largeness of their generosity, especially since neither the daughter nor the husband had the slightest inclination toward me; and rightfully so. It was my dear old friend, Tracy, who MADE this happen. I will always remember her family's fisheyes as I invaded their world. Eyes that said, "What on earth is this disheveled man doing in our house?"

The first indication that I was going to get well came when I asked Tracy to take charge of my checking account. Starting that week, my checks went directly to her and I had no access to them. I progressed from being a frightened 6-year old to an untrustworthy teen.

I had some sort of therapy session, group, AA meeting or drug rehab every single day—sometimes multiple times a day. I have had many therapists in my life, but none as wonderful as Roz Gilbert, my case worker from the Actors Fund. However, I was assigned an after-care group therapy session that was the opposite of dear Roz. A hostile and untrained overseer put us through unpleasant paces in a cramped and unpleasant room. Many bad times were had there. AA meetings in New York run the gamut from elegant to scary. I saw them all.

Under this constant supervision, I cautiously returned to my job in the Imperial Theatre. The stage door is on 46th Street between 7th and 8th Avenues. Now, 8th Avenue was the center of the drug trade in New York in the 1980s. Pre-Giuliani—good God, if Giuliani had been mayor during my dark days, I'd STILL be in jail. When I first caught sight of 8th Avenue looming in front of me, the entire world seemed to tilt as if I would slide off the edge of the planet. I was NOT expecting that.

My primary drug dealer, a very scary man named "Red," with big muscles, a huge silver handgun and a bevy of prostitutes with black eyes and bruises—from him—lived right around the corner. He had taken to meeting me at the stage door to collect his money every payday. When the Company Manager sent me to rehab, I owed Red several hundred dollars. Red could have killed someone for $50 much less hundreds. I had no idea when or where he might appear.

There were so many places in the city where I dared not go, that I constructed a grid for myself with "safe routes" that would allow me to get places without going past old danger zones. The grid was VERY restricted since most areas of the city had bad memories attached—it would be a very long time before I could go back to Greenwich Village.

All my fears quickly disappeared when I walked inside the Imperial Theatre. I was embraced by Joe the doorman, and many cast and crew members. I was presented with a huge floral display from Richard Jay Alexander and Cameron Macintosh—Mr. Macintosh is the biggest producer in the world—with a card saying, "It's so nice to have you back where you belong" —a lyric from *Hello, Dolly*. But, the thing that amazed me the most was that the ushers baked me dozens and dozens of cookies. The USHERS! For years afterwards the ushers from the Imperial would embrace me in the street whenever they saw me. This is the kind of thing that gives one hope about humanity. Why on earth would they be so generous? Because they were, they just were.

I had done something like a thousand performances of Thénardier at this point, but so much had happened and my poor brain and body had been through so much. I had no idea what was going to happen at that first show. But things went surprisingly well and the atmosphere was SO supportive. It was a very beautiful experience.

I wish I could say that was the end of my trials, but it was not. I quickly began to understand why people don't recover from serious addiction. When you've done that kind of damage to your brain and body, there is no such thing as a spontaneous regeneration. Your brain chemistry has been altered. All the producers of dopamine and serotonin and the myriad ingenious bodily productions that make life pleasurable are burned out and used up; so there is no joy to be found in normal activities for a very long time. Things like reading, listening to music, looking at trees and flowers do not elicit the normal reactions in early recovery. It's easy to see why people say, "Screw it!" and return to old habits.

I had reached the stage where my addiction had a personality all its own. It actually felt as if an entity would grab me by the front of my shirt and drag me out the door. There were occasions when I held onto the door handle of my apartment with both hands; just to keep from being dragged outside by my Golem. There was a ritual that I used to go through in my Greenwich Village apartment during the black days. When I was waiting for a drug delivery, I would hold down the intercom button and listen for footsteps in the street. As I heard someone coming, I would wait to hear if they came into my building. If they did not, I would beat my head against the wall until I heard the next footsteps. I could see myself doing this insane action while I was in the middle of it, but could do nothing to stop it.

Even after recovery, this level of obsession would take me over and sadly, I succumbed to it several more times. Each episode lasted only one evening, but they were extremely destructive to my process of recovery. I was unable to come up with 90-days of continuous sobriety.

The paradoxical thing about treatment is that they keep telling you, "It's up to you. You're responsible." But I would always say, "Yeah, but it was up to me before and look at the mess I made of it." Nevertheless, that's what they say, and that is, of course, the truth, no matter how little help it may be at the time.

After my third relapse, the Stage Manager called me into her office. I was not aware that she knew, but everyone in my life was quite tuned in to my condition by this time. She did not accuse me or berate me. I did not defend myself. She simply said, "You know how to get help. Get it!" When I returned home, Tracy's husband Austin asked me to join him for breakfast the following morning.

He took me and his 2-year old daughter to the corner diner. We sat in a booth and ordered breakfast. His eggs arrived and he said, "I'm not telling you that you have to leave. I'm telling you that I'm responsible for my home and for my family. I'm telling you that I don't know what to do." I took a breath and said, "If it happens again, you won't have to ask me to leave. I'll just go."

About a day later, I was following my prescribed safe-route home down 7th Avenue. When I crossed 42nd Street, I looked to my right and saw the old porno house where I so often bought drugs. It's not that I was thinking of going there, I was just allowing it into my consciousness. Then that very clear voice spoke in my head, the one that so often guided me during the previous three years. It said very clearly, "NO MORE ANGELS!"

Now you can call this whatever you like; dementia, schizophrenia, psychosis, you name it. But it was crystal clear, and it was quite startling—I had heard that voice numerous times during my addiction. This was the last time, and it was the last relapse. It was over.

Somehow, miraculously and instantly, that was the end of it. How this shift took place I will never fully comprehend. It gave me some insight into what "grace" might be. Deliverance and blessing through no merit on the part of the recipient—a gift which has not been purchased. It let me go. I had been in a deep dark pit for years, and suddenly...poof...I was out. It was invigorating and terrifying at the same time. I had no idea how I had done it, but there I was—out.

Eventually I was able to move freely around the city that had been my artistic and actual home for decades. Giuliani cleaned up 8th Avenue and I was able to walk there without seeing a single person or place from the old days. But the one area that remained off limits for me was Greenwich Village; where I had lost my beautiful apartment on Washington Place. Eventually I was required to run an errand that would take me to Christopher Street, only a couple of blocks from there, so I decided it was time to face my fear. I arrived at Christopher Street from Hudson Street on the West Side; so that I didn't have to actually pass my old home. This was the perfect timing for me to have the perfect punctuation for this period of my life.

As I passed a darkened doorway on Christopher just past Hudson, a shadowy figure stepped forward out of the shadows and headed right toward me. It was—the Lizard. He was a disheveled mess and when the light hit his face I could see that he had snot running out of his nose and down toward his lip. He was clearly stoned out of his mind. He reached out his arms toward me and I allowed him to embrace me. He gave me a big "Judas kiss" on the side of my face leaving a smudge of mucous. He asked me how I was and I told him that I was very well. I did not ask how he was; I knew how he was. I patted him on the shoulder and walked away. And that was that.

FORTY-TWO

Starting Over

(Circa 1991)

ONCE I GOT OVER THE shock of getting on with a life I thought had ended, I looked around and began taking stock. I owed money to virtually every person I had ever known. I made a list of them and began paying them back with checks that my dear neighbor, Tracy, would write out for me. I couldn't handle my own money for a year. You can imagine how shocked people were when they received a check from a third-party; for a debt that they never thought would be repaid; from a person they thought was dead. Many of them contacted Tracy to see if the check was real before they cashed it.

My favorite example of this requires a bit of background. When I was using, I called a famous conductor at about 3:00 AM one morning. His wife, a very sweet woman, answered the phone, explaining that her husband was out of town. I told her that my mother had died and I needed $100 to get to the airport. She told me to come to her home on the Upper West Side immediately and she would give it to me. When I arrived, she came downstairs in curlers and a chenille bathrobe; crossed her elegant lobby; forced three $100 bills into my hand; kissed me and said, "Here, just take this, you're going to need it." When she got back onto the elevator, I stood there thinking, that fire should come down from the sky and consume me for deceiving such a good person. However, it did not and I went out and bought $300 worth of drugs.

Her kindness lived inside me like a burning coal. It was almost unendurable. She was one of the first people I repaid. And of course, I sent a letter of apology, as if one could ever apologize for such a thing. A few days later, I went to my mailbox and found a letter from her that said, "I received this letter from you long ago in my heart." I just stood there at the mailbox, overwhelmed and thinking, "No one on earth deserves this kind of kindness, least of all me." I tried to tell her on several occasions what her gesture meant to me, but she never seemed to feel that what she had done was extraordinary—which is even more extraordinary.

It seemed totally impossible that I would ever make it through my list of debts, but as I went along, week-by-week, month-by-month, it slowly began to dwindle. There were a couple of people who died; and a couple who disappeared; but as far as I know, I eventually paid everyone back and apologized to the best of my ability. A few did not take my apology well—one even cursed me and wished me dead. I felt very strongly then and still do today, that if a person is going to do what I did, other people have every right to react any way they see fit in return. But, I must say, most people were generous, forgiving and kind in a way that was beyond imagining.

Once I had leveled that field, I began thinking about my career again, that is to say, my career that might or might not exist beyond *Les Miserables*. I knew I couldn't stay in the show forever—though it did seem as if it would last for eternity—but I didn't know if show business would allow me to continue. I was now 43-years old, washed-up, and I did not even have an agent.

I had been personal friends with my previous agent for many years—we had basically put my whole career together from scratch. But she was so upset by my behavior during the drug years that she dropped me both as a friend and a client. This was one of the few relationships that was never mended. I was a 43-year old actor with no agent. Not good.

I was so terrified of trying to start again that I went to a career counselor, told her my situation and asked her for guidance. She, a very straight laced woman of a certain age, was obviously appalled by my saga, but she took me on anyway. She suggested a new type of photo, a new type of resume, and rehearsed a kind of spiel with me that I would use as the basis for an improv I could do for an agency, to overcome the elephant in the middle of the room; "What is a 43-year old actor doing without an agent?" She even suggested which agency I should target; Abrams Artists. Not too big, not too small. I rehearsed my phone improv, dialed the number and set up an appointment.

I put on new clothes and set off to meet a new agent for the first time in two decades. When I arrived, it was a very cordial and pleasant office. I met a very cordial and pleasant, low-level agent. He approved me—and my carefully rehearsed speech—so I was sent to meet a higher agent. Then, I was called back to meet their literary agent. This was really looking good. I would even have someone to help me restart my writing career. At last, on my third appointment, I was to meet the head man himself. I was feeling confident by this time. So I got dressed, rehearsed my spiel in the mirror of my bathroom one last time and set off to become a new client of Abrams Artists.

I wasn't even nervous when I was called into the big guy's office. I sat there feeling cool and laughing and joking off-script. He was cordial and pleasant. Then, just as the interview was ending, he looked up and said, "Oh, by the way, 'so and so' is one of our favorite clients." The name—which I have just omitted—was the name of the actor in *Les Miz* who brought me up on charges and tried to have me fired. I knew perfectly well that this person had been calling her agent every day for the last year complaining about the horrors endured at the hands of an insufferable addict and begging for help to get rid of him. Her agent was the man sitting across the desk from me. I picked up my things and left, like Don Knotts doing an imitation of a whipped dog. I was done for.

I'm not saying it was the next day, because I don't want to make a story that is already dramatic seem overly so; but, within days of this event, my phone rang. It was a woman named Mary—whose voice I had not heard in many years. She had worked at the Ann Wright Agency when I booked that Captain Black Pipe Tobacco commercial during *Moby Dick*. She said that a candy manufacturer in Europe asked for me by name based on that previous commercial and she wanted to know if I had current representation. I took a deep breath and said, "I would love to come in and discuss that with you."

Mary was then working at the Epstein-Wyckoff Agency on 43rd Street, within walking distance of my little home on 36th Street. When I arrived at Epstein-Wyckoff, the story became even more implausible. When the European candy manufacturer had asked for me—a near impossible scenario since I had only done a handful of commercials in my career—Mary said out loud at her desk, "How on earth am I going to find Ed Dixon?" The young man she was interviewing piped in, "I have Ed Dixon's number." He was in the chorus of *Les Miz* and had my number in his cell phone.

Now here I sat in her office and the European candy manufacturer had somehow disappeared, but Mary was very happy to meet with me and wanted to know if I'd like to meet the head of the agency, Gary Epstein. She walked me around the corner and introduced me to Gary. We became fast friends and he is still my agent today (though the agency is now called Phoenix Artists

Management) and we probably will remain friends until one of us dies—or perhaps even longer. The even more implausible thing; within days of that encounter Mary left the office and I never saw her again. Now, the fact that she materialized only to bring me on board at Epstein-Wyckoff may not be divine providence, but it's close enough for me.

I had sobered up, paid back my debts, and gotten a new agent. Now I just had to get out of *Les Miz* and back into the world. Not so easy. I mean, first of all, an actor is never put in the position of having to say, "Take down my picture from out in front of the theater and stop giving me this money." It's a new development since the advent of the very long run. It's a very hard thing to do.

The last several months of therapy that year were all sessions about how on earth I was going to quit. One day, after one of those sessions, I walked in the stage door of the Imperial and was told that Wally—the dear old doorman from the Broadway Theatre—had died. I put on my make-up and costume silently. I walked to my spot when "places" was called. The smoke billowed up around me, the orchestra sounded, the lights hit me. But when I made the first sound in the opening scene, I began to cry uncontrollably. I cried through the entire show. All night long people would ask me what was wrong and I would just blubber, "Wally died." The usual response was, "I had no idea you liked Wally so much." There was no way to explain what he had done for me.

Shortly after that event, we had an Actors Fund Benefit performance, the first I'd had since my return. The audience went wild and it was extremely gratifying to raise money for the organization that had so tirelessly worked to keep me alive. The divine Laurie Beechman was at that performance and sought me out afterwards. She had come back from death's door several times to play Fantine as she battled cancer. I had done the show with her on more than one of those comebacks, but it was obvious that on this day she was losing her battle again.

I had never had much interaction with her because I had never been well enough when she was there previously. But on this occasion, she grabbed me by my lapels, pulled her face into mine and whispered forcefully, "You are so wonderful! What you have done is so incredible! You must go on doing it!" Then, she released me and was gone. I knew I would never see her again and I knew she had spoken to me directly out of her knowledge of fighting for her own life.

Eventually, my doorway out of *Les Miserables* was provided by my old friend Mark Bramble—writer of *42ND Street* and *Barnum* and *The Three Mus-keteers*. On a lark, he was directing a musical written by an ophthalmologist and wanted me to be in it. Oddly enough, a lot of doctors write musicals—they have disposable income and huge egos, so if they want to put up their musical opus, who can stop them? I have actually done TWO musicals by dentists. I can't say with certainty that all musicals by medical professionals are odious, just the ones in which I have participated. Nevertheless, I signed the contract to do the eye doctor's musical in Massachusetts and turned in my notice.

The cast of *Les Miz* had a ritual of singing the theme song from the Roy Rogers TV Show "Happy Trails" whenever a cast member would depart. I have always hated that song and forbade it to be sung to me. Instead, they sang "Auld Lang Syne" which is one of my favorite songs, so I cried like a baby. I honestly didn't know if I could live without *Les Miz*. I was about to find out.

FORTY-THREE

A New Life

(Circa 1992)

THE MOST INTERESTING THING ABOUT the ophthalmologist's musical was that it put forth the premise that since Christopher Columbus set sail for the new world on the day that the Jews were expelled from Spain, Columbus was a Jew. And therefore, America—was discovered by a Jew. This deadly earnest yet hilariously funny piece of theater had me playing Torquemada, the Grand Inquisitor, and saying wonderful lines like, "And when you pray, do you wear—a little hat?" We also had amazing parties at the ophthalmologist's mansion, on his yacht, in his helicopter, etc. However, all this merriment soon ended and I was returned to the perpetually recurring state of most in my profession—unemployment.

I began teaching and writing again. The first subject that I addressed was a sketch that I made just before my life fell apart, based on the early short stories of Willa Cather. I had sketched out the entire piece—on blue graph paper for some reason—and when it became clear that disaster was imminent, I put the pages into a plastic bag and gave them to a friend to keep for me in case I should ever be able to resume my life. When I first reclaimed the bag, I expected it to be filled with unintelligible chicken scratching. But, to my great surprise and delight, when I scanned the pages, they seemed quite cogent and very promising.

I set about composing *Cather County* in a frenzy—as is my wont. A first draft was done rather quickly and it immediately began to take on a life of its own. Mark Bramble, once again to the rescue, flew me to London where we did a presentation that included John Barrowman—now famous for *Dr. Who* and *Torchwood*—and Cleo Laine's extremely talented daughter Jackie Dankworth. When I came home, Nicholas Martin—now a well known director—presented it to Playwrights Horizons, and *Cather County* was shoehorned into their season. The entire experience there was one of my favorite ever with any of my works. The cast included: Judy Kaye; Brent Barrett; Alice Ripley; Sal Viviano; Glory Crampton; Brigid Brady; Mary Stout and Herb Foster. Rarely has such a talented group been assembled in one room. Drew Scott Harris directed and Stan Tucker was the musical supervisor. They both lavished attention on the project as if they had written it themselves. Rehearsals were an absolute joy.

Actors are very fond of the expression, "It's not brain surgery." One day, we were working so diligently on the opening chorale, and the balancing just went on and on—more tenor, less alto, less soprano, more bass—when at last, after much intense fine tuning, it landed very powerfully. And Mary Stout exclaimed, "It *IS* brain surgery!"

Herb Foster, a very wonderful and very experienced actor, paid me a marvelous compliment when we finished putting the very complex finale together. I was seated at the back of the house. Herb began walking up the aisle to speak to me. When he was almost to the last row, he got out, "That finale..." and burst into tears. No actor has ever complimented me so eloquently.

Brent Barrett and Alice Ripley were so dynamic in their segment that there was never a dry eye in the house at its conclusion. Brent died in her arms and eight times a week, you could hear people openly weeping. Judy Kaye popped out a high D in the big ensemble at the end of act one that any soprano at the Met would have killed for.

All the composers of the day came to see *Cather County*. I reconnected with Jones and Schmidt—*The Fantastics*; Ahrens and Flaherty—*Ragtime*; hell, even Wright and Forrest—*Kismet* showed up. It was truly a wonderful time for me. The entire project seemed to have been designed to begin a new segment of my life and to provide healing on all fronts.

Shortly after *Cather County* closed, I was sitting in my apartment and the phone rang. I picked up and a voice said, "Hi, Ed, this is Pete Gurney. Want to do a musical with me?" The great A.R. Gurney—Pete to his friends, (*The Dining Room, Love Letters, Sylvia*) had seen *Cather County* and was asking me to adapt an early play of his into a musical. The play was called *Richard Cory* and had originally starred Christopher Reeve. Pete had the fantastic idea that the leading character of this musical would not sing. All the other characters would sing every line—a very novel idea. The fact that *Cather County* was through-composed (everyone singing all the time) had given him the idea. I thought it was an inspired concept, but could I do it?

(About my composing process: I always start with the words first, so if I'm writing my own libretto, I begin with an outline and sketch out the entire piece, beginning, middle and end. When I'm working with someone else's book or play, I edit their piece down until I feel it's the size of a libretto (the play of Richard Cory was much too long for a musical) and then sketch in the lyrics where I feel the songs should be. Then I sit at the keyboard and stare at the words until I hear music. When I hear it, I write it down. It's almost like taking dictation. Where does the music come from? Your guess is as good as mine.)

With *Richard Cory* there was an additional problem. Every time the tortured leading character spoke; the music would stop. How to deal with this disjointed methodology and still have a cohesive piece? I had the idea that I would end the musical line before Richard's with a chord or motif that would hang in the air while he spoke and then the music would resume when he finished; giving the impression that the score was seamless. I sat down and hammered out the first three or four scenes in this fashion and then called Pete. I was very nervous because in order to make the concept work, I had to truncate his work pretty radically. He came to my house and sat silently as I played and sang several scenes. When I finished he exclaimed, "That's exactly right. I give you carte blanche." This was better than I could have imagined.

Pete also assured me that he could get Christopher Reeve to reprise the title role because it was a non-singing part. Sadly, poor Christopher had his terrible riding accident before this could come to pass.

I got a job playing Sammy Wurlitzer in *Happy End* at Center Stage in Baltimore. So, I packed up my portable keyboard and set off for a few months into the world of Brecht and Weill. During that time, I completed *Richard Cory*; notating it by hand, with a four-octave plastic piano, in my little bungalow across the street from Center Stage.

We did a reading of it at "Playwright's" when I got home, with a cast that included Judy Kaye and Ruth Williamson. Playwright's awarded me a grant from the Harold and Mimi Steinberg Charitable Trust to work on the piece further. It eventually played at the Eugene O'Neill Theater Center in

Connecticut; on the Premieres Series at Lincoln Center and at Lyric Stage in
Dallas—where it was nominated for a Leon Rabin Award.

During this wonderful time at Playwrights Horizons, I also adapted a
short story by Washington Irving into a musical of the same name, *The Spectre Bridegroom*. This piece also eventually made its way to Lyric Stage. I also
created an original one-woman play at Playwrights called *Norma*, which
received a beautiful reading by Carole Shelley.

During this period, I was also in several new works by other authors at
Playwrights Horizons. I went to Tennessee Repertory Theatre for the premiere
of Sheldon Harnick's *It's a Wonderful Life*, and recorded it. Sheldon was one of
the creators of *Fiddler On The Roof*. All in all, it was a pretty remarkable year—
and, given my circumstances, utterly unbelievable.

It occurred to me that all my life I had been taking three steps forward
and two steps back. It was truly enlightening to see for myself that only moving in one direction—and not tearing down all of the work accomplished at
the end of the day—really made things happen in a hurry. I'm sure many people have realized this simple concept in a much easier fashion, but I was happy
to be in possession of it, no matter the cost.

I had a real "moment" at Tennessee Rep. They gave me a beautifully
appointed apartment in a nice area. After rehearsal one night, I got into the
king-sized bed, pulled the heavy down comforter up under my chin and began
reading a newly purchased book. Suddenly I stopped reading and put the book
on my chest. I was completely happy. I wanted and needed nothing more in
the entire world. I was completely satisfied. I had never had any such experience previously in my life. Change really is possible.

FORTY-FOUR

Back on Broadway

(Circa 1993)

I DID HAVE ONE NIGGLING little question at the very back of my mind. Would I ever again be on Broadway? That question was very quickly answered. The biggest producer in Holland; Joop van den Ende, decided to bring over a production that had broken all records in the Netherlands, *Cyrano – The Musical*. He had just done a television deal in Holland that netted him $600,000,000 and he was longing to use that money to conquer the Great White Way.

I wanted to play the role of the Baker, so I retooled the lyrics of Stephen Schwartz's "Style" from *The Magic Show* to be about baking bread and took it to the audition. May God and Stephen Schwartz forgive me. This is something that I have often done with his song. I love "Style" and have skewered it in many different directions for many different auditions. I'm sure Stephen would agree with the word, "skewered." It was an immediate success and I was hired forthwith to play the Baker in *Cyrano – The Musical*.

From the minute word broke in the press about Joop van den Ende's plans for Broadway, the New York press began gunning for him. "Who the hell does he think he is, coming from Holland to meddle in our playground?" He had two other multi-million dollar productions in addition to *Cyrano* waiting in the wings and was anxious to produce them here, as well. It was amazing to watch the press try to shoot him down. I just kept thinking, "What if this was any normal town anywhere in America and some businessman came into town wanting to dump millions of dollars' worth of revenue into the local economy. And the press tried to drive him away? What would the people *there* do to the press?" But this was the Big Apple.

In spite of the fact that we were the brunt of all kinds of jokes from the moment we began rehearsing. The show, the crew, in fact the entire experience, was absolutely delightful. Joop van den Ende was a gentleman's gentleman, a true mensch. He showered us with presents, parties, dinners, toasts and roasts. He gave us picture books of Holland. And rafts of tulips; real ones, ceramic ones and ones carved out of wood. He gave us free show tickets to *Cyrano* for our friends and had show-jackets made for us. Never, and I mean NEVER has any producer ever been so generous and benevolent. I can't even recall how many times he took us all out to Gallagher's Steak House down the street from the Neil Simon Theatre where we were playing; and Gallagher's is NOT cheap. One night, after many, many cocktails, Bill Van Djck, our star, got in a fist fight with Albert Finney, who had also clearly had more than a few. How many shows can boast that?

The director, writers, and technical people were all Dutch and all had the most charming accent. To my ear they all sounded identical. I got very used to it, and could even do my own version. This was going to come in very handy later. Also they were extremely hard drinkers. This is not a generalization. They all drank with gusto as identical as their accents. They all chain smoked as well—and not some sissy over-the-counter brand—they hand rolled their own cigarettes; even the women. They reminded me of America's Southwest fifty years earlier when such behavior was de rigueur.

Mr. Van Djck, our Cyrano is a luminary in Holland and a very dear man who is friends with me to this day. Almost everyone in Holland has Dyck (*pronounced "Dike"*) in their name somewhere. He was wonderful in the part. But the press was, how you say, not disposed kindly toward him, "Have we no Cyranos' in THIS country?" Anne Runolffson was Roxanne. She is the woman for whom I coined the expression, "She can sing the ass off a donkey." (Anne and I were also in *Les Miz* together.) We also had Tim Nolan from the Metropolitan Opera and the very handsome Paul Anthony Stewart from the world of soap opera. I shared a dressing room with the multi-talented Paul Schoeffler—Paul's grandfather, also Paul Schoeffler, was one of the greatest dramatic operatic baritones who ever lived. Besides being a great singer himself, Paul the younger, is hilarious. It was a great group.

This was the time in musical theater history when the great English operatic musical had been ruling Broadway for a decade and an entirely new breed of singing actor had emerged. People were doing things vocally that had not even existed when I first came to New York. For instance, Anne Runolff-son at one point, stood at center stage, threw her arms open wide and belted a high D for a page and a half. She did this with such ease and grace that it appeared to be the most natural thing in the world—and believe me, it is NOT. She then turned right around and produced an operatic high B flat in the big love duet that would have been welcomed on any operatic stage in the world. There was a tenor in a small but pivotal role who trilled on a high C and then sang a sustained high D, eight times a week. My own number went from a low G to a high B flat and had a cadenza which I had improvised myself. It was truly thrilling to be in the middle of that group of singers.

The sets, costumes and lighting were more elaborate than anything I had ever experienced. It was glorious to look at. When I made my entrance into my bakery; the ovens came up out of the basement hydraulically, the walls flew in out of the flies, and a giant staircase lowered down to the floor with me at the top of it wearing the largest chef's hat anyone had ever seen. I used to joke that all I had to do was put on that hat and all my work was done for me. It was a FANTASTIC hat.

In my opinion however, the book and music were not good. I once expressed this view on a panel many years later and an audience member nearly attacked me physically; it had been one of his favorite shows. But, as I said, "IN MY OPINION, the music was not tuneful and the book concentrated on unimportant parts of the play and left out some of the most essential elements." These are the kind of flaws that you observe from inside a production and wonder how the hell they could have withstood the long gestation process. I thought later that I might have been too harsh in my criticism. But recently, someone sent me a pirated recording, and alas, I was not.

Opening night was televised, and the host for that event was none other than Christopher Reeve. It was one of his last appearances before the accident. Some of that opening night footage surfaced recently on Youtube.com. It made me extremely nostalgic. In spite of all, *Cyrano – The Musical* was a truly wonderful and memorable experience.

FORTY-FIVE

Reconstitution and Memorabilia

(Circa 1996)

ONCE THE SMOKE CLEARED A bit and I realized that I was not going to fall off the edge of the world again, I started to notice some of the belongings I had lost. It is an amazing thing to report that almost none of the items from my old apartment had any pull on me whatsoever. There were a few notable exceptions, however. I really missed my theater posters; many of them extremely rare and all of them very personal. Whenever I looked at my bare walls I would think of those lost treasures and how they could never be recaptured. Then of course, there was the signed piece of music from Bernstein's *Mass* and worst of all, the handwritten letter from Birgit Nilsson.

It was very interesting to learn that it's not as easy to eradicate a life as one might think. One by one, items returned to me. Someone would say, "I have this play of yours" or "I just found this poem you wrote" or "Do you have a copy of this song you gave me?" Before I knew it, I had put most of my personal library back together. Some things were lost yes, but so much returned.

Then one day I got an idea. At first I was afraid to even believe that it might be possible. I went to Triton Gallery—the famous framing shop that has been handling theatrical posters for decades—and inquired about the possibility of finding replacements for some of my lost posters. To my utter amazement, they had almost everything I was looking for—even the extremely rare shows such as *King of Schnorrers*, and *Very Good Eddie*. Before I knew it, I had almost my complete body of work surrounding me on my walls again.

Two notable exceptions were the poster from Leonard Bernstein's *Mass*, which had been an extremely limited edition and *The Student Prince*, which never opened in New York; so the posters only existed on the road. However, I was eventually given programs of both shows, had them blown up poster size and framed. It would be impossible to describe the sense of joy it gave me to stand in the middle of that collection of artwork when it was complete again.

The Birgit Nilsson letter was another matter. I had first written to her when I was a young man in my 20s—so full of hope and naiveté—when she was the greatest opera star in the world. Now, she was retired and turning 80 and I was, much schooled in the ways of the world. Whatever I would write to her would not be the same kind of letter and it could not possibly receive the same response.

I sat down and very carefully constructed a composition that referenced the circumstances of my first letter to her and what she had said to me. I told her, with as few words as possible, that her first letter had been "lost" through a great "hardship." I also tried to capture a few of my favorite moments with her; both on and off stage. I wanted to give her some idea of what she had meant to me over several decades and how she had impacted my life. I sent the letter to her in care of the Metropolitan Opera—where she had not sung in many years. I expected no response.

About a week later, I found myself standing at my mailbox holding a large letter from Sweden with very bold handwriting on the front and an address scrawled on the back—she gave me her home address. Inside was a handwritten letter from Birgit Nilsson and a recent photo inscribed, "To my dear Ed" with a heart drawn below it and her signature. The letter, in a very bold and firm stroke said:
"Dear Ed,
Thank you, thank you for your unbelievably beautiful letter.
You made not only the day but the whole month!
Many good wishes, (*another drawn heart*)
Birgit Nilsson."

I took it directly to Triton Gallery and requested that the envelope, letter and photo all be matted into one frame. From the day that I received it, she has been on my wall looking down at me from just above my work station. My most prized possession.

Over the next several years we developed a writing relationship. I have something like a dozen letters from her. I also ended up on her Christmas card list; something that simply astounded me. Is it really possible to create a relationship with your favorite historical person just because you desire it? Yes it is. She always answered my letters promptly. And I tried on many occasions, to explain to her what witnessing her monumental work on stage had done to the landscape of my psyche. For whatever reason, it was of tantamount importance to me that I convey this to her.

Eventually, after many more letters, I felt that I had actually informed her exactly how important I felt she was and what my interaction with her meant to me. This letter, accompanied by a hand-painted silk scarf with a dragon on it a la *Turandot* (her signature role), was not answered in a timely fashion. Many weeks later I received a letter from her hospital bed. She apologized for her tardy response and said that she was, "Not liking to be in hospital." She then said that oddly enough she had just lost her favorite scarf and that mine was now her favorite. At Christmas, I sent her a very large box of Godiva chocolates. She never responded. Many weeks later her family finally released the news that she had died—on Christmas Day.

I have never in my life cried the way I cried that day. Not for the death of anyone or anything I have ever known. I cried so loudly and so long that I feared my neighbors would call the police. Not a little "boo hoo hoo" with tears leaking out of my eyes; a loud sustained wail at the death of a great time in history, a great woman, and a great touchstone in my own life.

It's hard to talk about anything else after the passing of the great Birgit. But there was one other singer who played a big part in my life. I first saw Alfredo Kraus, the great Spanish tenor, in the middle 1960s in Tulsa, Oklahoma. He was on tour with Roberta Peters in *Rigoletto*. He tossed off the high flying lines of The Duke of Mantua with an ease that few singers will ever display. Over the next several decades I saw him many times; most notably, in a truly remarkable performance at Carnegie Hall of *La Favorita* in which he performed all of the impossible score in the original keys. The audience's response to "Spirto Gentil" the big aria—in its original high key—was the stuff of legends. He simply stopped the opera dead in its tracks for many, many minutes while the audience screamed, clapped, stomped and yelled.

At the height of my drug addiction—or rather, at the nadir of it—I was a destroyed creature, virtually a bum, a hobo who by some insane twist of fate was still employed on Broadway. In that condition, I was wandering down Seventh Avenue when I saw a poster about Alfredo Kraus coming back to Carnegie Hall for a solo recital after an absence from the New York scene of many years. I stood in front of the poster, bleary-eyed and unsteady, and had an epiphany. I would see that concert before I died.

Now to give you some idea of the impossibility of this, I had no clothes left, only some sweat pants, a couple of t-shirts and a pair of tennis shoes. In order to go to the recital, I would somehow have to save enough money from my drug money to get shoes, socks, pants and a shirt. I would have to buy a ticket and I would have to show up on the correct day. Another miraculous thing; the concert just happened to be on a Monday, my Broadway night off.

At this point in my life I couldn't save $5 for a sandwich, so how could this possibly happen? So great was the pull of this man on my shattered existence that I somehow—and I will never know how—overcame all these obstacles and found myself clothed in black and seated in the orchestra section of Carnegie Hall for Alfredo Kraus's return to New York.

He must have been in his late 60s by this time (unheard of for a tenor in his repertoire). He walked out; an extremely dashing, fit man—he always was—and stood at center stage in a gorgeous set of tails that had obviously been designed specifically for him. He put his head down briefly and when he raised it, he opened a door into another world that only he had the ability to unlock. In an instant, he pulled the entire audience of Carnegie Hall into a previous century when the vocal arts had been at their height. It was like being at La Scala in the nineteenth century hearing the work of a great Bel Canto master.

By the end of his first phrase—a phrase so gorgeously shaped and detailed and nuanced that it had no equivalent in the current singing world— I was in tears. I cried through the entire program, which was all of equal beauty. (*You might think to read this little opus of mine that I do nothing but cry; I can assure you, I spend just as much time laughing: ask anyone.*) At one point, I was so mesmerized by this exquisite performance that I had my eyes closed and was being moved back and forth in my seat by his indescribable artistry. I thought to myself, "Snap out of it, man, you're making a fool of yourself." But when I opened my eyes, all the rows in front of me were waving like a field of wheat in a summer wind.

Years later, I was describing this event to my friend Jane Parham and telling her that I credited him in part for my recovery, because that performance so reawakened something within me. It was shortly after this recital that I found myself in treatment and on the road to a new life. Jane set her jaw firmly:

"You must tell him this."

"I'm not about to write a letter to Alfredo Kraus and tell him that I saw him when I was a hopeless drug addict."

(Long pause.)

"Well, you have to find a way. You have to!"

And so it was that I found myself staring at a blank sheet of paper and looking for the words to tell a man from another country, whom I had never met, who spoke another language that he had helped me to recover from drug addiction. Eventually, after many tries, I explained a bit of my history with him; how many times I had seen him over many years. I explained that I saw him when I was "very ill" and thought I was going to die. I explained to him that he had touched me so deeply that I had begun to heal and that I was writing to him, at that point, a well man. Eventually, I thought I had phrased my letter in a palatable way and sent it off to the Metropolitan Opera; as I had done with Birgit's letter.

A few weeks later, I received the following communication from Madrid, in Spanish:

"Querido Sr. Dixon: (Dear Mister Dixon:)

"Gracias! Sus palabras son para me una de las mayors satisfacciones recibidas en mi vida artistica." (Thank you! Your words are to me one of the greatest satisfactions I have received in my artistic life.)

"Si de verdad le he podido ayudar a superar sus dolencias me siento profundamenta satisfecho. (If it is true that I have had the power to help you overcome your suffering, it gives me profound satisfaction.)

"Siga adelante y yo guardare su carta come un significativo recuerdo." (Move forward and I will keep your letter as a significant remembrance.)

"Un abrazo y de nuevo muchas gracias por sus carinosas palabras, Alfredo Kraus." (I embrace you and once again thank you for your dear words, Alfredo Kraus.)

Shortly after I received this amazing communication from Señor Kraus, he passed away from cancer. I had no idea he was sick. If I had waited any longer to communicate with him, it would have been too late. Jane Parham, who had insisted that I write to him, was the daughter of my beloved voice teacher, Elisabeth Parham. Of course it would be her.

As everyone knows, the world can be extremely unkind. Even very good people who stay firmly within the bounds of accepted behavior can be met with terrible hardships; much less people who have behaved horribly and made egregious errors in judgment. But the kindness and generosity of people and of life can be equally extreme. I have been the recipient of such kindness and generosity. There are those events and interactions that can only be called miraculous. I can never again look at life and pretend that it is not miraculous.

That being said, it would not at all surprise me if the Leonard Bernstein music returned to me someday. It hasn't, so far, but then, there really are miracles. There really are.

FORTY-SIX

Sunset Boulevard

(Circa 1997)

WHEN *SUNSET BOULEVARD* WAS STILL in London, I got the album and heard Max's song for the first time. I knew right then and there that I was going to play the part. I got the sheet music and began to work on it daily. It became part of my routine, like brushing my teeth.

By the time I had my first audition for the role of Max von Mayerling in *Sunset Boulevard*, I had sung it every day for a year. At my first audition, it exploded out of me like a loaded pistol left on a hot stove. I could hardly believe it myself. Peter Lawrence, the Production Stage Manager, told me later: "Actors walk into the audition room and TELL YOU which part is theirs. And that's just what you did."

While waiting for my contract to materialize, I honored a previous commitment and went to the Goodspeed Opera House in East Haddam, Connecticut, to play Boris Adzinidzinadze in a new version of *Can Can* conceived by Martin Charnin. (Martin wrote *Annie*) I always thought that the original Abe Burrows book of *Can Can* had become unsuitable for modern audiences—too long, boring and overly plotted—and that someone should revamp it; since the music (by Cole Porter) is terrific. Yet Martin managed to come up with something equally long, boring and overly plotted. By the time we were ready to open, this was all too clear to everyone—except Martin.

So, it was with a bitter sense of irony that I received a phone call asking if I was available to step in, on virtually no notice, for George Hearn—who was playing Max in *Sunset Boulevard* on Broadway—so that he could take five weeks off to shoot a movie. I would go in at the exact same time that Betty Buckley was replacing Glenn Close; we would debut together. I would have to leave immediately for New York.

But *Can Can* was opening the next day and I had no understudy. I had signed an ironclad union contract. There was nothing to be done. I had to pass. Hanging up the receiver at the end of that conversation was hard—very very hard.

Can Can opened to the press and none of us faired too well. It was the first time I was ever called "portly" in print. Hardest hit was the new version of the book. One local paper ran the headline, "CHARNIN TRIES TO REVAMP *CAN CAN*...CAN'T." We gritted our teeth and soldiered on with the run.

As soon as I returned to New York from Goodspeed, I was indeed hired for the first National Tour of *Sunset Boulevard*. This meant that I would get to rehearse the part properly instead of being thrown in with a big star and virtually no preparation time. I couldn't wait to find out what star they were getting for Norma Desmond on the tour. I had heard rumors of everyone from Cher to Ann-Margret, so it was with some trepidation that I learned it was to be Linda Balgord. Who the hell was Linda Balgord? Whatever feelings I had about that subject were immediately quelled the moment I met her. Linda was and is fantastic.

She was a great favorite of Andrew Lloyd Webber, and in fact, he had flown her to London to do the demos for the original production and to do press events. She was, in a word, fierce. We would also soon become great friends and playing opposite her would be a great joy. She also could belt like very few people on earth, so all the keys were restored to their original high versions a la Patti Lupone. It was awe inspiring.

The creative staff did a marvelous trick when we first started rehearsals at 890 Studios. They separated Max, Norma, Betty (played by the fabulous Lauren Kennedy) and Joe (the handsome and talented Ron Bohmer) from the rest of the cast. I never really met the rest of the ensemble until we staged the scene where they all come bursting in with the police at the end of the show. That first invasion was fantastic. We had been rehearsing our scenes like a very small play in a private room, and suddenly, here were all these strangers bursting into our private sanctuary. Just like in the story.

Max's big aria, "The Greatest Star of All" is a very hard blow. It goes from the lowest to the highest notes, with the loudest and softest dynamics and takes enormous breath control. I had been working on that for a year. But before we started rehearsals, I also worked up the script and was completely off book before we started. So, when the four of us got together to hear the script aloud for the first time, I sat in a folding chair with the unopened script across my lap and gave a totally delineated performance—complete with tears.

I should explain that the role of Max was the first part since Shylock that felt like a perfect fit for me. I was certain that the life-journey I had been on had prepared me to play this tortured character with a depth of understanding fairly unique to me. In the movie, the camera pulls away from Max to focus on other people and events. But in the stage version, he is always there, brooding in some dark corner, putting out a tortured, maniacal energy; a really interesting assignment.

Sunset Boulevard was huge. In order to tour the enormous and unbelievably lavish production; eighteen giant trucks were required to carry the scenery. A normal show might fit into five or six trucks. We had eighteen.

When we arrived in Denver, our first city, we went to a rehearsal studio for the first orchestra read-through and learned that the orchestra was almost as large as the set. It's very unusual for a touring show to have such a full orchestra. *Sunset Boulevard* did. I was so overwhelmed with emotion at that first orchestra reading that I burst into tears during "The Greatest Star of All." Okay, I know this crying thing is getting annoying, but that's what happened. There was no way I could stop and explain to the whole room why this was all so emotional for me. They had no idea that I had been absolutely certain that I would never again play a big leading part in a great big musical, much less one of the biggest musicals of all time.

Needless to say when we went back and started it again, I made damn certain that I finished it. However, I had forgotten that Denver is not at sea level. It is, after all, called the "Mile High City" and with good reason—it's 5,280-feet above sea level. Holding out those final pianissimo pitches in "The Greatest Star of All" was quite a trial, but I never again lost control of my emotions during it. I continued to do daily breathing exercises. There were backstage bets going about how many seconds I would hold the final note—I think the record was eighteen seconds. The Denver Center Theatre kept tanks of oxygen in the wings that I often made use of as I left the stage.

There are few thrills in the theater that could equal riding onto the stage atop Norma Desmond's flying mansion. It was suspended on two gigantic scissor lifts; the kind on naval destroyers to lift jet planes onto the deck. Except these didn't just go up and down, they moved forward and backward as well. This allowed the enormous mansion to seemingly fly through the air and come to a perfect landing on the very lip of the stage with me atop it. It was awesome!

The mansion by the way, was designed by John Napier—the designer of *Les Miz*—with such detail and accuracy, that even when standing on it, it appeared to be real, down to the slightest detail. There was an organ on the stage that even had names on the stops like a real concert organ. I was to pretend to play a Bach toccata on this prop. Since Napier had been so detailed, I actually learned the Bach toccata so that my fingering would look correct as I played along with the recording.

The clothes by Anthony Powell—a truly great designer who looks and acts like a British Santa Claus—were so beautiful that I often found myself in the wings watching "Let's Have Lunch" just to see his costumes. As for my own clothes, they were some of the finest I had ever worn. I had a handmade bow tie for the New Year's Eve sequence that cost $500. When the tour ended, Anthony gave me the custom made tails. They cost a good deal more than $500.

The tour of *Sunset Boulevard* was a dream production. We all knew that we were on the tail end of the mega-musical train and treasured every moment. *Sunset Boulevard* was crowded with marvelous memories. My dear old high school drama teacher, Mabel Ritzman, then in her 80s, drove by herself to Denver for the opening night of the tour. The Denver Center Theatre threw a spectacular party with a 40-foot high gold Oscar in the middle of the proceedings and a fake Joe Gillis floating face down in a swimming pool, just like the opening of the movie. I got a review from Variety that sounded like it had been written by my closest friend for my memorial service.

Easily, the most moving event of the entire tour was that my beloved voice teacher, Elisabeth Parham, who I had not seen in years—she was now a tenured professor at California State University, Northridge—flew to Chicago on Mother's Day to see me in *Sunset Boulevard*. We went sightseeing, ate in wonderful restaurants and took lots of photographs. She then returned to California and passed away. I will always be grateful for that farewell.

The enormity of *Sunset Boulevard* caused it to have to shut down for a week at the end of each city so that it could be transported; while the cast remained on full pay and per diem. An engagement would end and you would hear someone say, "Where shall we go this week? How about Puerto Rico?" It was a great gig. However, the enormous expense of the tour caused it to close at the end of the first year. I would have been happy to continue with it for ten more.

While the tour was in Minneapolis, I began one of my more unconventional relationships with a stripper turned car salesman. When the show finally closed, my former stripper and I flew first class to the Greek islands, and stayed there for two weeks in a private bungalow poised on the side of a cliff looking down on the Aegean by a dormant volcano. Over the next decade we would literally travel all over the world together. First stop Santorini; a very nice conclusion to a very nice year.

FORTY-SEVEN

The Scarlet Pimpernel

(Circa 1997)

I HAD NO SOONER RETURNED to New York when I found myself auditioning for a new musical version of *The Scarlet Pimpernel*. This was the first time I had met Peter Hunt, the director; he was an heir to the Hunts tomato fortune, and related to Helen Hunt. Peter laughed easily and loudly in the audition room, something that directors rarely do. When he laughed, his face would turn extremely red and blotchy. It may not have been a sign of good health but it was very amusing and Peter was enormously fun to be with. He always seemed to have just come from a cocktail party. Perhaps he had.

I auditioned for the role of the villain and since I was feeling on top of the world at that moment, I was sure I would book it. However, the role of the villain went, once again, to Terrence Mann. I was offered the role of Robespierre, a tiny and uninteresting little part. I turned it down. They came back with a better offer. I turned it down, again. They came back with an even better offer. Finally, they were offering me as much to do this ridiculous little part as I had made to play Thénardier in *Les Miz*. I thought to myself, "I don't like the book, the music or the lyrics. It's certain to close in a week. So, why not take it, put the poster up on my wall and move on?" I said yes to *The Scarlet Pimpernel*.

We had finished the negotiations for Robespierre. The contract was prepared and had already arrived at my agent's office to be signed. That's when I received a call from Gary Epstein telling me that they were now offering me a different role; Ozzy, the Pimpernel's sidekick. In other words, they were offering me

200

a role which I had not auditioned for, sung through or looked at, with the same terms previously negotiated for another part—I've simply never heard of such a thing.

I reread the script and still didn't like it. But the role of Ozzy—while not a great part—was more interesting than Robespierre. I felt it showed promise for a comic turn, diametrically opposed to what I had just spent the last year doing in *Sunset Boulevard*. So once again, I said, "Yes" and entered the world of *The Scarlet Pimpernel*.

It occurred to me that if they got a big enough star, preferably someone from Hollywood, it might run for 6-months. However, on the first day of rehearsal, I found that the title role was being played by an actor I had never heard of Douglas Sills. "Lost, lost, all lost," I cried! Famous last words. By the end of the first day I was completely convinced that Doug Sills could do ANY-THING, maybe even save *The Scarlet Pimpernel*.

Also on the first day, the door to the rehearsal room opened and in walked the most ravishing woman I had seen in many years. "Why, she looks like Christine Andreas," I thought. But she couldn't be Christine Andreas. I hadn't seen Christine for thirty years, since we were both starting out at the North Shore Music Theatre. There was no way this young and gorgeous creature could be Christine Andreas. Well, it was. There she stood; a completely beautiful leading lady, who was almost my age. I was just about to turn 50. She actually looked better than she had thirty years earlier. Amazing!

Rehearsals were very creaky and the material never improved. Peter Hunt laughed a lot, but we never seemed to get around to the work that really needed to get done. Some numbers were never staged and had to be cut. We were constantly waiting for rewrites that never materialized. There was one good thing however, apart from Doug Sills' constantly mesmerizing performance. If you could think of something funny, Peter put it in the show. The role of Ozzy grew and grew as I had hoped it might, and turned into a very interesting turn, complete with a little drag bit when Ozzy dressed as a woman to escape the guillotine. This quick change happened in something like 10-seconds on top of a huge boat.

The show was received by the New York critics just about as well as I had thought it would be—which is to say they nailed it to the wall, ripped it down and then nailed it back up again. Except for Douglas; there, everyone agreed that someone remarkable had burst on the scene. He got nominated for a Tony and we all ended up doing "Into the Fire" on the awards ceremony at

Radio City Music Hall. You can see a bit of my Ozzy on the YouTube clip. Doug did not win that night, but it's my contention that he absolutely should have. He delivered a very great performance.

During the run of *Pimpernel*, my *Cather County* opened at Lyric Stage in Dallas and was a great success with the local critics. It was named one of the best events to take place in Dallas that year and won the Leon Rabin Award for best new work. I was released from *Pimpernel* to attend the opening and it was a great pleasure for me. Steven Jones, who created and runs Lyric Stage, became a lifelong friend and has been a great supporter of my writing and composing.

My experience in Dallas inspired me and when I got home I had the revelation to turn the old naughty book *Fanny Hill* into a musical. It literally leapt off the shelf at me one day. And I wrote *Fanny Hill*, the musical—in a frenzy—sharing it scene-by-scene as it arrived from wherever these things come from, with my fellow *Pimpernel* cast members. (I just noticed that this is the third time that I've used that "in a frenzy" line in this book. I'm starting to think that if I'm writing anything, it's probably in a frenzy.)

One of the wonderful events of the Pimpernel experience was that I became friends with Nick Cavarra, a young man who expressed interest in my writing. He had aspirations to become a writer, so I offered as much encouragement as I could. Little did I know how much this small kindness would be repaid to me. Not only did Nick go on to become a very creditable writer of screenplays, he became a producer and is responsible for the New York productions of *Fanny Hill* and *Richard Cory*. He is also the producer of this book. It started in his producer's blog which is how I found the nerve to write it at all. He has remained my dear friend long after *Pimpernel* faded away.

The Scarlet Pimpernel hemorrhaged money from the very beginning. And soon our very wealthy producers had lost all the money that they could stomach. So they turned it over to even wealthier producers who could afford even greater losses. I don't know how many millions the thing lost in total, but it was a lot. I assumed that it had all been some sort of tax dodge since no other explanation made any sense to me. It seemed to me that somebody needed to "lose" some cash, and lots of it. If someone has another explanation, I'll stand corrected.

At the end of the first year (the first year!) the new management brought in a new director, Robert Longbottom; to revamp the show at even greater expense. Mr. Longbottom seemed to feel that there was too much levity in the show and set out to cut all the funny bits that Peter Hunt had allowed to creep in. He showed me this edited version of the script, minus most of my part, and said that he hoped I would stay on. I declined.

By the time I arrived at my final performance, Doug Sills had pretty much turned the show into his club act. On the stage he could say or do anything he felt like and the audience was wild for him. Since it was my last day in the show, Doug stopped the ballroom scene; in which the entire cast was standing around in formal period attire. Doug grabbed me by the arm and pulled me down to the footlights to pay a little tribute to me for my year of manufactured merriment.

When we arrived at center stage on the lip of the orchestra pit, we adlibbed for a bit and then he turned to me and announced, "There once was a man from Nantucket... " He then made a gesture with both hands as if to say, "Take it away, Ozzy!" The audience roared with laughter thinking I was stuck with the famous limerick. When the laughter died down, I turned stonily to him and replied, "And here I stand without a ducket!" At which point I gestured back to him which signaled, "Get yourself out of this one, Pimpy!" The audience adored all this horseplay and gave me a fabulous send off.

I was no sooner out of *Pimpernel* when the Eugene O'Neill Theater Center National Playwrights Conference produced *Richard Cory* and The Goodspeed Opera House announced the premiere of *Fanny Hill*. It would be years before Nick Cavarra and I—through ceaseless efforts—would get both of them to New York. But fortunately we didn't know that at the time.

FORTY-EIGHT

The Iceman Cometh

(Circa 1999)

I WAS LUCKY ENOUGH TO be cast in Mary Zimmerman's deconstructionist version of *A Midsummer Night's Dream* at the Huntington Theater in Boston. Now, this may sound like a normal occurrence. But in actual fact, I had never done a play in my adult life, not one time. Not since high school when I performed *Six Characters in Search of an Author* of which I understood not one line. When I first got the audition for the role of Nick Bottom— which is one of the greatest parts in the English language—I didn't take it too seriously since actors with an entire resume full of musicals (even if they are some of the most interesting roles in the genre) are not usually considered for big juicy Shakespearean parts. However, at the first audition for Mary Zimmerman, we seemed to hit it off. And by the call back, I was starting to feel that I might actually get it. I did.

Mary's version of *Midsummer* was a great success and I had a great time doing it. But during the middle of the run, I got the most interesting phone call. My agent said that Jay Binder; one of the biggest casting directors in New York, wanted me to fly in from Boston to audition for a Broadway revival of *The Iceman Cometh* with Kevin Spacey; the same production that had made such a splash in London. My response was not what you'd expect. I just laughed and said, "No fucking way." I wasn't about to spend hundreds of dollars on a last minute plane ticket to New York and lose my only day off to go on a "fool's errand." There was no way on earth that a guy who was in the middle of the first straight play of his career was going to get cast in the biggest play revival of the Broadway season for his second. My agent passed on a paraphrased version of this exchange to Mr. Binder, who nevertheless insisted that I come in for *The Iceman Cometh*. I conceded.

When I arrived, I found that the director Howard Davies, was not in attendance. In other words, I had worked up all the material for General Wetjoen complete with the Dutch accent mimicked from all my co-workers in *Cyrano – The Musical* (I told you that interaction would come in handy) and flown into New York, just to audition for Jay Binder, who already knew my work. Not so. It turned out that Jay wanted to put me on tape and send my audition tape to California where Mr. Davies was doing another project. This is NOT how auditions work and I was sure there was no possible way that I could get the part under such circumstances. Jay overnight expressed the tape to L.A. And a day later, I was in *The Iceman Cometh*. You'd think I would have learned by now that nothing is ever "the norm."

Howard Davies is a great director. And if you will kindly note, this is not an expression that I have ever used previously in this book. The play was five hours long, or five and a half; neither seems possible. Howard had an idea for every moment from the beginning to the end. And not just some arbitrary idea, an ironclad and clearly thought-out idea that he had the ability to communicate to a roomful of actors.

And what a roomful of actors it was. The parts in *Iceman* are all in pairs. Each role has a counterpart with whom he shares his O'Neill adventure. My partner was Patrick Godfrey, a man in his middle-sixties who had spent the bulk of his life in The Royal Shakespeare Company in London. He was one of the few Brits who had been retained from the original production on the West End. He was absolutely brilliant. Every breath, every gesture, every posture and every inflection he made was in some way a reflection of the text. It was simply divine to work opposite him, and he was a very nice man to boot.

Tony Danza was a revelation. It has often been my experience that meeting someone who is a very well-known personality can be very different from what one has been led to believe. This was true of Tony and in a very positive way. Far from being the "dems and dos" guy from Brooklyn—as he has so often been represented on television—Tony is extremely well-educated and a voracious reader. Any moment when he had a second to himself, he had his nose buried in a book. This included his time during performances, when I would often see him in the wings with a tiny flashlight stuck in an open book. He worked like a Trojan and was quite good as the Bartender, a really difficult role. When you're the bartender in a play full of hopeless alcoholics, you're going to have a very busy night. He did it with great charm and style. He's also in the best physical condition of any man his age I've ever seen. We are the same age—I look like his grandfather.

Kevin Spacey, of course, is a terrific actor; very famous and quite rich. And I do think he is brilliant. In fact, I believe he's a Rhodes Scholar. But he was obsessed with being fresh in the part all the time, so he steadfastly refused to ever repeat anything. This meant that very good choices that showed up on Tuesday would not be seen on Wednesday. In fact, they would never be seen again. Personally, I would have preferred more technique and less bravado, especially in the final monologue. But then, he's Kevin Spacey and I'm not.

Paul Giamatti, on the other hand, followed Kevin's big speech in the last act with a brief and searing monologue in which his guts seemed to explode all over the stage every evening without fail. It was almost impossible to watch him, it was so painful. This was before Paul's big movie career materialized, but it was pretty clear that something huge was about to happen for him. It did.

My part actually started during half hour. I would stumble out onto the stage while the audience was being seated. After checking out every glass and bottle on the stage to see if there was even a drop of alcohol left; I would trip, fall under a table on the lip of the stage, give up, and just stay there. This made my show a half hour longer than everyone else's. This is why I thought of the five hour play as five and a half. Ah, it comes back to me.

Once the marathon play finally began, the actor who had the opening monologue—I refuse to type his name—was so boring that it was impossible for me to stay awake. I had been lying on the floor "passed out" for a half an hour by the time he started speaking. Now, he thought he was a GREAT actor and delivered the first volley with such syrupy, plumy panache that it knocked me right out. (He also went around giving everyone notes—strictly verboten.) I would literally pinch myself to keep from falling asleep. But every performance, he would put me out like a sedative, and I would begin TO SNORE. Eventually, he would sidle up to me and give me a kick to shut me up. I think he may have thought I was acting. He certainly wasn't.

During the third act, our characters had all failed in our attempts to sober up and leave the bar and we had to sit there with the shakes while Kevin did his big blow. This was maybe the most difficult part of the play for me because it caused me to have to—so vividly—recall my addiction for a sustained period of time. I would just sit there, not even in the light, shaking and crying; it was exhausting and debilitating.

We got so tired as the gigantic play went on—we did two performances on Saturdays; eleven hours on stage—that we stopped returning to our dressing rooms and just sank down onto the floor in the wings as soon as we left the stage. One day, I was lying on the floor off-stage left next to Paul Giamatti, groaning. Suddenly, the door to the house swung open and a couple of Secret Service guys swept in with Bill Clinton. There I was, lying on the floor next to Paul Giamatti, both of us dressed as bums with grease in our hair and dirt smudged on our faces, looking up at the leader of the free world. The Secret Service guys burst out laughing. Paul and I leapt to our feet and Bill exclaimed, "Heck, I could do THAT fer a livin'!" I'm sure he could. It turned out President Clinton and the Secret Service were looking for the bathroom. They found it.

We held the curtain for a half an hour that night waiting for Hillary to arrive; she never did. We surmised that at the last moment someone reminded her of the plot of *The Iceman Cometh*—the leading character has been cheating on his long-suffering wife for many years and finally kills her out of guilt. I don't think she needed to see our play at that moment in her life.

I had a "photo op" with the President after the show. I reminded him that I had been one of the people who sang "One Day More" to him at the Meadowlands the day before he was elected for his first term. What I did not say was that the events of the last several years had turned him into another person. When I looked into his eyes, it was not the same ebullient person looking back who had made eye contact with me as he shook my hand the night before his first election. It made me sad. I got a great photo, though.

This was the first time since *No, No, Nanette* that I had shaken hands with a sitting president. And the first time since then that "everyone who was anyone" came to see a show I was doing. Every night was a parade of stars. Of course, they were all there to see Kevin, but we all benefited from that. During one 3-day period, I met: Harry Belafonte, Sidney Poitier and James Earl Jones. I hung out with Liza Minnelli in the waiting area and passed Jason Robards in the wings.

One night I saw Kevin peeking out the curtain before act two began—a real theater no-no—and thought, "There must be someone REALLY famous out there tonight to cause him to do something like THAT!" Afterward as I was exiting the theater, I saw Kevin talking to a pretty blond woman in the wings. When I got a little closer I realized that it was Meryl Streep. I could see that they were deep in "after performance" conversation, so I walked by them without speaking. She reached out, grabbed my arm and blurted out, "I watched you all night!" Then she suddenly seemed to realize that she had made a faux pas and snapped to Kevin, "When I wasn't watching you, of course." I burst out laughing and said something about how much I loved her. But she did what all great people do; she kept turning the compliment back on me. That one moment alone was worth my whole career.

The show extended two extra weeks, but I had to leave because *Fanny Hill* was opening at Goodspeed and I HAD to be there. As I came in the stage door for my final performance I saw a gigantic floral arrangement blocking the entryway. I asked the doorman who they were for. "They're yours" he laughingly replied. This thing was the size of a small tree. I looked at the card and it was a farewell gift from Tony Danza, who was out in California visiting his children and missing my final performance. What a gent!

As I crossed the stage—staggering under the weight of the giant arrangement—I passed Kevin who asked me who it was from. I told him that Tony had sent it to me. Moments later, Kevin's assistant brought me a little fruit basket—that had obviously been sitting in his dressing room for weeks. Hilarious.

Emanuel Azenberg our producer, had a reputation for not only being wildly successful, but for also being a real gentleman in business—a very unlikely combination. He promised all of us that if there were profits made on our extremely limited engagement of *The Iceman Cometh,* he would split them with the cast. Okay, first of all, it's impossible to break even on a limited run of a play with a huge cast. Secondly, no producer ever splits profits with an actor, period. I no sooner arrived at Goodspeed to take care of *Fanny Hill,* when a check arrived from Manny Azenberg. Not only did the show turn a profit (impossible), he actually split the abundance with the actors (even more impossible). Now, that's something worth writing about.

FORTY-NINE

Gore Vidal's The Best Man

(Circa 2000)

WHEN I LEFT *THE ICEMAN Cometh*, I went directly to Goodspeed in East Haddam, Connecticut. Gabe Barre directed a lovely production of my *Fanny Hill* starring Nancy Anderson. She was fantastic in the part and though she was in every scene and had most of the lines and songs, she never put a foot wrong. She was extraordinary. I wish I could say the same for the rest of the cast. It's hard to get people to go to East Haddam; it's hours from New York and the salaries are low. We had to make do with what we could get. Some of it was very difficult to watch.

I have often read in the biographies of writers and composers; sagas of the torments that they undergo while watching their works being performed. When I was young, I did not understand these accounts. I certainly understand them now. I can personally attest that watching your work be performed is really, really, really hard.

Every missed cue, muffed line, incorrect rhythm, incorrect pitch, dropped cue and missed entrance is like acid on your head. And then there is the audience; every candy wrapper, trip to the bathroom, conversation with a spouse, coughing fit, dropped program and cell phone ring is absolute torture.

There is a moment toward the end of *Fanny Hill* when all the jokes in a two-hour evening come home to roost. The last ten minutes of the play is one joke after another and the payoff for the whole journey. One afternoon at Goodspeed, at that exact moment in the play, a woman two rows in front of me got a cell phone call—and took it. As she chatted away with her head ducked, every matronly patron around, shushed her and asked her to stop. But on she went. I could not physically reach her, so I got up in the aisle and told her to hang it up. She did not. I told her again to hang it up. She did not. So I waited for the show to end, confronted her in the aisle and called her every name that a man is not allowed to call a woman in public or in private. It was awful. And, if I had it to do over again, I would do exactly the same thing. I was never able to sit in the audience again. I started watching the show from the rafters. No not the balcony; the rafters. There were some steel beams above the stage—and that's where I sat.

Critics are not allowed at Goodspeed for their developmental shows. However, a critic from the United Kingdom, who writes for a theater magazine called *Masquerade*, got in anyway and wrote the most spectacular review of *Fanny Hill*. Yet, somehow, we were not able to get the kind of important money people, who might have moved it, to show up in East Haddam, Connecticut. And my beloved *Fanny Hill* closed without a future in sight.

When something doesn't go the way you want it to go, there is that period of confusion immediately afterward when you're not quite sure if the tide may yet turn in your favor. Eventually, it dawns on you that you truly have not accomplished your goal. If this kind of dawning has the ability to stop you in your tracks, show business is probably not your career.

I returned to New York and found myself auditioning for another straight play—the revival of *Gore Vidal's The Best Man*. Gore, at age 80, was clever enough to have his name inserted into the title of his fifty-year-old political comedy so that he would be acknowledged properly in every print advertisement. It was being directed by Ethan McSweeney, a wunderkind who had directed me in a workshop of a musical. This was the musical that would introduce me to Kathie Lee Gifford, but I'll get to that in a minute.

I auditioned for the role of Senator Carlin, a Southern blowhard. And, if I'm not mistaken, it was the first time in my entire career that I ever used my actual Oklahoma/Texas accent. And so it was that I, maven of the period musical, found myself in yet another straight play on Broadway. By the way, the subject matter of the play was the closest in proximity to the present day that I had ever assayed. Most of my roles have been rooted in the nineteenth century or earlier.

The cast included Chris Noth (*Law and Order, Sex and the City*); Christine Ebersole (Queen of Broadway); Michael Learned (Ma Walton, no less);

Elisabeth Ashley (countless plays and movies); Spalding Gray (king of the monologue) and Charles Durning (too many movies to count). A rather glittering assortment of folks.

My first shock—after finding out that I was hired—was that I was expected to not only do my part, but to stand-by for Charles Durning. I informed the management, via my agent, that I had no interest in standing-by for Charles Durning, who had the starring role of the former President of the United States. I was counter-informed that standing-by for Charles was non-negotiable. If I wanted to play Senator Carlin I had to stand-by for Charles Durning. It was "take it or leave it." I took it.

On the first day, at the "meet and greet," Gore Vidal addressed the company. It became immediately evident that age, and massive alcohol consumption, had not dulled his intellect or his wit. He told many political stories and revealed a talent I would never have guessed he possessed. Gore Vidal is the most extraordinary mimic. As he told us amazing stories of all the famous political figures he had known, many of whom are parodied in *The Best Man*, he gave astonishing reproductions of their voices and mannerisms. He regaled us with his Lyndon Johnson, Ladybird Johnson, John F. Kennedy, Jacky Kennedy and a host of other perfectly replicated icons.

At one point, he turned to me. At first I couldn't believe that he was actually addressing me during his opening remarks since the room was filled with famous people. But I soon realized that indeed he was. He said, "And you, young man, have the only line in the play that was actually given to me by John F. Kennedy. He said to me (*and here he took on Kennedy's voice*) "Whenever a politician is going to stab you in the back, he always prefaces it with, 'let me know if there's anything I can do for you.' And then he pats you on the back." And indeed, I did have that line in the play immediately before I stabbed the candidate in the back. By the way, it was very charming that Gore called me "young man." I suppose to an 80-year old, I was.

At the first rehearsal, we learned that Mr. Durning was in the hospital recovering from an operation and would not be joining us for a while. So I began rehearsing *The Best Man* as both Senator Carlin and President Hockstader. Sometimes I would finish a scene as one character, turn around and come back in as the other. Both roles were very interesting and the whole assignment was very, very enjoyable.

Eventually, after weeks of rehearsing without him, Charles During finally joined us. I walked in and saw him sitting at a table reading the paper, so I walked over to introduce myself. When I spoke to him, he slowly, slowly raised his eyes to meet mine. When he finally made eye contact, I was very shocked. Charles had just gotten out of the hospital and he looked sick. He looked very sick. This was the first time I realized that I was actually going to be going on in the role of President Hockstader. I was very grateful to have had weeks to get to know the Company, and the lines. However, I was now officially worried about Charles.

The first rehearsals with Charles were very rocky. He had not looked at the script in the hospital and couldn't remember any of his lines. I got more worried for him—and more worried for myself. However, the rest of the cast was an absolute delight and I loved my strange double-role assignment.

Michael Learned is a wonderful woman, a fact that is obvious from observing her on film and television. But she has a surprising ability to use blue language like an ancient mariner. One day she recounted a story of some youthful indiscretion, peppered with language that was several leagues beyond "salty." She saw my face go slack and quipped, "Well, I'm not really Ma Walton, ya know!" I loved Michael Learned.

Chris Noth was hilariously funny and most of the time seemed to have just wandered off the set of *Animal House*. He has the personality of a naughty fraternity boy, with stories to match. The most surprising thing about him was his great love of show tunes, highly unlikely in a man with his urbane personality and sexy profile. It was highly probable that you would hear Ethel Merman belting out a song as you passed by his dressing room. Surprising.

Spalding Gray was also a bit of a surprise. It turned out that the "king of the monologue" was terribly dyslexic and had to transfer all his lines onto three-by-five cards in order to memorize them. Whenever you saw him, he always had his head buried in his cards and was shuffling through them as if hypnotized. He was shy to the point of being sociopathic. It was almost impossible to imagine how he had launched a solo career on the stage.

The surprise of the whole event was the unbelievably delightful Christine Ebersole. From the moment we met, we were like long lost brother and sister. We simply could not stop laughing and talking, even backstage during performances. This was very unprofessional, but we simply could not stop ourselves. Several times Chris Noth took us aside to say that he could hear us laughing in the wings while he was onstage performing and we were driving him crazy. I'm ashamed to say that even this did not stop us. We also developed this insane way of interacting where we would speak in the highest, squeakiest voices we could muster—she always won, of course. So you can only imagine how annoying this was to other people. I, however, never failed to find it hilarious and always ended up in stitches. We still do this on the phone.

At the first preview, Charles went blank several times and had to call for lines; with a sold-out house. I expected to go on at any moment, so I began drilling his part ceaselessly. However, as previews went on, Charles just kept on chugging along and eventually he made it to opening night. I won't say that the opening went without a hitch, but we did get rather good reviews. The fact that George W. Bush was up for his second term at the exact moment that we opened our political diatribe did not hurt sales. There was a line early in the play in which a politician said, "I think a lot of people feel safer voting for a stupid man than a smart one." The laugh from that line went on for a full minute.

The day after opening while arriving at the theater from 8th Avenue, I stopped at the light next to a dumpy couple who were obviously from out-of-town. The marquis of our theater was clearly visible from our vantage, proclaiming *Gore Vidal's The Best Man*. The husband, who was right next to me, turned to his wife and said loudly, "Gore Vidal, idn't he a fag?" I calmly turned to them and intoned quite deliberately, "Fuck you, you stupid pieces of shit!" I expected a fight. Instead they just stood there like slack-jawed statues as I strode grandly into the stage door. It wasn't until I got inside that the joke hit me. With my show jacket and shock of white hair, the poor stupid couple thought they had been cursed out by Gore Vidal himself. I would have laughed about that all night long had it not been for what I learned when I got to the call board.

Charles Durning was out. It was half hour and I had no warning whatsoever about taking over his part. Charles was not sick, his brother had died. So he flew out to the funeral but missed the return flight. I didn't have time to think about Charles; it was the night after our official opening, and all members of the Outer Critics Circle were in the house. I who had not had a rehearsal of any kind since Charles joined the company, was on.

There were no costumes for me. I could use my gray Senator Carlin suit for most of the play. But there was also a black tie and tails scene and there was no way I could be put into Charles' tux. So an assistant went rushing to my house with my keys to fetch my own personal tux to wear in the show. Then the director and stage managers began trying to shove the newest blocking changes at me—it had changed enormously since those first couple of weeks of rehearsal—I listened at first, but then realized that it was more important for me to be going over my lines than learning new blocking. So I ordered everyone out of my dressing room—Charles' room. I told them that I was just going to do the old blocking and the other actors were going to have to accommodate me. End of story. It was very nervy, but I knew that it was the only way to save my ass.

Everyone was very kind and supportive. But when it came time for my first entrance, I was in a kind of terror that I hope most people will never know. The cue came and I opened the door. This is where Charles would be greeted with massive entrance applause. There was dead silence. I had expected nothing less, so I was not taken aback; but it was not the least bit welcoming. As I hit center stage, I began to get my equilibrium and very quickly I launched off into the first big speech in which President Hockstader is recounting a meeting with Clarence Darrow. It is high oratory.

Now Charles Durning is a very great actor, but his illness and lack of a full rehearsal had made this opening speech rather tentative. I had been rehearsing it day and night and it exploded out of me as I believe had been Gore's intention. When I left the stage there was an ovation. I can't tell you the satisfaction that applause gave me after the stony silence of my arrival. The rest of the evening went fantastically for me. It was perhaps the single most exciting moment of my career to date.

Eventually President Hockstader died on stage and the play ended. I was met with such raucous appreciation at the curtain call that I was simply knocked out by it, center stage among that glittering array of stars and personalities. My agent was there; along with my old friend Tracy, who had dropped everything to race to the theater. There was high jubilation in Charles Durning's star dressing room after this simply amazing event. The director told me that he felt he had FINALLY seen his play on the stage. And I received a note from Shirley Rich, a very famous casting director, telling me that my performance reminded her of why she went into the theater in the first place. It was a very joyous night.

The next day, I had an audition for *Judgment at Nuremburg* for Tony Randall's National Actors Theater. I was high as a kite. I walked into the room with John Tillinger and Tony Randall sitting behind the table and made a great tactical error. I was just too happy. I said that I had had the most wonderful week. When they asked me why, I informed them that I had just opened a very exciting political revival on Broadway and that I had gone on for Charles Durning in the leading role.

Tony Randall's face turned ashen. "What happened to CHARLES?!" he demanded. I realized instantly the error of my jubilation. "His brother died," I quietly replied. "OH, MY GOD!" exclaimed Tony with the greatest distaste! I could feel the whole room turn on me. John Tillinger coldly asked for the scene I had prepared. I read it. They said "Thank you." The audition was over. But as I walked toward the door, John Tillinger added, "Well, here's another wonderful thing that happened to you this week, you met US!" Tony Randall gasped and looked away. The door closed behind me. It's very hard to stay on the pony ride in show business sometimes.

Charles Durning never missed another show. I continued to work on the lines, but never played President Hockstader again. I enjoyed playing Senator Carlin and I enjoyed working with Charles. He is a lovely man and after he learned the part, he was quite good in it. He also told the most wonderful stories and is quite a good singer. And believe it or not, an excellent dancer as well.

Spalding Gray was a bit of another story. Stage acting was really not his thing. I had a big scene with him and he always seemed to be distracted or only partly there. He had such a curious personality that it was hard to tell what he was trying to do with his role. He also had all the physical characteristics of an unmade bed. The hair and make-up people would try to clean him up, but five minutes later he would look like Pig Pen from the *Peanuts* cartoon strip again. He had hair coming out his collar, out his ears, out his nose, and the hair on his head was never where it was supposed to be. Even the giant photo on the stage for his character's presidential campaign had nose hair clearly visible.

At one performance, I was vainly trying to relate to Spalding on stage, but when I looked into his left eye, there was a wayward eyebrow hair right in front of the pupil that was driving me crazy. So I switched my gaze to his right eye, but it also had a cockeyed eyebrow hair in front of that pupil. I could never really concentrate during the whole scene and walked off into the wings beating myself up for not being able to rise above my own distraction. However, I had no sooner hit the wings when Charles Durning, a very level-headed man, came running up to me, clenched my arm and hissed, "What the hell's up with Spalding's EYEBROWS?"

The sad news is that after the show closed, Spalding lost a life-long struggle with depression and threw himself off the Staten Island Ferry in the middle of winter. I was told later that the kind of cold we were experiencing at that time causes a body to sink straight to the bottom when it hits the water. He was not found until spring. A very sad ending for a brilliant, if troubled man.

On the other side of the coin, I was able to maintain my friendships with Ethan McSweeney, Christine Ebersole and Michael Learned after the show closed. It's always unlikely that people with busy show business lives will keep in touch. Those three have been the exception to the rule. Still, it's hard to think of those lovely people without remembering poor Spalding. However, having seen into his life a bit, I can't help but feel that his problems and their conclusions—much like my own—were inevitable.

FIFTY

The Best Little Whorehouse in Texas

(Circa 2001)

I HEARD THAT THERE WAS about to be a tour of *The Best Little Whore-house in Texas* starring Ann-Margret. I said to myself, "I simply MUST be in this." I couldn't imagine anything more delightful than seeing the United States of America with one of the great icons of my generation. I decided that I had to play the Governor of Texas (Charles Durning played it in the movie). And since his song in the musical doesn't work well out of context, I sat down and penned a double entendre song called "Great Big Gun" (you figure it out) and started prepping it for the audition. The time came, I did my naughty song, they all laughed and I got to go to the whorehouse.

We rehearsed at 890 Studios with Thommie Walsh directing; he had been the co-choreographer with Tommy Tune of the original Broadway version. (He was also the original Bobby in *A Chorus Line*.) When Ms. Ann-Margret walked into the room, I was suitably blown away. I mean, there are famous people and then there are FAMOUS people. In my book, Ann-Margret is FAMOUS. She made me nervous like a prepubescent heterosexual. This never lessened even after we spent a year and a half together. However, her first entrance into the rehearsal studio was not quite what one might have imagined.

She had been in a motorcycle accident—both she and her husband, Roger Smith, of *Route 66* fame, love motorcycles and have several—and had badly injured her leg. While recovering from that, one of her cats had darted in front of her on their patio causing her to fall and break her arm. She entered the rehearsal room on crutches with an external fixator on her arm and wearing a turban that covered almost all of her head, ears, chin and neck, accompanied by very large tinted glasses. I assumed that she had had "some work done"—though I spent the next year and a half looking for signs of it and never saw any.

There was a great deal more dancing in *Whorehouse* than I had done in many, many years, so learning it was a bit of a challenge. Memorizing a lot of complicated dance steps is something that your mind has to be in the right mode for and believe me when I tell you I was not in that mode. I had one whole meltdown just over the steps in the highly choreographed curtain call.

In addition to this, at age 50, I was about to have my first solo dance number—ever. I had done a lot of dancing over the years and even some serious partner dancing, like in *Very Good Eddie*. But this was a solo. Me at center stage—all alone—solo.

I started to get the dance somewhat under control, but the ending was proving problematic. After a very complex beginning and middle, the end of the number just seemed to peter out. When I asked Thommie about it he said that the ending had always bothered him and we should try something else. I thought of my time in *Very Good Eddie* and suggested, "How about I end the number with the splits?" Thommie's eyes grew wide. "Can you?" he whispered. I thought it was still in my body from all those years ago and gave it a shot. Thommie fell out of his chair laughing. The splits were in.

That's how I began to tour America. In my 50s; doing the splits at the end of a big dance number; dressed as the Governor of Texas; in a pin striped suit; a bolo string tie and a giant white Stetson hat. It was hilarious. If you don't believe me, the commercial for the show is still on YouTube. There I am in the promo, doing the splits. It's listed under "Ann-Margret commercial."

On the day of the first performance, I was dressed early and loitering anxiously in the central hallway backstage. The star dressing room opened and out came Ann-Margret for the first time looking like—Ann-Margret. She had that famous Ann-Margret hair and that Ann-Margret make-up and was wearing a $10,000 Bob Mackie gown specially designed for—Ann-Margret. She moved across the corridor in a swath of marabou feathers and very expensive perfume. I have never smelled anything like her one-of-a-kind personal fragrance. It was dark, dense and well—overwhelming. It smelled like money and sex with a little bit of the jungle in it.

She headed straight toward me without a word. I gathered that she was going to wish me luck, but instead, she continued forward and crashed into my chest burying her face in my lapel. Almost unbelieving, I put my arms around her. She was scared out of her mind. It finally dawned on me; the great Ann-Margret had somehow managed to do her entire career without ever performing a live musical comedy. Of course she had done many movies and a very famous act, but this was her first time to step onto a stage as the lead in a great big musical.

I looked down at the top of her head disbelieving. All I could think was, "THAT'S ANN-MARGRET!!!" A really great moment. Then she pulled herself together and went on. I felt very honored to have been standing there at that particular moment.

The Best Little Whorehouse in Texas is not a great show. The score is terrific, but the book is a mishmash of improvs from the Actor's Studio. This version of it was not any great shakes, either. The set had been in storage for years after the last bus and truck tour had shut down years before. It had been slapped up onto the stage with not so much as a coat of paint, just to save money. The giant curved staircase that came down from the upper level was so rickety that it shook like a shantytown stoop when Ann-Margret put her high-heeled foot down on it for her first entrance.

Here was a great star, making her entrance in her first stage musical ever and the set was shaking just from being touched. The entire tour depended on her presence. And she had a recently broken arm and leg. In fact, her injured right arm was still in an external fixator when we opened—Bob Mackie disguised it to look like part of the costume. Ann-Margret on a rickety staircase? Yup. That's how it was.

So off we went, on a less than first-class tour with a first-class star. A lot of people came to see what she looked like at age 60. And let me tell you, she looked GREAT. I often saw her in her dressing room in a wig cap without a speck of make-up and she looked absolutely amazing. Her skin literally looked like a baby's bottom—perfection. I never stopped looking for any telltale signs of work having been done. Whoever has laid hands on her has been the greatest living artist at his craft. No signs whatsoever.

This tour was long after her big accident—a famous and much publicized fall during her Las Vegas act in 1972. Scotty Salmon, my high school chorus teacher, (remember him?) was dancing in her act at the time and said that her fall was the worst thing he ever saw in his life. Google reports that she fell from 22 feet. But I have been told that the actual number was more like 40. She was standing on a gigantic Genie's hand that collapsed, dropping her on her face.

It was a hair-raising moment as told to me by Roger Smith; how he kidnapped her against doctor's orders, got her on a private jet and flew her to a famous doctor in L.A.—a doctor he knew could save her face as well as her career and her life. He operated through her mouth rather than cutting her gorgeous face. I saw her comeback in Las Vegas after that event quite by accident, and long before I knew her. She was ravishingly beautiful and I will never forget it. Nor will I forget having the famous disaster reported to me by the very people who lived it.

What surprised me was how many people didn't remember Ann-Margret. Our society has become so instantly disposable and fame has become so ephemeral that anyone under 30-years old seemed to have no idea who she was. This icon; who had even been made into her own cartoon character (Ann Margrock in *The Flintstones*); the paramour of Elvis; the fantasy girl of a million men's teenage years; forgotten by the most recent generation while she was still beautiful and vibrant.

I used to think Andy Warhol was a fraud and that his pronouncement of, "In the future everyone will be famous for fifteen minutes," was a load of crap. But no, he had it right. And even in Las Vegas, where Ann-Margret had been a superstar a mere twenty-five years before, she was forgotten.

On the other side of the coin, many people across the country DID remember her and enough of them turned out to keep us afloat. It was a great joy to see how she treated all those people. First of all, she treated everyone the same; doormen, cleaning staff, fans, co-workers. I never saw her behave less than perfectly with anyone. I used to joke that it was like traveling with Buddha. She simply gave love to everyone she met.

The closest I ever saw her come to losing her temper was at a company photo shoot on stage one afternoon. It went on for a long time, and of course, no one wanted to take any photos of anyone but Ann-Margret. And when she finally struck a provocative pose against the proscenium, the photographers all went crazy snapping shot after shot after shot. She finally got tired of this after a very long time, and asked if they were done. They all cried, "Just one more! Just one more!" She let out a long world weary sigh. That was it. That was her version of a fit. Amazing. The thing that I found so amusing about her behavior was that of all the people I've ever worked with, I've never known anyone who would have been given more leeway had she chosen to misbehave. I mean, she was ANN-MARGRET fer Cripes sake! But no, she chose to behave perfectly. Very impressive.

Playing *The Best Little Whorehouse in Texas* in Dallas was amazing for several reasons. First of all, when I made my entrance as the Governor of Texas in front of a giant state flag that covered the entire stage, the audience of Texans came completely unglued. It was a very fun thing to experience that on a nightly basis. Another thing that transpired was not so pleasant. Ann-Margret lost her very beloved mother after the first Tuesday performance in Dallas. The next afternoon when we came in for the matinee we learned that our star had taken a private jet back to L.A. for the funeral.

At the presenter's insistence, Ann-Margret—who had been totally joined at the hip with her mother for her entire life—flew back to Dallas on Saturday morning (the funeral was on Friday in California) to do four sold-out shows: two on Saturday and two on Sunday. I happened to be standing outside the theater when she arrived in a limo; dressed in black including big hat and a veil. She was almost too grief stricken to walk. I remember thinking, "How on earth is she going to do the show?"

I was standing in the wings when she made her entrance. As she pronounced the first line, her voice was so filled with inexpressible pain that I burst into tears. Yeah, you know I do this all the time, but so did everyone else. She was unbelievably strong through the entire performance but when she reached the end of the show and the new song that had been written for her by Carol Hall, she came to the end of her rope. The song was called "You Were a Friend to Me." It is about losing someone you love. It was very moving under any circumstance, but on this day, words fail. She made it all the way to the last line in which she had to repeat the title line once more and she just lost it, breaking down in sobs.

The totally choreographed curtain call started immediately at the end of her song. As part of that curtain call, Ann-Margret would storm angrily up to me, give me a shove and say, "You shut me down!" since it was the Governor's fault that her establishment was eventually closed. On this day, she walked straight toward me eye-to-eye, said, "Aw, I ain't mad at you, honey." and kissed me right on the lips. I don't recall how I got through the rest of it.

There was one more noteworthy event in Dallas. One of the producers of *The Best Man* lives near Dallas. He came to a performance and waited for me afterward at the stage door. What he had to tell me was rather surprising.

It seemed that *The Best Man* had won the Outer Critics Circle Award. All of the Outer Critics Circle had attended the show the night I played President Hockstader. He wanted to tell me that he credited me with that award, the only one the show garnered. It was a very generous gesture from him and a grand moment for me.

About a year into the tour, when we were in St. Louis, I heard that Chita Rivera was in the audience. It gave me untold pleasure to think that I was dancing in front of the great Chita Rivera. And that I was finishing my number with the splits for this great dancer and great lady of the theater. She came backstage afterwards, wearing a gray pant suit and looking like a million dollars. She walked dramatically toward me as I tried to tell her how thrilled I was to meet her, but she exaggeratedly staggered, pretending to faint and fall into my arms. Then she recovered and pretended to faint, again. She did this three times. Thereafter, no matter how much I tried to praise her and tell her what an honor it was to meet her, she kept turning the conversation back to me and my splits. It was one of my favorite memories of the entire tour.

Another favorite memory happened while the show was in Vegas. I met a Puerto Rican marine after the show—who seemed very impressed that I was the Governor of Texas. I, of course, was very impressed that he was a Puerto Rican marine. We ended up at the Aladdin having the date which simply would not end—it went on and on and on and on. Finally I was reduced to a dishrag and unable to move or speak. At which point, my marine slapped me on the shoulder and said, "Now THAT'S how you treat the Governor of Texas." One for my scrapbook.

A couple of cities later, I came in to warm up before the show, did my usual stretches and went out to do my number. But when I dropped into the splits, something snapped. I had violently pulled my hamstring. I finished the number somehow but was in pretty bad shape.

I went to a young sports doctor who asked me how I had sustained such an injury. I told him that I did the splits in a dance number in *The Best Little Whorehouse in Texas*. His face went slack as he asked incredulously:
"Why?"
"Because it's funny,"
"Well, can't you find some humor that's more—AGE APPROPRIATE?"
I did not return to that doctor. I continued to do the dance number for the rest of the tour, but unfortunately, the splits were out. I had done the splits 8 times a week for a year. But alas, I think my splits shall not resurface again—but then I've so often been wrong.

The show eventually arrived in southern California where I had one of the only reunions I ever had with my Bible toting mother. She and a group of ladies from her church put on their clip-on earrings and plastic pearls and came to see *The Best Little Whorehouse in Texas*. I had dinner with them beforehand—and to say that it was odd would be a great understatement. I only saw my mother a couple of times in my adult life. The insanity of my Bible Belt upbringing was a sin I never forgave her. So to meet her again at *The Best Little Whorehouse in Texas*—was odd. One of the church ladies took me aside at one point:

"If ya don't mind me askin', I was wonderin' why you and yer mother don't speak that often?"

"Things were kind of unpleasant in our home back in the day."

"Uh huh. Yeah, that's what I thought."

Ann-Margret greeted them all after the show as if they were good friends and treated my aging mother like a family member. She was beyond gracious and the church ladies were suitably impressed. Afterwards, as I walked the women to their van, one of them turned back to me and said, "This was the greatest day of my life." Fame is a powerful thing. I never saw my mother again.

FIFTY-ONE

9/11

(2001)

WE DID A POORLY ATTENDED week in Green Bay, Wisconsin and set off for Kalamazoo, Michigan on a bus. It had to be loaded onto a ferry boat across Lake Michigan. By the time we landed in Michigan and made the long trek to Kalamazoo, we were all exhausted. I checked into a very nice Renaissance Hotel, turned the air-conditioning on high and pulled the covers over my head.

The next morning my phone began ringing at about 9:00 AM. I assumed it was the maid wanting to make up the room so I put a pillow over my head. The phone rang again twenty-minutes later, so I called the front desk and told them to tell the maid to leave me alone. They said that the maid had not been calling my room. The next time the phone rang, I picked it up.

Hal Davis, who was playing Edsel in the show was on the line:

"Have you heard?

"Heard what?

"We've been attacked! The World Trade Towers are down to the ground. We're at war!"

While I tried to become conscious, he told me that everyone was meeting in a room across the hall to watch the coverage on television.

By the time I got into my clothes and stumbled across the hall, most of the cast was gathered in one room glued to the TV and weeping. I watched enough of the news to get some idea of what was happening and eventually made my way back to my own room to collect my thoughts. Later, in spite of

224

everything that was happening, daily life intruded and I realized that I needed some toiletries and was going to have to go to a drug store. It seemed insane to do something so ordinary at such an extraordinary time, but it had to be done. I took the elevator down and when I got to the lobby, everything was in a state of standstill. People just stood around in clumps watching televisions that had been pulled out of offices into common areas. No one spoke. No one moved.

When I went out into the street, storeowners had pulled TVs out of stores onto the sidewalks and people were huddled around them. Eventually I found a big drug store and went inside. The news was being broadcast over the loudspeakers. It truly seemed insane to be buying toothpaste. I made it to the checkout stand and an adolescent boy said to me, "And how are you, Sir?" He said it as if he was reading it from an instruction sheet from the management. I looked him in the eye and said calmly, "I'm not very well, actually. They've just bombed my hometown." To which he replied in an equally monotone delivery, "Well, you have a nice day." It couldn't have been weirder in a David Lynch movie.

When I got out into the street—a closed mall-like stretch of the shopping district of Kalamazoo—one of the girls from the show spotted me in the street. She was a very pretty, very full figured African-American girl in the bloom of youth. She was extremely upset and when she spotted me, she ran toward me, flouncing like a slow motion figure in a perfume ad on TV. She collided with me, threw her arms around me and wept for a minute or so. Then she kissed me and went on her way. As she departed, I looked down and saw a withered old African-American man sitting on a park bench next to us holding onto his cane. He looked at the girl; looked me up and down and croaked, "Well, YOU do all right!" Even at a moment like that, it was funny.

The management cancelled the next couple of shows since it was simply impossible to perform *The Best Little Whorehouse in Texas* with the entire country in such despair. I developed a terrible habit that continued for many months—sitting in front of the television watching CNN all day. I would watch the latest news flashes and listen to sound bites all day; fall asleep watching it and wake up in the middle of the night to start watching it again.

It just seemed like there would have to be some resolution of some kind. Someone would be caught. Someone would be punished. Something would make it better. As we all know now, this would not happen. And as we all know now, many people would eventually be punished, imprisoned, bombed and killed, but none of them would be the responsible parties. It would be a decade before Obama would finally kill Osama. We had entered the darkest days in my country's history and I was in Kalamazoo in *The Best Little Whorehouse in Texas*.

The World Trade Center had been a pivotal location in my New York life since its inception. As a young man I used to go down to the site when the foundations were being laid. I knew that something monumental was happening. In those days, that part of the city was completely deserted after dark and I used to go down there alone, late at night and look at the amazing construction. Often I was the only person there.

Once while I was down there around midnight, I heard someone playing a trap drum set like Gene Krupa on speed. I wandered around the deserted neighborhood looking for the sound of the amazing drumming and eventually found myself at the base of a tall pre-war building. This building by the way, survived the collapse of the towers. There was only one light on in that building, or in fact, in any building in the environs. The sound was coming out of an open window on the 15th floor. I just stood there in the dark listening to the drummer jam. I don't know why the memory has remained so strong; other than the fact that it was a bit like a scene from a Fellini movie and it had a frozen other-worldly quality. I always associate it with the World Trade Centers and I always look up there when I'm downtown. The towers are gone, but the Gene Krupa window remains.

When the towers were first finished, I thought they were ugly and put them out of my mind. But a few years later in the 1970s, I got a terrible case of hepatitis. For ten days I was very bad off and had the distinct feeling that I was going to die. When it finally broke and I was well enough to walk, a friend of mine came and picked me up in a cab. He wouldn't tell me where we were going. He took me to the top of the observation deck at the World Trade Center and we stood there, on a gorgeous day, looking out at the world in all directions. It was a beautiful and memorable gesture; a new start.

In the 1980s I received a surprise birthday party at Windows on the World—the restaurant that was at the very top—and who should be playing piano there but Judd Woldin, the composer of *King of Schnorrers*. He asked me what he should play for my birthday and I said, "All the Things You Are." He played it first as written, then as a Bach chorale and finally in his own unique jazz style. It was very beautiful and very memorable.

In the 1990s my old high school drama teacher, Mabel Ritzman, was in town. I took her to the observation deck knowing full well that in her late 80s, she was beginning to fail mentally. I wanted her to see the view before it was too late. There was a long line for the elevator and as we talked I looked up and realized that we were standing in front of a giant photo display of *The Scarlet Pimpernel*. We were standing directly in front of a 10-foot tall photo of me in full *Pimpernel* costume and wig. So, here I stood with the woman who had launched me in the theater, standing under a giant photo of myself on Broadway. A real moment. Shortly after that she lost her battle with Alzheimer's and was gone—still alive, but gone.

I also stood at the top of the World Trade Center after Philippe Petit's amazing climb up the side of the building and saw the place where he had signed his name on the lip of the ledge. It made me physically ill to see his signature on the rim of that terrifying precipice. I mention all these things just to point out the long and complex relationship that I had with the World Trade Centers and how devastating it was to me personally to have them obliterated in an instant. The fact that I wasn't even in my hometown for the largest event in its history was also very difficult. It was for us all.

Eventually, the show did have to go on, but the show that went on was weird and so was the audience. During the curtain call, Ann-Margret stopped the applause and led the audience in "God Bless America." It was devastating. The audience stood with their hands over their hearts. I saw men who had obviously been soldiers in World War II standing at attention and weeping. I, needless to say, was a hot mess. We did this practice for some time afterward and I don't think I ever got out a peep during "God Bless America." It was just too emotional; the way the audience looked, and the fervor with which they stood and sang.

Imagine what our next plane trip was like; a huge group of motley show-folk traveling one-way only days after the attack. No one knew when the next attack would be and the airports were awful—no, they were unbearable. There was one poor young man in the show who was a dark-skinned Sicilian with a perpetual five o'clock shadow a la Richard Nixon. He had a hell of a time.

Some surly guard forced Ann-Margret to remove her turban in one crowded airport. Her hair wasn't done—that's why she was wearing the damned turban in the first place—and it was very embarrassing. Roger Smith was livid. They traveled to the next couple of cities in a limo. God, I wish I had been with them. The tour lasted 6-months past this point.

Things eventually calmed down and touring life got more normal—if that word can be used to describe touring America in a musical comedy, about a whorehouse. I finally weaned myself off CNN when I realized that nothing was going to happen. And that every story they aired was nothing but a sound bite designed to get me to watch one more segment and see one more commercial. I had my cable service disconnected back in New York—permanently.

When the tour was finally over, we had covered all of America during a crisis; made a cast album and interacted intimately with an American icon for a year-and-a-half. On my birthday, Ann-Margret met me at the stage door, grabbed me by the lapels and sang "Happy Birthday" to me a la Marilyn Monroe with her face about an inch in front of my nose. I felt like I was in an MGM movie. During the whole journey there was constant talk of us coming to Broadway with the show. But in the frozen Canadian wasteland we finally learned that dream was not to be and the tour was over. I loved playing the Governor of Texas. I loved getting to know Ann-Margret. She gave me one degree of separation from Elvis and I cannot think of her without a smile.

FIFTY-TWO

The Persians

(Circa 2003)

WHEN WHOREHOUSE ENDED, I GOT a phone call from Ethan McSweeney who had directed *The Best Man*. He wanted me to be in *The Persians* at Tony Randall's National Actors Theater. I thought this was hilarious, given my last encounter with Mr. Randall. So I was going to score an end-run around the rude Mr. Randall and end up in his company without his permission. Hallelujah! Then came the bombshell. Ethan wanted me to be in the chorus. I told him in no uncertain terms that I hadn't been in the chorus since *No, No, Nanette* in 1970 and I had no intention of going back there now or ever.

He then patiently explained that it was the "Greek" chorus he was referring to; in the oldest play in recorded history. In Greek plays, members of the chorus are often the largest roles in tragedies and that was the case here. Furthermore, in this new translation by the very talented Ellen McLaughlin, she had divided the chorus up into several heads of government: The General, The Admiral, The Secretary of State, etc. They became very interesting parts in a very interesting endeavor. Presto! I was doing Greek Tragedy.

The plot of *The Persians*—5,000 years old, by the way—is rather shocking. The leader of the most powerful country in the world achieves his position in an unmerited fashion by being the son of the former ruler. He leads his mighty country in an unjust and unwarranted war against a much smaller and weaker country. But through a series of blunders and errors caused by his own incompetency, he utterly decimates his mighty nation. Hmm.

229

Put that plot together with the fact that Bush had just launched his war against Iraq, and that the Pace Theater, where we were performing *The Persians* was only a few blocks from the site of the World Trade Center's ruins, and you had a recipe for some rather highly-charged drama. People had a lot of trouble believing that the play was actually as old as it was or that Ms. McLaughlin had not manipulated her translation to fit the world situation. She had not. The play worked like an atomic bomb. At the end of the evening when the destroyed Councilors sank down, defeated, into the blood red sand that covered the entire stage, beating their breasts and smearing themselves in blood, the audience was staggered. So was I. It was utterly devastating to perform and to witness.

One of the great perks of the show was meeting the divine Roberta Maxwell, a classic tragedian of the old tradition. She played the inconsolable queen of Persia to raging perfection. She had been one of the founding members of the Guthrie Theater and was in the original company of *Equus*. I often found myself seated on the floor of her dressing room while she made-up, listening to her stories and sharing some of mine. We became fast friends.

When I was in my own dressing room with the other Councilors—alias "The Greek Chorus" —I was surrounded by a group of the most fantastic old geezers imaginable. Yes, I was now officially an old geezer. We calculated that between the eight of us we had about four hundred years combined stage experience—quite a formidable group. And the laughing; we would laugh ourselves silly in the dressing room, then joke all the way to the wings. At which point, we would pull ourselves together and go out to play the most devastating tragedy imaginable. I used to think to myself that all that laughing was our way of dealing with the devastating truth of the play.

The ghost of the dead King Darius was played by Len Cariou (*Sweeney Todd, A Little Night Music*). I had somehow managed to go my whole career without ever being in the same room with him, so it was a great pleasure to rehearse with him. He was, however, a bit of a tough nut to crack. In the beginning, he kept very much to himself. Then, several weeks into rehearsal, we found ourselves seated in a big circle in the theater lobby with Mr. Cariou regaling us with stories about rehearsing the premiere of *A Little Night Music*.

He said that he had been promised a song at a certain point in the script, but Sondheim and the other creative staff had not been able to come up with it. So he and some of the other actors did an improv on the topic and the writers went off to try and come up with something. A couple of days later, Mr. Sondheim announced to Len that he had good news and bad news. The good news was he had written the song. The bad news was it turned out to be for someone else. Mr. Sondheim then sat down at the piano and played for the first time anywhere "Send in the Clowns."

When I mentioned this story to Roberta, she said, "Yes, but what he didn't tell you was that we were living together at the time." (Who knew?) And that he had come home from rehearsal at the end of that day; closed the door behind him and said to her, "I have just heard the most remarkable thing!" He then proceeded to encapsulate the entire song for her without one mention of the fact that it had gone to Glynis Johns; just amazement at the beauty of the creation.

Not all the stories were as nice. We were at the beautiful New 42nd Street Studios—my favorite studio ever—about to do our first run-through. As I walked out into the hallway on the break immediately before the run, I ran right into Tony Randall. I said hello to him and he walked past me as if I was invisible. Roberta then reported to me that he had done the same thing to her. Apparently he only acknowledged those who he considered to be of equal rank. A very small group, mostly deceased.

Roberta's first entrance as the Queen was a very big to-do preceded by a great deal of build-up: there was much carrying on from the Councilors, a gigantic lighting effect, much music and sound effects, and the raising of a gigantic gate. It took a long time and a great deal of coordination. Here we were doing this enormous pomp and circumstance for the founder of the company for the first time. And just as we got to the very moment of Roberta's first line; the gigantic gate flew up, Roberta raised her arms to speak and Tony's cell phone went off.

We all froze, waiting to see how this would play out. And to everyone's dismay—he took the call. I thought Roberta's eyes would pop out of her head. Eventually he finished the call, mumbled something—not an apology—and we went back to the beginning.

For the second time, the company launched off; the Councilors carried on, the lighting effects and sound cues were called, the gates flew out, Roberta entered and raised her arms to speak, and Tony's cell phone went off *again*. The room was speechless. At least this time, Tony had the grace to leave the room to take the call. After the laughter stopped, we went on without Mr. Randall.

During the performances, there were often bomb threats due to the general consternation in the city about terrorist attacks and also due to our close proximity to Ground Zero. Many times during the run we found ourselves standing out on the street in full costume and make-up, waiting for the all clear to sound. Given the subject matter of *The Persians*, it all seemed to just add to the whole ambience of loss and destruction. A great theatrical experience.

FIFTY-THREE

Here Lies Jenny

(Circa 2004)

I HAD REMAINED FRIENDS WITH Bebe Neuwirth ever since we had done *13 Days to Broadway* more than twenty years before. It is thrilling to watch someone you know put together a really big career coup. Bebe certainly did that in a very big way and on both coasts. So, you can imagine how happy I was when she called me up and told me that she was putting together a theatrical event and that from the very beginning she had always imagined me being in it. The piece to which she was referring was to be an evening of Kurt Weill music entitled *Here Lies Jenny*.

Her old friend Roger Rees (the original *Nicolas Nickleby*) was set to direct. The choreography was to be by Ann Reinking, former protégé of Bob Fosse and one of Broadway's premiere dancers and choreographers. The cast was to be just Bebe, myself and two superb male dancers from *Chicago,* Greg Butler and Shawn Emamjomeh. The venue was to be the fantastically rustic Zipper Factory Theater, which had the ambience of a bombed-out cellar in the Weimar Republic. A more fantastic location or group of cohorts could not have been found. Plus, we were going to open the show doing only late-night performances when all the other shows in town had shuttered for the evening. A pretty heady brew.

Roger was everything one could want in a director: smart, funny, perceptive, creative and bright as a penny. As for being choreographed by Ann Reinking—not something I ever thought I would experience, by the way— what can I say? I played the old beat up bartender and confidant of Bebe. At one point, we were to have a tango together; me in my 50s and well into my poundage, tangoing with one of Broadway's premiere dancers. Wow.

At the first rehearsal, I was simply terrified that I would step on Bebe's foot during the complicated choreography; complicated for me, I hasten to say, not for her. At one point when Ann was putting it together, I was doing the combination first with her, then with Bebe, then with Ann, then with Bebe. At the climax of this amazing interaction, I yelled to no one in particular, "Do you fucking believe who I'm dancing with?" My career has often landed me in places where I NEVER expected to be—this was definitely one of them.

The show got an unbelievable amount of publicity due to the star power of Bebe and the creatives; but the odd nature of the piece also got a lot of attention. Rare theater songs by Kurt Weill in a bizarre and intimate environment at midnight really caught people's attention. The rich, the famous and the pretentious filed through the doors in an amazing procession for our late night repast. It was nothing to see Dame Judy Dench, Renée Fleming, Isaac Mizrahi, Alec Baldwin and Patti Lupone in the same weekend. They all stayed after the show and had drinks at the bar with the cast. Standing around after a performance having a club soda with Judy Dench is the stuff dreams are made of. Having Patti Lupone tell you she really likes your voice is not bad either. Just between you and me, she said it twice, to make sure I heard her— I heard her the first time.

Before the show ended, I met half of show business. I finally came face-to-face with Elaine Stritch. She was exactly what I expected—exactly. I finally met Joel Grey, whom I had seen in *Cabaret* the first week I arrived in New York. He told me stories about Lotte Lenya; she came to Joel's wedding! I had the great pleasure of meeting Tyne Daily, who was as delightful as any star could possibly be during an after show meeting. I kept trying to tell her how happy I was to meet her, but she just kept telling me how happy she was to meet me. Classy.

Eventually, the management decided to open up the run to a wider audience and started scheduling performances during regular theater hours. This may have been good for the show financially, but it was not good for the cast artistically. The audiences that showed up for the late night performances of a rare Kurt Weill evening were not the same audiences that showed up at the regular 8:00 PM shows. Those regular audiences tended to have a lot of non-theater folk who didn't understand why they were in a zipper factory; why we weren't singing songs from *Chicago* and why Bebe wasn't acting like Lilith from *Cheers*.

Most of my part was in German. I sang most of the German sections of music and most of my dialogue was also "auf Deutsch." I even improvised in German while I entered through the audience as a drunken, irritable old curmudgeon. I would stand at the back of the house waiting for the cue to start the show and then I would begin swearing and carrying on in German to the confusion of the patrons.

I entered behind a row of seats at the rear that were traditionally sold at a discount by TKTS. They were perfectly good seats, but they were in the back and went for cheap; very cheap. The patrons who sat there—having paid less than anyone else in the place—always caused the most trouble. I got very tired of watching their annoying antics with the House Manager—a very pleasant young man—night after night as I waited for my entrance.

On one particular evening, three disgusting harridans came in together. From the moment they arrived they made everyone's life around them hell. They complained about everything from the temperature of the room; to the sightlines; to the padding in their seats. Finally, their attacks on the sweet young House Manager were so out of line that I could bear no more. I shouted out from behind them. "Hey! Fuck you! Fuck you! And Fuck you!" They were stunned into silence for a second. At that very moment, the lights dimmed, the House Manager called out, "Places. Have a good show." Then I began yelling at the rest of the audience in German as designated in the script. This may not have been good manners or proper stage etiquette, but it was one of the most enjoyable moments in the run for me. Nobody ever gets to tell a disruptive audience member to go fuck themselves. I highly recommend it.

The show was definitely NOT for everyone. Bebe had a whole number in French with no translation. I had a lot of German and even the English numbers by Kurt Weill cannot be understood by certain audience members under any circumstances. Some people went out hoarse from screaming "Bravo!" And others left scratching their heads in confusion. Yup, that's Kurt Weill for ya.

On stage, Shawn and Greg were the epitome of swarthy machismo; backstage, they were two of the most hilarious people I've ever worked with. We were all crammed in one small dressing room on the 2nd floor with no bathroom and no sink. In the entire time we were together there was not one moment that was unpleasant. I don't know when I've enjoyed dressing room camaraderie more. And what a work ethic—there was no slacking for these boys. Before most of the late night performances, they had already done at least one performance of *Chicago* on Broadway, sometimes two. I never once heard either of them complain—if you only knew how miraculous this was for dressing room decorum.

Early on in the play Bebe arrived in my broken down bar after being beaten up (perhaps raped and being left broken and abandoned). In a scene with no words, I helped her get herself together, took her coat, offered her a seat at the bar and held up a silver drink platter like a mirror, so she could fix her make-up. Without a word, we set up the relationship that would run the entire length of the play. It always broke my heart and it was really great to play it every night with my old friend.

FIFTY-FOUR

Under The Bridge

(Circa 2005)

HOW DID I BECOME FAST friends with Kathie Lee Gifford? Let's see—A mega-famous television icon noted for her "slightly right of center" politics and born-again Christianity joined at the hip with a formerly drug addicted gay pagan—highly unlikely. But then, it's not always possible to predict how things will turn out, is it?

I was workshopping a musical by David Friedman based on an ancient French fable. Directed by Ethan McSweeney of *Gore Vidal's The Best Man*. David was long-time friends with Kathie Lee and had done arrangements for one of her albums. He had even written some songs with her. (Kathie Lee writes songs? Yes.)

David was looking for some investors to move his show forward. So Kathie Lee offered up her Connecticut home for a backer's audition in front of some of her wealthy friends and acquaintances. When we arrived by car service, we were buzzed through a large wrought iron gate onto a private peninsula jutting out into the bay of Greenwich. (She has her own peninsula? Yes.) She and her dog Regis, met us at the door. (She has a dog named Regis? Yes.)

From the first moment we arrived, she was absolutely delightful. She gave me a guided tour and proudly showed me through her recording studio. (She has her own recording studio? Yes.) She showed me the wine cellar. I would have expected that. But then, she showed me the theater in the basement. (She has a theater in the basement? Yes.)

At one point, we were in this miniature elevator that connected the recording studio to the theater and it stalled. Now, this was an elevator that was maybe 3-feet square, and the two of us were crammed into it, nose-to-nose. All I could think was, "I'm trapped in a miniature elevator with Kathie Lee Gifford; this is going to make a fantastic anecdote." Unfortunately, one of her employees heard us yelling and got the elevator running before the situation turned into a really good story.

We rehearsed all day while Kathie Lee played hostess. She fed us and took care of us like we were her own personal guests—or relatives. It was a gorgeous day. The house was gorgeous, the view was gorgeous and I was having a gorgeous time. After Kathie Lee had watched rehearsal for several hours, she took me aside and told me that she wanted to show me something. She took me by the arm and walked me up the main stairs to her bedroom and shut the door. "Well, this is going to be a much better anecdote than the elevator one," I thought.

She started fishing around in her bedside table; what on earth was she doing? She then pulled a bound script from the drawer and handed it to me while whispering:
"I want you to be my Armand."
"Huh?"
"Ed Dixon—I want you to be my Armand."
I took the script from her. It appeared that she had written a musical and wanted me to play the lead in it. (Kathie Lee wrote musicals? Yes.)

I went home that evening and read Kathie Lee's script. It was based on an award-winning children's book called *The Family Under the Bridge*. The lead character was an old broken down alcoholic curmudgeon who hated children and dogs—I was starting to see her logic. The plot concerned his journey from dissolution to transformation. I closed the script and said to myself, "I am going to play this part in New York if I have to pull the Sun out of the sky to do it."

Before long we were doing a backer's audition for *Under the Bridge*, as it came to be called. We did it at Chelsea Studios with Eric Schaeffer directing. Now, Eric and I had become fast friends when he came in to restage *Whorehouse* on the road. After the first backer's audition, I heard him say to Kathie Lee, "He IS this part!" and so I was. I knew perfectly well that I had a grounding for Armand that would be hard to match.

I became a cheerleader for the show and did everything that I could think of to move it forward. When no venue seemed to be forthcoming, I called the management of the Zipper Theatre and suggested that they look at the property. Their basic reaction was, "The Zipper Theatre, known for edgy, naughty, out of the mainstream, in-your-face theater, do a children's musical written by Kathie Lee Gifford? Are you out of your mind?" But that's exactly what they did.

Since there were a couple of children's roles in the show, Kathie Lee asked me if there were any kids that I particularly enjoyed working with. I had just done two productions of *The Sound of Music*. In the first production, I loved the children and they loved me. People were constantly saying to me, "I had no idea you were so good with children!" In the second production, I hated the children and they hated me. People were constantly saying to me, "Oh, I had no idea you were so bad with children." I suggested the children from the FIRST production and they ended up doing the show. The second cast of children is probably in juvenile detention somewhere.

For the first time in my life I was billed above the title. When the giant marquis was installed in front of the Zipper Theatre it read, "ED DIXON in UNDER THE BRIDGE." This is an experience everyone should have at least once—with your own name, of course, not mine.

I should mention that working with children is one thing but performing FOR them is quite another. They scream, they cry, they wet their pants, they fight with their siblings, eat things and make noise with cellophane wrappers that you wouldn't think possible. Oh, yes, and they talk to you while you're performing. They answer questions that you've posed to other cast members. They sing along. It is, how you say in English, "The hardest fucking thing in the world."

However, like so much of life, in spite of everything, in spite of all the obstacles and barriers and difficulties, it was a swell time. The cast was great and I had a great time being Armand and there was a LOT of publicity.

Tony Danza came to see *Under The Bridge* and invited me as a guest on his talk show. Both backstage and on the air he treated me like his long lost brother. He is truly a mensch. If you haven't performed a big song from a musical in which you're starring on live television at 8:00 AM with about 60-seconds of technical rehearsal; it's pretty indescribable. Tony made it seem almost normal.

My interaction with him and Kathie Lee taught me something that I would never have known otherwise. There is a kind of personality in the American public that has become famous in such a way that they become reduced to being a sound bite. Both Tony and Kathie Lee are such people. Whenever you hear of them discussed in any arena, the same catch phrases are always applied, without exception, and by people who do not know them. If I hadn't gotten to know these two people myself, it would never have occurred to me to question the situation. I would simply have accepted the sound bites like everyone else does. Here are two fine, decent people who are always referred to in the same dismissive way. It's really unconscionable.

The New York Times mentioned Kathie Lee's personal catch phrases in their review of *Under the Bridge!* Sweat shops and infidelity in a theater review; in THE NEW YORK TIMES! I might have expected it of The New York Post or possibly The Daily News, but The Times? This was really shocking. And speaking of reviews, they were very kind to me and very mean to Kathie Lee. Sound bites.

When it was all over and the smoke had cleared, I mentioned that I was planning to take a vacation once the show closed. Kathie Lee chimed in:
"Why don't you stay in my house on Key Largo?"
"But I'm going for two weeks."
"Take my house, I hate to have it sit empty."
And that's how I found myself in Kathie Lee's sprawling mansion on the water in Key Largo; complete with staff. In the course of the two weeks I was there, two different friends of mine flew in from different parts of the country just so they could see it with their own eyes. I figured this little gift that she so blithely offered me; was worth about a $100,000 for the two weeks. Not bad for a sound bite.

I got one more amazing perk out of *Under the Bridge*. Kathie Lee asked me to sing for the Johnny Mercer Society Benefit at the Rainbow Room at Rockefeller Center to honor Cy Coleman. Now I hadn't seen Cy for years at this point and I was thrilled. Then I found out that I was sharing the bill with Chita Rivera, Glenn Close, Brian Stokes Mitchell, Adam Guettel and the great Tony Bennett—Cy and Tony performed "It Amazes Me" my favorite Cy Coleman song, not 10-feet away from me. It was a simply one of the greatest nights I've ever experienced. I got a one-on-one photo op with Cy. And just like old times, he was cracking me up the whole time. It was a completely joyful night and I went home on a cloud. The next day I picked up the paper and Cy had passed. After I got over the shock, I thought, "Wow, there are worse ways to go than after being fêted at the Rainbow Room high atop Rockefeller Center. And how many of us get to leave behind his kind of musical legacy?

FIFTY-FIVE

Richard Cory and Fanny Hill

(Circa 2005)

I RETURNED FROM A BRIEF tour of *Doctor Dolittle* (don't ask) in time to see *Richard Cory* at the New York Musical Theater Festival (NYMF). My old friend, Nick Cavarra, had produced my show. It was directed by Jimmy Brennan, who I had known since Surflight Summer Theater in 1968. It won the Festival Prize; The Audience Award and Lynne Wintersteller got a Best Actress nod for her performance as the long-suffering wife. Of course, A.R. Gurney was there, since it was based on his original play. But the real surprise was that Stephen Sondheim came. Can you imagine having Stephen Sondheim come to a musical you wrote? I couldn't. It was fantastic.

The offshoot of this success with *Richard Cory* was that we got the impetus to finally get *Fanny Hill* off the ground and into New York City. Nick Cavarra worked tirelessly to put a team of producers and fund raisers together. And we got the support of the York Theatre with whom I had a very long-standing relationship. They put the show on their schedule and we began moving forward to open *Fanny Hill* in New York.

I can't speak for anyone else, but judging by my own experience, mounting a show in Manhattan, dwarfs all other previous adventures. It made everything that had gone before seem easy, and I'm including everything. I'm not saying it wasn't joyful. It was. It was also very, very, very hard.

It started with auditions at Ripley-Greer Studios. I had to pick from people I knew and loved, one over the other. Feelings were hurt. I had no one to pawn the blame off on. It was my show. People whom I had worked with in better days came in on their last legs and made scenes. One guy, whom I'd known for years, literally got down on his knees and begged for the job—and this was a very low-paying job, mind you.

Jill Haworth, the original star of *Cabaret*—who I had seen on Broadway the first week I arrived in New York—came in dead drunk and made a simply dumbfounding scene. No one knew how to react. We just sat there stunned until it was over. Every actor should sit on the other side of the audition table at least once. It's a steep learning curve.

Eventually we put together a really good cast. I was out-voted on one choice, which I regretted later. And one unanimous choice proved to be, if not disastrous, very unsatisfactory. But we had Nancy Anderson in the leading role and she once again, never put a foot wrong. Of course, she was desperately ill on the night that The New York Times came; but that goes with the territory.

Everything was going along swimmingly. Michael Bottari and Ronald Case designed fantastic sets and costumes. This was attested to in every review with numerous awards and nominations. The cast was working hard together and everything was coming together. Then, about two days before Christmas, one of our investors pulled out. Leaving us $40,000 in the hole.

Now, $40,000 may not seem like a lot of money in the great scheme of things, but we had used every connection we knew and overturned every rock we could find to raise the quarter of a million dollar budget. We had nowhere to turn, NOWHERE. The source we had counted on to be our main fundraiser turned out to be a complete bust. And here sat Nick Cavarra and I—just before the holidays—with an incomplete budget, and unless something changed instantly—no show.

In absolute desperation I turned to some very wealthy friends and said the words that rich people hate to hear above all others, "Will you give me some money?" It was humiliating to ask and even more humiliating to be turned down flat. What to do, what to do, what to do? I went to my computer and began composing a mass email. It began, "This is not a Christmas greeting…" I then poured out my heart about the shortfall and the unbearable position that we found ourselves in and sent it to everyone in my address book. Unbelievably enough, this revolting email raised $40,000. The show was back on.

Rehearsals were very exciting and the cast and crew worked tirelessly. I'm not saying they didn't complain about the slave wages and difficult conditions, but they did their jobs tirelessly. The reviews were wonderful. We had many, many wonderful quotes that could have been used to create quite a stir, but we didn't have the money to take any ads to publicize the reviews. We had only been able to raise enough money to OPEN the show, nothing more. We were busted.

To cap off the situation, one of our main producers and fundraisers left the country and went on a European vacation. While the show circled the drain, Nick Cavarra was left to keep the sinking ship afloat single-handedly. And when it went down, it was he alone who had to do all the final closing of accounts; stave off the last of the creditors and see to it that the cast got their last checks.

When the show closed, I had some great production shots; some fantastic reviews; one Drama Desk Nomination; one Drama-Logue Award; two Dean's List Awards and a shattered dream. The show that had taken me almost ten years to get to Manhattan was washed up and washed out in spite of excellent reviews. Nick Cavarra got a job offer in Los Angeles, and closed up his New York apartment to move to the other side of the country. This was like losing my brother and my right arm. I could not imagine ever trying to write again. I felt bad. I felt very, very, very bad.

FIFTY-SIX

Mr. Dixon Goes to Washington

(Circa 2006)

I HAVE LONG SINCE LEARNED that when things look completely bleak, if you just keep breathing and/or walking, something will happen. And, of course, it did. The phone rang and dear Ethan McSweeney offered me another production of *The Persians*, this time at the very prestigious Shakespeare Theater in Washington, D.C. No sooner had that call happened when Eric Schaeffer rang up and offered me the role of Lindsay Woolsey in a big, glorious production of *Mame* at the Kennedy Center. I was able to console myself that no matter how disappointed I was about *Fanny Hill*, it's a very rare thing in show business to have people call you up and just offer you jobs. It's always good to work. So, off I went to Washington.

Of course, I had worked in D.C. many times, but this time I saw it with completely new eyes. There's something about totally giving in to your fate that is very enlivening. The Shakespeare Theater put me up in a beautiful apartment right above the theater. From that lovely apartment I had access to all the monuments and museums of D.C., which are open to the public for free. For the first time I fell in love with our nation's capital and I just happened to be there in cherry blossom season. Really something worth experiencing.

I was the only holdover from the original production of *The Persians*. It was a very interesting process to learn the same show in a different part with a different cast. Originally I played the General, now I was playing the Secretary of State. The overall effect of the play was equally as startling as the New York production. Previously, we were just beginning the war with Iraq. In D.C. we were completely engulfed in the quagmire that it was to become. The tragedy seemed to have grown more teeth.

One of my favorite events of the run involved a cast member who ran into a Republican congressman after the play. The congressman castigated him and the cast for creating *The Persians* to humiliate our president. The cast member simply reminded him that the play was 5,000 years old and is in fact, the oldest surviving play in Western literature—a fact that was mentioned in the prologue. If we had created the production to humiliate "Dubyuh," we did it in a time machine.

The amazing thing about my stay in D.C. was that the two gigs, *The Persians* and *Mame,* lined up so perfectly that I was able to do them both in perfect sequence. They overlapped by three weeks. So I was rehearsing *Mame,* the quintessential American Musical Comedy, all day and doing *The Persians,* the quintessential Greek Tragedy, at night. I seriously doubt that any actor in the history of the theater can make this claim. The day after *The Persians* closed, *Mame* went into tech rehearsals. It's a wonder I didn't get the theatrical equivalent of "the bends."

Mame was as joyful a theatrical experience as I can ever imagine. Christine Baranski, (*The Good Wife*) someone I'd always wanted to meet, played the title character, and Harriet Harris, (*Thoroughly Modern Millie*) an equally marvelous and zany character actress, was playing her drunken best friend, Vera. Now, Lindsay Woolsey is not a great part, but as Mame's literary agent, he's in every apartment scene, standing right between Mame and Vera watching them fire one-liners back and forth at each other like great tennis pros being observed from the center net. Standing next to Baranski and Harris when they were lobbing laugh lines into an audience was like watching showgirls throw grenades into a pool of fish. The accuracy of their delivery was something vastly beyond the human. One would like to think one might learn something from such observation, but I'm afraid it was more awe inspiring than instructive.

I talked Eric Schaeffer into letting me play Uncle Jeff in the Peckerwood section of the play as well. So, in the New York portion of the endeavor, I was the extremely erudite and sophisticated Lindsay Woolsey and in the Deep South section I was the exact opposite. This made the engagement a great deal more fun than either part would have been alone.

The brilliant Gregg Barnes gave us all jaw-dropping costumes to make our characters work as simply as possible. He dressed Lindsay Woolsey like Diaghilev and made Uncle Jeff look like Colonel Sanders. Both were hilarious visually and a ball to inhabit. Walt Spangler's larger-than-life sets were both wonderful to look at and be engulfed by.

Oh, yes, and I once again had a big dance solo at Peckerwood that preceded the title song, dressed for all the world as Colonel Sanders, goatee and all. The choreography was by the completely brilliant Warren Carlyle. There I was down center in front of all his glorious young dancers, dancing my little post middle-aged heart out. How do these things happen? As Sweet Charity would say, "Fickle finger of fate!"

I had a wonderful moment as Lindsay Woolsey in Mame's apartment in the second act. I was standing right between Christine and Harriet when older Patrick (Max Von Essen) arrived and delivered a completely heartless and utterly Republican line. Harriet and I shared a glance with each other that was so knowing and so filled with disappointment, sorrow and anger that for my money, it was worth the entire trip to Washington. I looked forward to that moment with Harriet every night.

It was crystal clear to everyone from the beginning that *Mame* was moving to Broadway. Jerry Herman, the show's composer/lyricist (as well as *Hello, Dolly, Dear World, Mack and Mabel, Milk and Honey, The Grand Tour* and *La Cage aux Folles*) was with us the whole time. It was perfectly obvious that the show was being prepped for a transfer to the Palace Theater as soon as we closed at the Kennedy Center. However...

"The best laid schemes o' mice an' men (and musical comedies) gang aft agley." A couple of big critics came to review the show before we were ready to open and both of them shot a gaping hole into the side of our ship of state that nothing could repair. Just when we thought that we might survive those blows—as the favorable reviews poured in later—it turned out that the set was too large to fit into the Palace Theater. It would either have to be totally rebuilt or put in another space. Of course, no other space was available and rebuilding the current set was a financial impossibility. How do these things happen? "Fickle finger of fate." Show business can really kick your butt. Seriously.

At that very moment, Kathie Lee Gifford called and suggested that I do her new musical, *Saving Aimee*, about the famous evangelist, Aimee Semple McPherson. I would play Brother Bob, an evil and unscrupulous rival-revival minister who was a dead cross between Jerry Falwell and my father. How could

I refuse? On top of everything else, it was to be directed by Eric Schaeffer at his own gorgeous and newly-constructed Signature Theatre just outside of— Washington, D.C.

What better antidote to the poison of my youth than to invest a caricature of Jerry Falwell, with a smidgeon of my dear old dad, and drag him out on stage to be a laughing stock in front of a cheering crowd of theater-goers. At one point I even brandished a giant Bible that was a dead ringer for the Morocco bound, red-letter edition, gold-leaf-paged King James Version that my dearly departed Papa had pounded in the pulpit. The feel and smell of it gave me the deep dark creeps and I infused it into my performance. That character was one scary—and funny—motherfucker.

My performance of Brother Bob got me a Helen Hayes nomination, the highest acting award D.C. has to offer. Jerry Falwell died while I was flogging him on stage at the Signature Theatre—I would be hard pressed to tell you which was the greater honor. Of course, I know which one was; I would just be hard pressed to tell you.

The press was, as usual, very mean to Kathie Lee. There were promises of a recording. The title role was played by the incandescent Carolee Carmello, who DEFINITELY deserved to be recorded; and a move to New York. But these fell through for all the usual reasons. Same old, same old. Things finally came to a halt in my D.C. adventure.

I would be remiss to leave the D.C. chapter without mentioning that the entire time I did all three gigs at three different theaters in our nation's capitol, I was "consorting" with a Hispanic stripper who barely spoke English. (And just when I was certain that my social status was "retired.") We cut an unlikely swath from the Outer Banks to New England for the next two or three years—you simply cannot make this shit up.

FIFTY-SEVEN

Scenery and Pirates!

(Circa 2007)

IT'S ONE THING TO HAVE a director call you up out of the blue and offer you a part. It's quite another thing altogether to have a director call you up out of the blue and offer to star you in a production of a play you wrote. That's the event which came on the heels of my D.C. excursion.

David Glenn Armstrong, an ebullient director who had staged me in *The Great Big Radio Show* at the York Theatre, had, without my knowledge, managed to get a production of my play *Scenery*, on the next season of the Mason Street Warehouse in Saugatuck, Michigan. *Scenery* is a two-person play (a "two-hander," as they say) and David wanted me to star in it opposite the multi-talented Lynne Wintersteller, who had starred off-Broadway in *Closer than Ever* and played opposite me in *The Great Big Radio Show*. All I had to do was say, "Yes." All the arrangements had been made without me lifting a finger. I said, "Yes."

Then it dawned on me, I had never before acted in a two-person play. I certainly had never acted in a two-person play of which I was the author. And I certainly had never done both of those things in the middle of Michigan with no friends and co-horts to support or encourage me. Besides, it's a very political and psycho-sexual play about aging, raging, drinking, philandering, the desire for fame and the insanity of ego. What the hell would people in the middle of Michigan make of me and my self-revealing play? Even if they bought the topics and/or me, would they think that *Scenery* was funny? I was about to find out.

Jim Morgan from the York Theatre, designed a fantastic set that perfectly captured the feeling of the backstage play; The Mason Street Warehouse built and lit it perfectly; David Glenn Armstrong directed it with great wit and understanding; Lynne Wintersteller was the perfect co-star—I believe that people have a tendency to think of her as "a nice lady" because she's pretty and has a gorgeous voice; but the truth is, she's as nutty as I am and is seriously talented—Seriously.

Playing *Scenery* at the Mason Street Warehouse was an absolutely delightful experience. And you know what? People got it. People from another part of the country; from a different geopolitical background; from different professions, mores and values came and cheered on the daffy anti-heroes in my zany play. The reviews were fantastic. We even attracted the Chicago Tribune, which wrote us a love letter. I guess I wasn't quite finished with writing after all.

The day we closed, I flew directly from Saugatuck to the Goodspeed Opera House in East Haddam, Connecticut to play the Modern Major General in Nell Benjamin's new adaptation of *The Pirates of Penzance* called *Pirates!* I had auditioned for it with "The Nightmare Song" from *Iolanthe,* which I had performed at the Huntington in Boston. *Iolanthe's* Lord Chancellor is one of the greatest roles ever written; only topped by Major-General Stanley (The Modern Major General).

After they heard my "Nightmare Song" they not only hired me for *Pirates!,* they interpolated that song into the show as the opening of Act Two. "The Nightmare Song" is the hardest of all the Gilbert and Sullivan patter songs and is called "Nightmare" not only because that is its topic, but because that's what it is to perform. The song, "I Am the Very Model of a Modern Major-General" is also difficult, but it has lots of repetition, and the chorus chimes in periodically to let you get your breath and your bearings. "The Nightmare Song," goes on for several minutes at breakneck speed without a single repetition and no chorus. If you miss one syllable, the whole thing collapses into a giant train wreck. It is—a nightmare.

I learned the Modern Major-General song and reinstated "The Nightmare Song" into my memory banks while I was doing my two-hander *Scenery.* This was very stressful on my post-middle-aged brain. I haven't mentioned before what happens to one's memory over many decades in the theater. Well, perhaps I should say "my" memory since it's the only one of which I can honestly comment. It has been my experience that each year that passes I find it harder and harder to do my memory work and I have to constantly invent new tricks to coax things into my head. Every time I assay a new role I always have this sinking feeling along the lines of, "How am I ever going to remember all this stuff?"

I always type out scripts, songs, and audition pages into my computer and rearrange them on the screen as my mind grasps the information, breaking up sentences and paragraphs to help me formulate my interpretation of the material. I emphasize certain ideas by making them bold faced or a larger point print. This has nothing to do with my eyesight—a whole other situation—which demands that I use 18 point font print at auditions; so as not to be forced into wearing reading glasses while hawking my wares. If I make the same word mistake several times in a row, I put that particular word in 72 point font for a while, to make my mind retain it in a different way. I italicize certain words, colorize some and underline others, etc., etc., etc.

All of this is to say that learning and relearning the *Pirates!* material while performing a very talky two-person play was maddening. Then I got the rewrites. Nell Benjamin changed the period of *Pirates!* moving it a hundred years earlier in time which made many of the references anachronistic or downright impossible. So, she rewrote and I relearned the material. She rewrote again. I don't know how many times I relearned The Modern Major-General's song and "The Nightmare Song" before I arrived at Goodspeed, but it was—several. By the way, it was one thing to relearn The Modern Major-General Song, which I never performed. It was quite another to relearn "The Nightmare Song" which I had been singing at auditions and benefits for a decade. And which had been the hardest thing I'd ever learned in the first place.

Gordon Greenberg directed the production with great wit and charm; John McDaniel, one of the most "in demand" conductor/arrangers, did fabulously original, whimsical arrangements and Warren Carlyle, one of the best choreographers I've ever met, staged it beautifully. Did this stop me from being nervous? No. I never stopped going over the lyrics from the beginning of rehearsals to the end of the run. I would go over the material several times during the day. I kept my motor-scooter up at Goodspeed and I would putter around the Connecticut woods doing first the Modern Major-General song and then "The Nightmare Song" for all the local fauna.

When I arrived at the theater, I would do the Major-General's song for the first 45-minutes until my first entrance with that ditty and then, come intermission, I would begin drilling "The Nightmare Song" until it opened the second act. Only when that was over could I begin to relax. One might have considered all this a burden were it not for the fact that performing that role is one of the great pleasures of my entire career. It was worth whatever it took to make it happen.

The audiences and critics alike went nuts for *Pirates!* We soon attracted several groups of producers; young, old, independent and connected. Perhaps there were TOO many, since they could never come to a decent coalition. We closed without a firm offer to move the show, but with a second engagement booked at the Papermill Playhouse. Since it's so close to New York City, I assumed that the Papermill production would catapult us onto Broadway. We certainly seemed to have the backing.

Then the Papermill Playhouse went bankrupt. So, not only did it suddenly look as if our production might not happen there, it began to appear that the historic Papermill Playhouse might shut-down altogether. This was not my first big disappointment with them. A few years earlier, they scheduled a $2,000,000 production of my *Fanny Hill*, and even produced a workshop of it starring Kristen Chenoweth, for whom I had originally written the piece. But, before the show could go into rehearsal, they fired all their top staff and cancelled my production, crying financial hardship. Did I mention that show business can be frustrating?

Gordon Greenberg worked tirelessly to raise additional funds and to find a way to make the Papermill *Pirates!* a reality. He succeeded. By the most amazing corner cutting and cost slashing, he managed to mount a spectacular production of our dear Gilbert and Sullivan classic, revamped. The reviews were over the moon. It seemed inevitable that we would move straight to Broadway. We did not.

The more one knows about how difficult it is to produce a Broadway show, the more unlikely it seems that anything ever gets done. Because I knew all the players in the *Pirates!* drama so well, they shared many personal insights about the obstacles of our forward motion with me. I won't go into any of that privileged information, but let me tell you, "Beltway politics" has nothing on us. Yet, somehow shows like *Dracula, the Musical; Dance of the Vampires;* and *Lestat* get produced. A conundrum.

FIFTY-EIGHT

Dr. Seuss' How the Grinch Stole Christmas

(Circa 2007)

AT AGE 59, IT SEEMED to me, that my stock value seemed to be falling. *Pirates!* was stalled; I didn't seem to be on the A list and I was not being considered for things that I would have previously considered a "shoo-in." I thought to myself, "Well, I don't suppose anybody sends you a telegram when it's over. You just wake up one day and there's no pony ride."

So I should have been thrilled when my agent called with an audition for *Dr. Seuss' How the Grinch Stole Christmas* on Broadway, but I said, "No frigging way." I had auditioned for them the year before and found out afterward that the part was already promised to John Cullum—who is ever so famous. Why should I waste my time jumping through that meaningless hoop a second time? My agent insisted that the part was indeed open; that John Cullum was not doing it again and that they had, in fact, asked for me specifically. I didn't really believe any of that. But for whatever reason, I showed up at the audition.

From the moment I walked into that audition room at Telsey Studios, it seemed apparent that they were going to hire me. There is a feeling in a room when people are tuned into you. And I have an almost infallible sense of how things are going at an audition—governed by decades of audition experiences. I usually call my agent on the way home from an audition and tell him whether we'll be hearing from them or not. It's a mysterious and highly mercurial science. For instance, just this week, I had an audition go south for no discernible reason. It was simply clear from the very moment I arrived that they didn't see me in the role and vice versa. But, that day for *The Grinch* things were clearly happening.

I still had to go through the formality of a callback, but I knew what the outcome was going to be. However, never willing to leave anything to chance, I did write a piece of special material for the second call. I knew that there was a bit of dancing required for the part and I had no intention of going through a dance call, so I wrote a soft shoe number called "You Can't Teach an Old Dog New Tricks." I choreographed it myself. I was, after all, auditioning for the role of Old Max—a dog. I did my song and dance; got the part and began rehearsing a truly life changing experience.

It wasn't until after I had the part that I realized I was going to be playing the historic St. James Theatre, a hallowed hall which I not only had never played before, but was the site of one of my earliest and most profound New York memories. It was the theater where I saw the great Ethel Merman perform *Hello, Dolly* from the last row of the tippy-top balcony. I was about to stand center stage in the great theater where she had held forth FORTY YEARS earlier.

I made my entrance through the audience and up the aisle—just as Ethel had in *Gypsy*. I ascended the stairs and addressed the audience of excited children. Since Old Max was the narrator of *How the Grinch Stole Christmas* I addressed them directly. Very early on in the opening monologue, I talked about the high mountain where the Grinch had lived many years ago. As I described it, my eyes wandered upward and fell on the row where I had been seated—in the upper balcony, forty years earlier. Here I was standing on the very spot where I had once looked down upon the great Ethel Merman. It was an amazing moment for me. It was amazing at every single performance. And since *The Grinch* often played four shows a day, it was amazing A LOT.

I had of course, often performed for children, but this gig was for thousands of them. There were times when the screaming, crying, yelling, eating, puking, fighting and running up and down the aisles was so distracting, that it was literally impossible to hold a cogent thought. I had the distinct impression that I was being permanently altered and that I would never be able to be distracted by an audience again. Of course, that wasn't true, but that's how it felt.

In spite of all their annoying distractions, however, there were moments with the kiddies that were transcendent. At the end of the show, Old Max goes off to die. My final exit was up the aisle through the teaming masses of children. I begged the director not to make me run that gauntlet of kiddies; but to no avail. In the final analysis though, it ended up being one of my favorite parts of the show.

The children would reach out to touch me and I was amazed at how profound some of the interactions could be. Some found it funny; some found it terrifying; but I always found it extremely interesting. In the middle of the aisle one day, a haughty little girl pointed at my little suitcase and demanded angrily, "What's in there?" "My stuff," I replied. She was not impressed. My all-time favorite was a gorgeous little Hispanic boy of about 3 or 4 years who reached out, grabbed my hand and pressed it to his cheek like he was touching Mother Teresa. You know me; I cried all the way up the aisle.

We did 14 shows a week so there was no shortage of opportunities for interesting interactions in all manner of physical and emotional states. I've never been through anything like it. I swore that I would never claim to be tired during a regular 8-show-a-week schedule again. That turned out to be a lie as well.

It took two people to get me in and out of the intricate dog suit; very tricky if you have to go to the bathroom in the middle of the show—which, of course, I always did. Sometimes there was only about 45-minutes between shows. I could turn out the lights in my dressing room and lie on the floor comatose, until my dresser would return to shove me back into the dog suit. Sometimes I was standing center stage at the Saint James Theatre so tired that it was impossible to be anything but 100% real. I honestly think that my sense of being on stage was changed permanently by *The Grinch*. Who had ever stood center stage at the Saint James Theatre for 12-hours at a stretch?

While we were rehearsing *The Grinch*, I had an audition for the revival of *Sunday in the Park with George*. I had never been taken seriously for a Sondheim show in New York before, but somehow, I had a feeling it was going to be different this time. It was.

I remembered from my *Passion* audition many years before that Mr. Sondheim didn't care much for comedic songs at auditions—at least not the one I brought that particular day. I wanted to sing something that was Southern since I was auditioning for the role of Mister who is from South Carolina, but I didn't want my song to be funny. All my Southern material was funny. I got the idea that "Another Hot Day" from *110 in the Shade* would be a good way to go, but I didn't have the sheet music and every store in town seemed to be sold out of it. So I created an arrangement of "Another Hot Day" from memory, wrote it out and worked it up for the audition. I wrote to Harvey Schmidt, the composer of *110 in the Shade*, in Tomball, Texas, where he is retired and shared with him how much I enjoyed reconstituting his wonderful song. And he sent me a gorgeous lithograph in return—he's a superb artist as well as composer.

As I got ready to walk into the audition room at the 42nd Street Studios—with my handwritten song in tow—I kept second-guessing myself. Had I chosen correctly? Was I doing the right thing? Would Sondheim approve? Would he even look up when I came in? Sondheim is considered to be aloof and detached. So, you can imagine my surprise when I walked into the room and he greeted me with a big friendly, "Hello!" The same could not be said for James Lapine, the original director and librettist, who was so removed as to seem almost invisible. I was in very good voice that day and when I finished my self-created arrangement, Sondheim shouted out, "Great!" So much for aloof and detached.

I found out almost immediately that I had gotten the part. My agent reached me on my cell phone as I left rehearsal that day. There I stood in the middle of the street; a man who feared his Broadway career had ended only a couple of months earlier; in TWO Broadway shows at the same time—something that had never happened to me before. In actual fact, they overlapped by three weeks. I was going to have to rehearse *Sunday in the Park with George* while I was performing 14 shows a week of *How the Grinch Stole Christmas*. How the hell was I going to do that? Who cares? I was ecstatic.

Toward the end of the run of *The Grinch* a terrible crud started running through the company. A hacking cough and fluid-filled lungs were the symptoms that surrounded one on all sides, day and night. Children are petri dishes of illness. Eventually, I succumbed and found myself terribly sick as I entered rehearsals for *Sunday in the Park*. This is not how I pictured rehearsing my first Sondheim show in New York.

But here was the deal, *The Grinch* producers paid actors a bonus for every show above 8, and we were doing 14! So by the end of such a week, you had virtually doubled your salary. I did performances with two cough drops in my cheeks at the same time because I couldn't stop coughing long enough to get a single line of dialogue out. The whole top range of my voice dropped out; I found alternative notes in the songs. I wasn't going to miss a performance, not even if an arm or leg fell off. I was going to do every show. And so I did. I heard that John Cullum had the same crud the year before and he had prayed, "Oh, please God, don't let me die on stage in a dog suit."

As I limped into the final week of *The Grinch*, I found out that the entire creative staff including Jack O'Brien the director, was going to come to the final performance. This meant that while sick, on the 14th show of the week and with a full rehearsal week of *Sunday in the Park* behind me, I was going to have to give an opening night level performance. Either that, or be remembered by the creative staff as that sick and tired old guy who was supposed to be buoying up the dog part. I pulled energy reserves from someplace deep down inside—that would have preferred to be left undisturbed. By the curtain call I lost feeling in my right arm. I could not lift it. I thought I was having a heart attack. It was very scary. However, I know my penchant for over-dramatization, so I skipped the closing party, went to bed and resumed rehearsals for *Sunday in the Park* the next day.

FIFTY-NINE

Sunday in the Park with George

(Circa 2008)

THERE WERE SO MANY BEAUTIFUL things about *Sunday in the Park with George* that it's hard to know where to begin. For starters, Daniel Evans and Jenna Russell, the two stars who had come over from England, were so dear as to be almost other worldly. Not that they weren't delightfully naughty as well, they certainly were, but they were just so damn charming.

From the moment I met them, they were free, easy, unencumbered with ego and seemingly tireless. It's a good thing, since they carried the whole weight of the show on their tiny, cute little shoulders. There are no easy roles in *Sunday in the Park*, but theirs were real monsters; hard, complicated and LONG. They never missed and they never flagged.

The rest of the cast was made up of a bunch of showbiz "lifers" like Michael Cumpsty, who I had always wanted to work with; Jessica Molaskey, who was in *Les Miserables* with me back in the day and Anne L. Nathan, who I coached when she was a child and who was now playing my wife. Rehearsals were an absolute joy.

The day after *The Grinch* closed, we had a special event after the *Sunday in the Park* rehearsal that evening. There was a much touted Seurat Exhibit at the Museum of Modern Art that I had not been able to attend because it closed the same day *The Grinch* did. *Sunday in the Park* is, of course, about Georges Seurat. However, the next day, the museum invited the entire cast of

Sunday in the Park to an after business hours private showing of the Seurat Exhibit for a "photo op" with some of Seurat's paintings.

Of course, the painting at the center of *Sunday in the Park with George*, "A Sunday Afternoon on the Island of La Grand Jatte" was not there—it is on permanent display at the Art Institute of Chicago; but a study for the painting was there. Curiously enough, the study contained only the background without any of the people in it. So we staged a very clever photo with the cast members standing in their locations in front of the painting. It was an amazing thing to receive such treatment from The Museum of Modern Art. Very heady. I was most moved by Seurat's little sketch books, so intimate and personal—a truly rare experience to have them all to ourselves in a deserted museum.

Because we were already three-weeks into rehearsals by the time I finished *The Grinch*, it was no time at all before we were having our first complete run-through in the rehearsal space with Mr. Sondheim and Mr. Lapine in attendance. People were nervous. People were very, very nervous. As for me, there were many parts of the play that I hadn't even seen, because I had been over at the Saint James in a dog suit.

I was fascinated when Sondheim arrived. I watched him quietly open The New York Times and begin doing the crossword puzzle alone. No one acknowledged his arrival. He's just so famous, so austere and so revered that no one went over to speak with him. When James Lapine arrived it was pretty much the same thing, except that he and Sondheim cursorily acknowledged each other. Lapine then sat quietly waiting for the run-through to begin; sans crossword. There was dead quiet in the room. People were very nervous.

Interestingly enough, Sondheim seemed to go out of his way to make us feel comfortable once it started. When something was funny, he laughed long and hard. This was very helpful to the overall mood. Lapine on the other hand, never seemed to find anything remotely funny. And the one time he did, he turned his head to the side and covered his mouth so as not to make the tiniest sound.

In spite of all the nerves in the room, the performance really started to pick up steam as it went along. By the end, it became moving; extremely moving. I had never before been in the room when Jenna sang "Children and Art" in the second act. I was sitting off stage right, slightly behind her, waiting for my entrance. The number was unbearably emotional. I began to cry. I tried to stifle it. It was a very small room. It was really hard.

When Jenna finished the song, she exited right next to me and I unthinkingly reached out and grabbed her hand to say, "Well, done." This was a big tactical error. Because when my hand touched hers, the condition that she had created in the number seemed to flow from her body into mine and I began to cry uncontrollably. This seemed to unlock something in the entire room and everyone seemed to lose it at that moment. All the actors were weeping. To my great surprise, Sondheim and Lapine were weeping as well. The last time I had experienced anything like it was forty years earlier, at the first put-together of Leonard Bernstein's *Mass*.

I have always thought it was ridiculous that some ignorant critics and some ignorant laypersons as well, insist on referring to Sondheim's work as intellectual and unfeeling. Hogwash. I don't think there is a more emotionally charged creation in all of musical theater than *Sunday in the Park with George*. We were weeks into the Broadway run before I could sing "Sunday" without crying.

Just a few days later, we were finishing up in the rehearsal space and about to move into the theater. Management informed us that the cast had been invited to a party at Stephen Sondheim's house. Well, there's something I never expected. The information ran through the company like an electric current. It was roughly the equivalent to having Ludwig van Beethoven invite you to tea or Abraham Lincoln suggest that you stop by his cabin after work.

The topic, during every rehearsal break was how one should behave at Mr. Sondheim's party; how nervous everyone was and how insane it was that we were all so nervous. I mean, we're all highly experienced individuals, but this is a historic personage, someone who's not only famous, but a genius and extremely rich—and eccentric.

I had heard that he rarely makes eye contact and doesn't really enjoy talking to people all that much. So, as I prepared to go, I really did not expect to share even a hello with him. I had been unable to speak with him in the rehearsal room; too nervous. I hadn't felt anything like that since I was left alone in the wings with Leonard Bernstein in 1971. I didn't know it was possible for me to feel that way again.

We finished the run-through at 5:00 PM and were told to arrive at Mr. Sondheim's at 6:00 PM. Many people went to the bar next door to tank up. But since this was not an option for me, I began slowly making my way across town on foot. A couple of the girls from the show joined me and I was grateful for the company—and the distraction. We got there 15-minutes early. And since arriving ahead of the invitation was unthinkable, we went into a local drug store where I bought tooth paste; which seemed excessively frivolous at that moment. It reminded me of my drugstore moment on 9/11. As I paid the bill, the clock behind the register showed exactly 6:00 PM, so the three of us went to Stephen Sondheim's front door.

It was now past 6:00 PM, but no one had the nerve to ring the bell. We stood there for several minutes making inane conversation until one of the other *Sunday* guys arrived, who had had several drinks to loosen himself up—and perhaps, something else as well—he was VERY loose. He rang the bell. And the door was opened by Sondheim himself, who was extremely cordial—without making eye contact. The fellow who was feeling so "loose" began asking Mr. Sondheim ridiculous questions, like which of the items in his home was he going to will to the Smithsonian. "Just my corpse" Sondheim replied drolly.

We found ourselves by a small staircase leading to the next room and Sondheim began to speak—to no one in particular—about his old friend Burt Shevelove, with whom he wrote *A Funny Thing Happened on the Way to the Forum*. He mentioned what good friends they were and how he missed him. I got my nerve and piped in with, "You know, I knew Burt."

Sondheim's eyes grew wide as he, for the first time ever, made direct eye contact with me. He was very close. I took a breath and continued, "I was in *No, No, Nanette*." He then told me it only got produced because Burt had had a heart attack and was very depressed. Harry Rigby, the producer, trying to cheer Burt up, suggested that he direct the old clunker which everyone thought was going to be a bomb. Sondheim mentioned his huge surprise when at the Boston opening, it had been a smash.

I told him how astounded we all were when the audience stood up and threw their programs in the air. And I also told him that at the opening night party, Burt had gotten very drunk, and kissed me on the staircase. To which Sondheim replied, "Where exactly is your staircase?" Sharing a private joke with Sondheim on his own staircase? Priceless.

I then informed him that I had known Bernstein, as well. He asked me, "How?" And when I told him about the premiere of Bernstein's *Mass*, Sondheim recalled how "Lenny" had invited him down to Washington during previews and sat with him in the audience. At the end, Bernstein was crying. But Sondheim was sitting there thinking it was the most maudlin piece of trash he'd ever seen. As they walked out, unable to think of anything nice to say,

Sondheim suggested, "Maybe the whole the whole thing should have been in Latin." Bursting with laughter, he explained how that had not gone down too well with Lenny. I then told him the opening night story about Bernstein being rebuffed by Rose Kennedy for slobbering on her. Once again, Sondheim howled with laughter. This whole interaction was a great deal more than I had expected.

He said we could wander around the house; so a couple of us went upstairs. By the way, the house is in Turtle Bay—a part of New York that is so toney—I'd never even been there before and I've lived in Manhattan forty years. The house next door used to belong to Katherine Hepburn. The wood floors and paneling, the memorabilia, the furnishings, in fact the whole place is gorgeous beyond belief.

I climbed the hardwood stairs to the 2nd story—there are 5—and found myself in the room where Stephen Sondheim composes. The grand piano, a Baldwin, was willed to him by Leonard Bernstein. Apparently, Lenny had scratched his name into it somewhere but we could not find it. What we did find was empty music paper lying next to the piano bench with pencils and pens lining the top of the piano. The actual ones he uses when he's being the greatest composer/lyricist in the world—sitting right there—on Bernstein's Baldwin.

There was an unpublished score of a concertina for two pianos lying there, as well as music from *Bounce*, his latest musical. Holding these compositions in place were two brass signs (paperweights) that said "No Singing" and "No Dancing." I found them hilarious. Over the piano was original artwork by Larry Gelbart and signed music from "Lenny." On the opposite wall were numerous awards including several Olivier Awards. As to the location of the six Tony Awards—they were nowhere to be seen. The rumor is that he banished them to the basement after *La Cage aux Folles* won Best Musical over *Sunday in the Park with George*. Sounds right to me.

The house is totally filled with games of all kinds; a passion of his, particularly antique framed ones which are everywhere. His taste was exquisite throughout. There was only one area that looked lived-in; a black massage chair next to the piano in a corner with a coffee cup and some pencils next to it. It had the look of the most well-worn place in the house. I sat there, of course.

When I could take no more of this headiness, I decided to make my way home. I came downstairs and there was the man himself seated at an antique card table with several cast members just jabbering away—so much for not liking to talk. I walked right up to him, put out my hand and said, "Stephen, thank you so very much." I couldn't believe I called him Stephen. He looked up and said, "Say hello to Burt for me." I replied, "I will, tonight in my journal." And so, I did.

Nothing as big as that happened for the rest of rehearsals, although I sat in front of Sondheim for the orchestra read-through of the score and could hear him humming along with his own tunes. "Could this really be happening," I thought? Yes. During the orchestra read of "Move On" Jenna and Daniel, who are very good friends, became swept away with emotion and collapsed into each other's arms weeping like little children. That was pretty marvelous.

The opening night was exciting in the way that New York opening nights always are. In this case, virtually every director who works in the theater was present. No pressure! The reviews were full of the most purple-prose kind of praise. The show received 9 Tony Award nominations, including Best Revival.

The only caveat in all this delightfulness was that shortly after that glorious opening, public attention switched to "the new kids on the block" when both *Gypsy* and *South Pacific* opened; also to glowing reviews. Our producers, who I think had money in one if not both of those shows, pulled out all support and financial aid for our production. No ads ever appeared announcing our nominations. We became invisible on Broadway with 9 TONY NOMINATIONS. Astounding.

I was very blue about the downward turn of events. But in the middle of my blueness, three miraculous things occurred. First, my old friend George Connolly invited me to Barbara Cook's house. She was about to do her 80th birthday celebration with the New York Philharmonic and wanted to run through her whole set for a few people in her living room. I sat in a big armchair, just 3-feet away from her while she sang her entire program. Who gets that? Second, my old friend Roberta Maxwell—from *The Persians*—invited me to Zoe Caldwell's house. Zoe Caldwell is perhaps the greatest stage actress of all time. She was considering playing a speaking part in an opera at the Metropolitan Opera and Roberta, knowing how much I loved opera, wanted me to speak with her. I no sooner arrived at Ms. Caldwell's home than Roberta took off and left the two of us alone together. I spent the entire afternoon with Zoe Caldwell; just the two of us chatting about opera and everything else on earth. At one point she performed a monologue from *Antony and Cleopatra* just for me. Who gets that? Finally third, I got a call from Miracleor2 Licensing, the company that holds the stock and amateur rights to several of my shows. They had an idea for a musical "whodunit" and thought I was the right person to write it. I finished the first draft of *Whodunit... the Musical* in a matter of weeks. And as soon as it was printed out, the York Theater put it in their experimental reading series and 12 productions of it were booked all across the country. All of this happened while *Sunday in the Park* was still running. Who gets that?

When audiences finally realized that our limited run was truly limited, they began to turn out in droves. Our last weeks were packed to the rafters with enthusiastic Sondheim lovers. Of course, there were always a few befuddled spectators who wandered out muttering, "I don't get it." But then, some people have the most remarkable ability not to "get" anything.

When I got home from the final performance, I wrote the following entry in my journal:

"Just finished the most simply amazing final performance of Sunday in the Park with George. Everyone came in with such high spirits to begin with and we were all kissing and hugging each other and then suddenly at the end of the basement green-room area appeared the great man himself. I went over to say goodbye and thank him for the wonderful experience I'd had, and he was very gracious. Then I sat down but noticed that a couple of my colleagues found the nerve to ask him for a photo. I sat there knowing how he hates such things and thought, well, you can either sit here and honor his feelings or you can seize the only chance you will probably ever have to get a one-on-one picture with Stephen Sondheim. I went over and he was very gracious once again, though I really felt that I was imposing something fierce. Afterwards I was absolutely giddy at the thought that I now have a photo of me, one-on-one with one of the greatest artists who has ever lived. Unfortunately, my gesture caused an avalanche of people to request photos and Sondheim became displeased...noticeably. I was very happy to have gotten in under the 'gracious' wire."

The last show went fantastically from the first moment. The entire sold-out audience had a momentous sense of occasion and all, as one, came to say goodbye to us and to the show. They greeted every number with rock concert applause and laughed their asses off at the jokes. My entrance with my "wife," Anne L. Nathan, into the pastry eating scene, was met with an ovation including bravos. On our ENTRANCE! Playing that scene was the kind of thing for which you wait a lifetime—literally. Anne had been such a fantastic cohort on this adventure. We had never stopped working on the scene the whole run; in fact, we found a new laugh one week before we closed.

There were the kind of things you'd expect during the closing of a show like "Finishing the Hat" and "Move On" stopping the show. But even where there was no place to stop it, they stopped it anyway. The real event was the final moment when the cast began singing "Sunday" for the second time. We were to pause and then Jenna was supposed to sing, "In our perfect park..." At that moment she just broke down crying and the audience immediately began screaming and applauding. Then we all resumed singing and when we got to the first real physical movement in the song, on the word RIVER, the audience went nuts.

I was already crying from having to make eye contact with Daniel as we all tipped our hats to him, but the audience going wild at that moment put me over the edge. When we reached the finale of the piece, the point when we sang those amazing chords of "Sunday" three times, we had not gotten the first one out and the audience leapt out of their seats and began clapping their hands over their heads. It was pandemonium.

By the time we got off into the wings the actors were loudly sobbing. We could hear audience members openly weeping before we left the stage. The curtain call was as insane as you'd imagine. I was lucky enough to make eye contact with my friend Lynne Wintersteller, who was in the center of the fourth row—sobbing. We finally made it off into the wings after that bow when the audience demanded that we come back out. First Jenna and Daniel came out to sheer madness and eventually we all came back on stage for one last tumultuous bow. Very, very, very satisfying. This is what people think show business is going to be like when they wander into it. But as we all know—it ain't—not ever. That day it was.

Well, the closing of *Sunday in the Park with George* seems like the perfect time and place to bring this book to a close. Certainly I am not finished with my life, but I can't keep writing this forever.

So, to whoever is still with me, a moral, if you will: If there is anything you want to do—do it. Everyone will tell you that you can't and will explain the reasons why. Do it anyway. And, oh yes don't drink; don't do drugs and for God's sake don't smoke—smoking is the only vice I never embraced—and you should avoid it for that reason alone.

And one more thing—it's a very informative experience to write down what's happened to you in life. I heartily recommend it. It will surprise the hell out of you; to recount what you've seen on your journey. It certainly surprised me.

POST SCRIPT

(Circa Now)

THAT WAS TO HAVE BEEN the last line of the book, but since I wrote it, a couple of remarkable things have happened. I reprised the role of Max in *Sunset Boulevard* at the Signature Theater—14 years after the tour—and won the Helen Hayes Award. I revisited Judge Turpin in *Sweeney Todd* at the Barrington Stage Company and Mr. Sondheim came to the final performance. He told the artistic director, Julianne Boyd, that I was the best Judge Turpin he'd ever seen and that if he wasn't already married, he would marry me. I made her repeat that twice. When I got back to my apartment Mr. Sondheim had sent me an email saying, "I meant what I said behind your back. Steve."

I returned to Broadway in *Mary Poppins*—more than forty years after my debut on the Great White Way—and while I was there wrote *Cloak and Dagger*, a new musical which is just about to be launched.

And finally, I got in touch with a Mr. Mark Horowitz at the Library of Congress and briefly informed him of my lost music signed by Maestro Bernstein. To my great surprise, this total stranger in Washington, D.C. got involved in my problem. It turns out that Mr. Horowitz writes for the Sondheim Review and had, in fact, seen me in *Sunday in the Park with George*. He personally dug through endless boxes of Bernstein manuscripts until he found what he thought was the perfect replacement for my lost music. He picked for me the last page of the original composition of "Somewhere" from *West Side Story*. It is the page which contains the lyric—by a young Stephen Sondheim—"Hold my hand and we're halfway there. Take my hand and I'll take you there, somehow, someday, somewhere." At the bottom of the page it is signed:

"Leonard Bernstein"

CPSIA information can be obtained at www.ICGtesting.com
Printed in the USA
LVOW061745130213

319909LV00003B/414/P